IN SEARCH OF LEADERSHIP

HOW GREAT LEADERS ANSWER THE QUESTION "WHY LEAD?"

Phil Harkins
and
Phil Swift

New York Chicago San Francisco Lisbon London
Madrid Mexico City Milan New Delhi San Juan
Seoul Singapore Sydney Toronto

The McGraw·Hill Companies

1 2 3 4 5 6 7 8 9 0 FGR/FGR 0 1 4 3 2 1 0 9 8

ISBN: 978-0-07-160295-2
MHID: 0-07-160295-X

McGraw-Hill books are available at special quantity discounts to use as premiums and sales promotions, or for use in corporate training programs. To contact a representative please visit the Contact Us pages at www.mhprofessional.com.

This book is printed on acid-free paper.

Library of Congress Cataloging-in-Publication Data

Harkins, Philip J.
In search of leadership : how great leaders answer the question "why lead?" / by Phil Harkins and Phil Swift.
p. cm.
Includes bibliographical references and index.
ISBN 0-07-160295-X (alk. paper)
1. Leadership. I. Swift, Phil. II. Title.
HD57.7.H367 2009
658.4'092--dc22

2008011678

This book is dedicated to Cindy, Morgan, and Gabriel Swift for their unconditional love and support.

CONTENTS

INTRODUCTION **1**

PART I: Our Road Trip to India **7**

Chapter 1 The Journey **9**

Chapter 2 What Should I Be Doing? **15**

Chapter 3 The Leadership Discussion **21**

PART II: The Stories **29**

Chapter 4 Rising Above **33**

Leading Against the Grain: The Story of Ron Greene
Business as Sport: The Story of Claude Lamoureux
Were It Not for Kindness: The Story of Henri Landwirth
Life-Altering Events: The Story of John Hammergren
Her Father's Table: The Story of Rafiah Salim

Chapter 5 A Personal Mission **81**

A Human Enterprise: The Story of Mac Van Wielingen
I Did It for You: The Story of Jim Lewis
Beautifully Focused: The Story of John Lloyd
The Business of Sustainability: The Story of Hans Zulliger
Tenacity: The Story of John Coleman

Chapter 6 The Quest **129**

Seeker of Answers: The Story of Larry Strecker
Between a Handshake and a Bear Hug: The Story of Paul Brainerd
Climbing Mission Hill: The Story of Anthony von Mandl
The Optimist: The Story of John Keane
Believe in Justice, Pay the Price: The Story of Mary Robinson

Chapter 7 Someone Had to Do It **175**

Leadership by Candlelight: The Story of Rajaa Khuzai
Such a Life: The Story of Mikhail Gorbachev
The Conductor and the Lead Violin: The Story of Hal Kvisle
Leadership that Is Not Safe: The Story of Benazir Bhutto
Fathers and Sons: The Story of Ara Hovnanian

Chapter 8 Because It Was Right **227**

Teach One to Teach Another: The Story of Erin Gruwell
If Not Now, When? If Not You, Who?: The Story of Jane Simington
Teaching Power: The Story of Mike Towers
Becoming Swanee Hunt: The Story of Swanee Hunt
Say Yes, then Figure Out How: The Story of Pat Mitchell
Be the Change You Wish to See: The Story of Mohandas K. Gandhi

PART III: Conclusion **277**

Chapter 9 Leadership Insights from the Journey **281**

Chapter 10 Why Lead?—The Answer **289**

INDEX **301**

ACKNOWLEDGMENTS **309**

This is the true joy in life, the being used for a purpose recognized by yourself as a mighty one; the being thoroughly worn out before you are thrown on the scrap heap; the being a force of Nature instead of a feverish little clod of ailments and grievances complaining that the world will not devote itself to making you happy.

—George Bernard Shaw

I don't know what your destiny will be, but one thing I do know; the only ones among you who will be really happy are those who have sought and found how to serve.

—Albert Schweitzer

You make a living from what you earn, but you make a life from what you give.

—Winston Churchill

Do you know the difference between happiness and joy?

—Sri Narayani Amma

INTRODUCTION

What prompted us to write this book? It arose out of our personal journeys of discovery in leadership and life. *In Search of Leadership* began as an exploration of questions that every leader seems to face: *Why should I lead? When have I had enough? Should I continue to lead?* Then we focused on the questions: *Why do people lead at all? What keeps leaders going?*

It became clear that the question *Why lead?* was larger than just an inquiry into leadership. It involved searching for meaning and purpose in life and discovering a way to achieve that through a leadership role. It is a question that prompts others: *What should I do with my life? What is my purpose? If I do choose leadership, will I be any good at it? Will I make a difference? Will I be fulfilled?*

We learned that some people come to leadership by accident or on a path to another goal. Yet all leaders at some point must answer the question *Why should I continue leading?*

These questions took us on a journey literally around the world. We first traveled to India to reflect and to engage with a gifted spiritual leader who helps millions build better lives.

We then spoke with accomplished leaders from all walks of life. What light would be shed on our questions from their successes, struggles, hardships, and even failures? What nuances or new insights would we find?

When we asked these leaders *Why lead?* we often stopped them in their tracks. Some seemed to regard it as a loaded question. We realized that *leader* is a big word. By itself, it creates a pause. Most said they had never set out to be leaders. That was fascinating in itself. It could also offer encouragement to young people who wonder what they want to be, as well as for parents who wonder if their children will become leaders.

This research soon became a project and, finally, a book. The more we reviewed our notes after meeting these leaders, the more common themes we found. Certainly, everyone was interested in the question *Why lead?* It led us to others, like the age-old: *Are leaders born or made?*

We wondered, as we explored people's lives, why do they take on the challenges that sometimes seem so difficult—even through hard times—with no results in sight? We believe you will be as amazed and awestruck as we were after learning about these people's lives. They inspired us.

It prompted us to ask these people *Why lead?* and then patiently wait to discover what they had to say. We found that these remarkable leaders' life stories conveyed powerful reasons why.

Many of these leaders will be familiar. Others may be less so, but their stories are nevertheless moving. Each story has its own qualities, insights, and lessons, but we uncovered common and powerful reasons leaders keep going—especially once they have achieved their goals.

We organized these stories around the key insights we had gained to the question *Why lead?* Rather than sort, analyze, and crunch the data, we decided to let the stories speak for themselves. They speak directly to the heart of those who listen.

Unsurprisingly, none of the highly successful leaders we spoke to was doing it—leading—for the money. Once their financial goals were met, money had become invisible, circumstantial, and somewhat superficial to the question of why they lead.

One crucial finding from our work is that leaders who reach their goals can find even higher levels of satisfaction. We found that continuing to work for the reasons that originally brought them to leadership just wore leaders out. Leaders who continue to chase the same goal after they have achieved success often experience higher levels of dissatisfaction. Just getting more of the same doesn't always create more happiness.

All leaders face doubts in their leadership journeys. They question why they are still pushing on. Some answer these doubts by changing tack or by throwing themselves into new adventures. Ultimately, a more sustaining answer comes from a *transformational shift.*

Leaders must eventually change how they think and operate. Frequently, this approach was service oriented, in the sense they had found something *greater.* For our purposes and research, they had found a new reason to lead.

The highly successful leaders we interviewed transformed their leadership and reckoned with the concept that we call *enough.* These leaders reached their goals or achieved their dreams. They were able to raise the flag, declare victory, and move on. They found a greater happiness, almost a joy, in doing what they were doing. And they seemed to know what they were about. For many of these leaders, their renewed purpose brought a glow to their lives. They measured their results in different ways, as you will see.

As we neared completion, we received a poem that Warren Bennis had read in a eulogy for a great leader. Its first line was especially relevant:

"Did you get what you wanted in this life, even so?"

The way Bennis, the world's reigning leadership guru, reads that line, he will pause and say, "It's the comma and the 'even so' that are important in the lives of leaders."

The moral here is that leading is not easy. We all know that. The "even so" is about the twists and turns that leaders must withstand. We certainly found it in all of these leaders' lives.

We have written this book for a broad audience: the world of leaders in business, government, education, health care, nonprofit organizations, and religious institutions. These principles are relevant to those leaders, as well as to leaders of community organizations, coaches and mentors, and even parents. *In Search of Leadership* is meant for those contemplating becoming a leader, as much as for those early in their careers or at a career crossroads. You might see yourself in these stories. We hope that our book will help you find insights and answers into your own struggles and questions about leadership.

As we wrote this book, some of the leaders we interviewed changed roles. Some were affected by life experiences and changed direction. And at least one left this earth. We reached an important conclusion about the question *Why lead?* Leadership is first a choice and then a commitment. Once you're committed, you can't back down. Such a commitment forces leaders to move outside themselves, as it is no longer just about yourself. In the process of choosing to lead, you have already given that away.

Some leaders said they started out thinking they were just traveling down a path on a goal-directed mission to blaze a new trail, to prove something, or perhaps just to achieve. They, too, ultimately faced a leadership choice.

We conclude that most leaders are asked at some time in their journey to step up. This commitment changes everything because it is a declaration that requires stepping outside one's self.

All the leaders we talked to, especially those in this book, acknowledged that they reached a point where they were leading for others. Being a leader is not about walking in your own shoes, but stepping into others'. That was the case with Benazir Bhutto, who told us that she had to go back to Pakistan. We knew that this decision would put her in great danger. Although no question had been posed, she volunteered in a quiet tone, "I just have to." No more was said. It was clear. She was committed to her reasons for leading.

Once committed, true leaders cannot easily step aside. We found leaders who would occasionally take "time outs" and some who would defer to others. That's also part of being a leader. We believe leadership is a calling that requires stepping forward with both feet, despite the risks. Leaders turn fear into faith and create true fellowship. Their reflection is seen as a humble statement of service to others.

We hope you enjoy this book and that it provides a meaningful answer to the question *Why lead?* We also hope it helps you create more success and impact as a leader, while making the experience more meaningful and sustainable.

Simply put, this journey integrates the intellect with the heart and the ego with the soul. Enjoy your trip.

PART I
Our Road Trip to India

Chapter 1

The Journey

by Phil Harkins

The plane touched down just before midnight in Chennai, southern India's most populous city. Even in darkness, India lay awake and pulsating with life. In the taxi en route from the airport, the sights and smells piqued my senses. The humid air reeked of sewage. Flowers, spices, and perfume softened its pungency with fragrance. I was told that traffic was light at that hour, but it did not seem that way to me. Cars, taxis, and trucks cut across each other's path, jostling and beeping horns. Scooters and motorized rickshaws bleated like smaller, quicker animals, darting into open spaces that slammed shut only moments later. Buses barreled past. People hung from the buses' sides and sat on their rooftops.

The ramshackle buildings that arose at the edge of the road were dark. A trail of makeshift street-corner food stands, strung with brightly colored lights, suggested a healthy business with late night eaters. Old men stood in groups. They conversed through the smoke of thin cigarettes, through the steam of *chai.* Families camped under tarps in the crooks and crevices between buildings. The sights, sounds, tastes, smells, and textures of India were about to change me. I could feel it in my blood.

Weary from travel, I sat back in the car. I was dazzled by this cascade of sensory data. Even though it was not my first trip to India, its impact remained strong. There are over four million people in Chennai. Compared to high-tech Indian business centers like Bangalore, where a burgeoning middle class benefited from thousands of outsourced back-office support jobs, Chennai still seemed to exist in the Third World.

Why was I here? The short answer was that as a consultant and executive coach from Boston, I had promised one of my closest clients and friends that I would assist him on the next leg of his leadership journey. That client was Phil Swift. A founder and cochairman of the billion-dollar energy sector investment firm ARC Financial Corporation, based in Calgary, Alberta, Canada. He was to meet me in Chennai.

Swift, a pragmatic businessman, had come to a crossroads in his own leadership journey. No longer satisfied with the allure of more success in business, he had set out on a personal quest for greater meaning and satisfaction in his life.

I had seen highly accomplished leaders reach this stage in their careers before. It fascinated me that successful men and women who had achieved power and wealth continued to struggle with the fundamental questions about leadership.

As a lifelong student of leadership, with 30 years of experience, I could relate to the strains and difficulties that might inspire a quest for more depth. I had no doubt that counseling clients undergoing a similar journey would be of enormous benefit to me as a coach. I also wanted to use this time for serious reflection on the nature of leadership.

The car passed through the outskirts of Chennai and into the countryside. It would be three hours before I reached Vellore, a historic town of 400,000 built around a medieval fort. My destination was a retreat called the Peedam. It was founded by the spiritual leader Sri Narayani Amma.

Swift was already at the Peedam with his family, awaiting my arrival. We had planned the trip for more than a year, each of us with his own agenda.

I was in India primarily to help Phil Swift, but I was also drawn to the prospect of witnessing Sri Narayani Amma's work firsthand. Leadership comes in many different forms, but Amma seemed to be truly unique. At 28 years of age, Sri Narayani Amma had the presence and impact of a much older, wiser person. Enlightened even in childhood, Amma experienced a vision at age 16. Amma embraced the vision and brought it to the outside world by leaving home, moving to the site of the Peedam, and beginning to teach.

Although Amma's focus was spiritual, it was Amma's leadership ability that fascinated me. Swift told me that at the Peedam, Amma was engaged in a great development project. Thatched huts and spiritual temples were scattered around the 350-acre complex. In recent years, the work had intensified. Now there was a school, a modern hospital, and facilities to feed the poor. More ambitious plans were laid out for a university and a spiritual park called the Sripuram. Thousands of workers were engaged in the constant building process. Hundreds more ran the facilities under Amma's patient, often witty, and unfailingly calm guidance. I realized that I knew of no one—let alone a 28-year-old from rural India—who had accomplished so much in such a short time with so few resources. The vision was remarkable and the execution, by all accounts, was even more impressive. Operations at the Peedam required tremendous management skills and leadership acumen, and it all ran with the precision of a Swiss watch. I believed that this leadership merited deeper appreciation and study.

I thought about the first time I had met Amma. It was in New York City, at the home of a well-known physician from a renowned hospital. I joined people from all walks of life, including corporate leaders and others of substantial means. Looking around the room, I considered how remarkable it was that these influential leaders, some of whom were well-known public figures weighed down by great responsibility, were exploring the spiritual dimension of their busy lives. Truly, leadership was a multidimensional enterprise.

We waited patiently to meet with Amma privately. When my turn came, I found Amma seated on the floor. Amma greeted me with a pleasant smile, and a relaxed and peaceful air. *Such bright eyes in such a young face*, I thought, as Amma gestured for me to sit down.

Foregoing small talk, Amma asked what I did for a living. To avoid a complicated answer, I said that I was a consultant. This polite elusiveness did not satisfy Amma.

"What do you consult about?" Amma asked, more pointedly. I explained that I was a consultant and leadership coach. Leaders, I said, employ coaches to help them work through business challenges. Sometimes they need to analyze strategy or organizational structure. At other times, they need help making tough decisions about people or issues in their personal lives. Amma listened intently, seeming to indicate that it was all very interesting. Then Amma suddenly interrupted my explanation with, "Do you coach leaders on happiness or joy?"

The question brought me up short. *Happiness or joy?* What did that have to do with leadership? Perplexed, I paused to think.

"Do you know the difference between *happiness* and *joy*?" Amma continued, as though reading my thoughts.

"I'm not sure I do," I admitted.

As Amma explained further, I experienced a sense of recognition—a feeling that I had encountered such thoughts before in my work, but had not put them into words. "Leaders," Amma said, "need to spend more time in search of joy. Too many leaders are willing to settle for happiness."

Settle?

Amma explained that the longing for more and more was, ultimately, unfulfilling. "Happiness can only get you so far," Amma said, "but joy is unconditional. Joy requires letting go. It means that your role and purpose is no longer just about your own needs and desires."

It wasn't an easy contradiction to grasp, and yet it carried the ring of truth. Ambition, money, competitive fire, impact—there are as many different motivations as there are leaders. I believed that much of a leader's ability to nurture and constantly improve an organization is rooted in the elusive quest for personal happiness. Now Amma seemed to suggest that such a quest might not be enough.

High-impact leadership, I understood, was never just about achieving the leader's agenda. It was about helping others to achieve their own agendas in a way that synchronized with the leader's objectives. Yet this message of Amma's went deeper. Amma was talking about how leading others could bring joy.

But what did *joy* really mean? And how was it different from *happiness*? Was that what Phil Swift was looking for? Were other leaders searching for it too?

As we drove, dawn was beginning to overtake the darkness. Women and children walked along the edge of the road, unfazed by the traffic. They shared the narrow path with pack animals burdened by heavy sacks. Cows, which are sacred in India, roamed freely. There were only a few minutes left before my arrival.

Chapter 2
What Should I Be Doing?

by Phil Swift

The Peedam

My wife, children, and I were eagerly awaiting Phil Harkins's arrival at the Peedam. It was our second vacation in India. Although nine-year-old Morgan and seven-year-old Gabriel had visited many of the traditional destinations, the Peedam remained their favorite spot. For me, it was a testament to the authenticity of its people and the atmosphere around them. There was potential for rejuvenation in the peace and the simplicity of the Peedam. No blaring televisions and no interrupting telephones. We were free from stress and worry. The guest quarters were spartan but comfortable. Friendly faces greeted us. Amma had created an environment that gave me and my wife Cindy a feeling of mental and emotional strength.

I was enjoying the time and the space of the Peedam. This respite allowed me to do some thinking. I was eager to share my thoughts with Harkins, my friend and business coach, and to hear his impressions.

The night before I'd written in my journal: "What should I be doing with the next part of my life?" I had asked myself this question before, but still didn't have an answer. Over the past few years, I asked friends and colleagues in similar positions of leadership whether they had ever posed this kind of question to themselves. I was surprised at how many had.

When I reflected on my personal leadership journey, choices just seemed to happen. Things had started simply enough. As a boy, I'd been a solid but unremarkable student until an athletic coach taught me a basic lesson: The more effort you put into something, the more benefit you get out of it.

From that point forward, I tested my capacity in both sports and academics. I discovered that I excelled whenever I applied myself. I became fascinated with math and philosophy, which I studied formally in college. I carefully sorted through my opportunities in life. After graduation, I chose a practical route and settled on an MBA.

In the business world, I quickly progressed through the ranks. I first worked for a series of large corporations, but I felt as though my entrepreneurial instincts weren't thriving there. Next, I tried a midsized company, switching my area of expertise to finance. Once again, I excelled, yet I was still frustrated as an entrepreneur. But when I began to work for a small national investment firm, researching the energy industry, I felt in sync with my business environment.

My partner Mac Van Wielingen and I became the number-one-rated oil and gas securities team in Canada. We were later joined by a third partner, John Stewart. We moved to a large national investment dealer, where we burnished our reputation in investment research and corporate finance. We were in our mid-thirties with the best jobs we'd ever had. We were making more money than we had ever imagined. Then we quit. The new dream was to form our own company—a boutique firm that could expand its business plan from investment analysis and corporate finance to acquiring oil and gas assets and investing in the equity of junior companies. Sixteen years later, we had built a multibillion dollar company with hundreds of employees.

This summary makes my career sound like it was a straight ascent, which would not do justice to the many ups and downs I experienced along the way. Earlier in my career, with an abundance of confidence and a reckless disregard for risk, I managed to get into financial difficulty. It taught me some of the toughest and best lessons about tenacity and entrepreneurship—managing risks while pursuing the dream.

Over the years, my leadership evolved. Early on at the firm, I held ambitious and motivating goals: building the business, making projects succeed, and getting good returns. I needed to lead in order to make the firm perform well, but I didn't think about leadership beyond those parameters.

As my leadership evolved, I gained some interesting insights: Business is all about results.

Results arise from opportunity.

Opportunity arises from relationships.

Business relationships hinge on creating value for people by helping them get what they want. I thought about what I was doing to add value for the people with whom I was dealing. That meant not just the firm's customers and clients, but our employees and my partners.

It was a constructive framework. I realized that my significant opportunities came to me from relationships. I concentrated on what people wanted. If I could determine what drove them and what they hoped to achieve, then I could help them obtain it. Operating this way gave rise to a new level of business success.

More importantly, I recognized that there were other dimensions of leadership to explore. I started delegating everything I could from an operational standpoint. I became free to focus more on adding value through my relationships.

As time went on, the all-consuming success of each new deal lost its momentum. I felt myself losing the drive and the passion that had once consumed me. The stress of business and success took a mental, emotional, and physical toll on me. Where would more success take me? How much was enough?

By all objective measures, I had more than I needed. What was my motivation to keep going? Retiring wouldn't affect my lifestyle. If anything, it would improve things because I would have more time to enjoy life. But I knew that people who retired because they no longer needed to work usually tried to get back into the game a year or two later. They were still unsatisfied.

Seeking balance, I took more holidays. I spent more time with my young family. I tailored my work pace to accommodate my desire to enjoy life. But the question of meaning and intent lingered.

Meeting Amma in late 1999 switched my journey to fast-forward. Amma's messages were spiritual, but also universal and practical. Amma's insights led me compellingly into giving back through philanthropy.

At the time, I had been exploring ideas to mark the start of the new millennium. This led to one of the most important commitments we ever made as a family. We called it our "millennium project," which centered on contributing in a significant way to the building of a 150-bed general hospital in India. It was a very satisfying adventure.

Still, the questions *Why?* and *When is enough enough?* remained unresolved.

Later in 2000, I met Phil Harkins at the annual Global Institute for Leadership Development conference. We later engaged Phil and his firm, Linkage, to work with us in leadership development and our succession plan. As I made the transition from CEO to chairman, I realized that his experience could be invaluable in helping me with my personal transition. Beyond our business relationship, we had become friends. I was intrigued at the prospect of inviting Phil to India. There he could see firsthand my other interests and to explore these issues in depth.

As soon as Harkins was rested and ready to go, I gave him a tour of the Peedam compound. Its level of development and activity was a sight to behold. I enjoyed watching Harkins's growing astonishment. There were thousands of people involved in building projects, school administration, and readying the recently built hospital for its opening. Yet despite all this activity, there was always time for their spiritual ceremonies.

Even though Harkins was prepared for what he'd seen, he still couldn't fathom how all of it was happening under Amma's direction. As we walked through grounds that were once abandoned and fallow, we agreed that the Peedam was a leadership story in itself. As a consultant and executive, Harkins had seen impressive organizations in their early days of high energy and rapid growth. The Peedam had that kind of momentum.

Amma greeted us warmly, and asked Harkins about his travels. Harkins said it was pleasant to see Amma again. He said he felt like he was visiting an old friend.

Amma asked, "Are you still looking for answers?" Amma laughed lightly, seeming amused and curious at the same time.

Harkins confessed he was still thinking about the remarks Amma made in New York about the difference between happiness and joy.

"When it comes to success," Amma suggested, "it's not how happy you are, but how many people you make happy." Amma also said that the failure to discover joy eventually puts happiness at risk.

Harkins and I looked at each other. This felt like an important realization, a glimpse of a far-off destination. Amma, still smiling, said nothing more. The meeting had ended. Harkins and I left the room, knowing that we would spend the next days in debate and analysis before seeking further direction from Amma.

Chapter 3
The Leadership Discussion

That night, Harkins couldn't sleep. A remarkable energy had come over him. He went to the roof deck of the guesthouse and reflected for hours on the messages of the day. Somehow, Amma's comments had addressed a critical aspect of leadership rarely touched on by top leadership experts. Amma spoke of sustaining a leader's capacity and effectiveness while providing deeper fulfillment.

Harkins reflected on what he had learned from working with leaders as an executive coach. Could he connect their experiences to the concepts of happiness and joy? He knew that leaders are intensely motivated, with a great deal of focused drive. Whatever their field of endeavor, leaders tend to be relentless doers. They throw everything into their work and leave little of themselves behind. Paradoxically, leaders are usually seen as people of action, yet they are often introverted and curious. They have a variety of interests and think deeply about life. Their reflection is coupled with a drive for achievement and sometimes power. This drive is what distinguishes a leader from a poet, a professor, or a research scientist. Leaders are visionaries who don't work in isolation. They strive for goals by bringing others along with them. Yet Amma suggested that it was a paradox of leadership that the continued quest for more of the same could distance leaders from joy and ultimately limit their effectiveness.

The next day, while out for a run around the Peedam, Harkins told Swift what he had been thinking. It must have been an amusing sight: two Western businessmen jogging in the heat of the day perspiring, apparently for no good reason.

"Then what truly drives a leader?" Swift asked.

Harkins laid out some of the accepted theories. Psychologist David McClelland had observed that leaders are characterized by combinations of an achievement orientation, a power orientation, or an affiliation orientation. "People who are affiliators make good followers, networkers, and team players," Harkins said, "but leaders have a need to take charge or responsibility."

"So maybe the real questions are," Swift considered, "'*Why take on the roles and responsibilities of leading?*' and '*How can you know that you are right for leading?*' "

"It's as though some *have* to do it. They're unable to avoid the mess," said Harkins.

Swift laughed. "The other day, when I asked my son to clean his room, he said, 'Whatever, Dad!' and rolled his eyes. I laughed and thought how nice it must be to just shrug off responsibility. I never get to say 'whatever.' I always have to make things right."

"I've heard my share of 'whatevers' over the years from my boys," Harkins concurred, "and even from people I work with. It's such an easy expression of apathy, as if the person is saying, 'I have no purpose and you have no purpose and nothing matters.'"

Swift wiped his brow as they came up over the hill and back to the complex. "I bet there's a 'whatever' in every language in the world. We'll have to ask Amma for the Tamil version."

"*Leadership* is the opposite of *whatever*," Harkins said, as they reached the guesthouses. "Leaders can't say 'whatever,' no matter what situation they find themselves in."

Later that day, the discussion continued.

"The best leaders are the ones who are always looking for ways to make things better," Swift said. "You can't stand back and ignore things. You can never say 'whatever.' You have to be in the middle of the tension. You feel enormous responsibility. How do you recognize this early on? Can you see leadership traits and characteristics in children?"

"You *can* see leadership potential in some children," Harkins replied.

"It must be tough to raise a little leader," said Swift with a smile. "I don't imagine they take direction well. One of the most successful leaders I know refers to himself as virtually unemployable."

"If you're not careful, you can take away a child's sense of curiosity and the need to improve things," added Harkins. "It would be valuable if parents could assess whether their child was a leader in the making. It would give them a whole new way of interpreting their child's behaviors." After a pause, Harkins continued, "Why do we measure dysfunctional behavior with psychological tools more than high-functioning behavior? It's a question worth posing to my colleagues."

"I've seen people blossom into leadership roles late in life," Swift said. "It always made me wonder whether they had that potential all along or whether they needed particular circumstances to generate their leadership drive. Did Jack Welch's mother or Winston Churchill's grandfather look at those young children and realize they had that spark? Did they kindle the spark and fan the flame? I guess it's the age-old question: *Are leaders born or are they made?*"

Harkins thought about it. The easy answer came to mind first: Leaders are born. They have special capabilities and attributes that give them a knack for leadership. However, it was equally true that many leaders—individuals he had known and historical figures he had studied—grew into their leadership roles because of an historic opportunity, a difficult childhood, or the careful mentorship of a parent or a teacher.

"A leader's life journey," Harkins continued, "defines his vision and the path of his leadership. It becomes his passion. One of the most significant things Jack Welch ever did for leadership development at GE was to let Noel Tichy into Crotonville, where he created leadership timelines for the emerging talent."

"What do you mean by a leadership timeline?" Swift inquired.

"If you ask leaders to chart out the highs and the lows in their lives, and to indicate how high and how low those moments were, you get something like an electrocardiogram. All leaders have significant spikes up and down that they can attribute to really important moments in their lives. Some leaders' timelines look like a distant set of mountains with only a few life-changing peaks. Others have dozens of events, giving them a timeline that looks like a defibrillated heartbeat."

"So, it's not just a leader's natural capabilities that matter," Swift commented, "but also those peaks and valleys too?"

"A major impact," Harkins replied. "You mentioned failure. In fact, leaders' low points are as relevant as their successes."

"We learn many of our great lessons from our failures," Swift said. "That's always been true in my life. I believe that as long as you don't become bitter or defeated, the school of hard knocks will teach you things that might benefit you in the future. At ARC, we responded well to crises, but I don't think we really celebrated when we scored a big win or reached a new plateau. We tended to put our heads down, get back to work, and only reward ourselves momentarily."

"The other top leaders I've worked with have that characteristic, too," Harkins agreed. "When you're goal-oriented, you go for results. When you surpass that goal, you set a new one farther along the track."

"I can relate to that," Swift said. "I remember people saying that if I achieved my goals, I would keep moving the goalposts. I didn't believe them, but they were right. What I achieved went beyond my expectations, so I found myself reframing my goals and setting new objectives. This wasn't necessarily a bad thing, but it wasn't making me any happier. In fact, it started to take on a life of its own, full of stress, pressure, and obligations." Swift continued, "So when is enough *enough*? Isn't part of maturity knowing when enough is enough?"

They fell silent. Harkins sensed his friend's struggle with these psychological and spiritual dilemmas. Where was the greater purpose for leading, and how could leaders integrate it into their lives to create wholeness?

Swift said, "The usual advice on leadership doesn't seem to address the bigger questions. No matter how far along the leadership path you go, these questions are still there. And the farther you go, the better your answers have to become. They must be not merely words that sound right, but words that are deeply meaningful. Words that sustain you."

"One theme that is regularly explored at the annual Global Institute for Leadership Development conference is how leaders can find their voice and passion," said Harkins. "I believe it requires going deeper and engaging more of yourself. For leaders to achieve their potential, they must confront their values, beliefs, and, I'm beginning to realize, their spiritual purpose."

"These questions and issues don't lend themselves well to just logic alone," Swift agreed. "Maybe the answer lies deeper, in places that we haven't explored. Amma's message seems to be: Move from the head to the heart and then to the soul."

"Others have pointed in this direction," Harkins explained. "Vaclav Havel said, 'The power of authentic leadership is found not in external arrangements but in the human heart.' Authentic leaders in every setting—from families to nation-states—aim at liberating the heart so that its power can liberate the world."

Swift added, "And the great leadership theorist Warren Bennis said, 'The process of becoming a leader is much the same as the process of becoming an integrated human being.'"

"Are these elements that need to be integrated into how we think about leadership?" Harkins asked. "Will they help answer the big question, *Why lead?*"

Swift agreed that this made sense. "Doesn't it amaze you that Amma is always smiling?" Harkins observed. "There's no question that Amma operates from a place of joy."

Swift agreed. "Amma is busier than anyone I've ever known, yet always maintains a balanced perspective and simple grace."

"The joy in the Peedam is tangible, too. It's as though Amma is nurturing that feeling among everyone who serves here."

"No commitment or retention problems," Swift laughed. "Their motivation and rewards are internal, not external. It reminds me of that quote from George Bernard Shaw: 'I'd like to feel totally used up by a purpose. That would be a true joy in life.'"

Harkins looked down at his notepad. It was now covered in key words, circled over and over with arrows, loops, and scribbled half phrases. "I'm not sure if we've figured out where your joy in leadership will come from, but I'd love to learn how other successful leaders have done it."

"I'd bet we'd get some interesting answers," Swift agreed. "Successful leaders have differing visions and goals. I wonder if there's any commonality among them? How would the best of them answer these questions? What qualities, intentions, and expectations did they have that made them successful *and* able to sustain their commitment to leadership?"

"*Why lead?*" Harkins reiterated, echoing their discussion with Amma. "When is enough, *enough*? Ask leaders those two questions, and you'll get their leadership stories. Get their leadership stories, and you may find the answers you're looking for."

PART II
The Stories

This book will explore what we believe are some of the fundamental questions of leadership.

- Why are some people drawn to leadership?
- What keeps those people going?
- What makes them stop?
- What makes them change course and assert their leadership in entirely different realms?
- How does being a leader sustain, fulfill, or enrich them?
- What makes leadership worth it, after you've added up the benefits and costs?
- Why lead?

We looked hard for the answers to these questions. We knew that any truth we found would have to come from leaders who had personally experienced the trials of that role and would answer candidly. To that end, we decided that our best approach would be simply to interview a great number of leaders extensively and write down what they had to say.

But who should those interviewees be? We know remarkable, high-achieving business leaders around the world, but feared that if we focused only on limited aspects of leadership, the picture would be half-formed and the data skewed. We sought out leaders with a broad spectrum of viewpoints, experiences, and fields of endeavor.

At first, we thought about who we would like to interview in an ideal sense, without any restrictions of access or circumstances. Contemplating that felt like the conversation game in which people ask each other, "What famous person, living or dead, would you most like to have dinner with?" Immediately, many historical figures leap to mind: great political leaders such as George Washington or Winston Churchill, great spiritual leaders such as Mohandas K. Gandhi or Martin Luther King Jr., and great business leaders such as Thomas Edison or John D. Rockefeller. How illuminating it would be to talk with such individuals about the tests, rewards, and truths of leadership!

When we returned to reality and considered the leaders available to us today, we were not disappointed by our options. History assigns greatness to a leader, but not all great leaders are remembered by history. In their own time, leaders engage in a quiet struggle that may not be recorded or even noticed. That does not make them any less worthy. In fact, it probably makes them more valuable.

We spoke to leaders with varied experiences and backgrounds. We boldly knocked on doors to ask these very busy and important people for their time. In the end, we chose 26 leaders from various fields, including politics, grassroots organizations, Fortune 100 companies, entrepreneurial enterprises, health care, and education. We also considered the nonprofit realm, the international arena, and the world of religion and spirituality. Some of those people will be familiar to readers through news accounts: Mikhail Gorbachev was an agricultural engineer who eased a dying empire into democracy and Benazir Bhutto chose to lead her Islamic nation at great personal risk and tragedy.

Other leaders we interviewed will be less recognizable, but their stories are moving nevertheless. As broadly as we define leadership, certain areas, such as intellectual leadership (leadership through ideas), we were not able to cover.

Despite the broad range of life and cultural experiences among our interviewees, everyone engaged immediately with the questions we were asking. The discussions resonated on a deep, meaningful, and ultimately spiritual level. The answers to *Why lead?* were not as simple as we might have anticipated.

In the end, we found clear and concrete lessons that resisted any attempts to be tagged with pithy business book slogans. We also found categories that our leaders *sort of* fit into, having straddled multiple categories at different times. We also found astonishingly universal ideas about the spiritual dimensions of leadership and its larger significance.

Rather than sort, analyze, crunch, cross-reference, and churn that data into a bland purée, we let the stories speak for themselves. They are too magical and precious to alter. They stand on their own, speaking directly to the heart of the listener. We believe that these insights are compelling, since they were revealed through the interviewees' personal struggles and triumphs. That's the power of showing versus telling.

These stories are organized into five themes that describe what draws these individuals to leadership:

- Rising Above
- A Personal Mission
- The Quest
- Someone Had to Do It
- Because It Was Right

What we found from these stories were fascinating insights into these leaders' lives. The stories were enriching on many levels. They offered insights into a leader's character, as well as the "how to" of leadership—although this was not our principal focus. The insights and answers to the question *Why lead?* were as varied as the leaders themselves.

Chapter 4
Rising Above

The stories in this section are both happy and sad. Some leaders, we discovered, were driven by their passion to lead from early childhood. It ignited the spark that focused their drive to achieve.

In some cases, they may be compensating for something that was lost—as you may see in Henri Landwirth's story. For others, it is an awakening to new possibilities. Rafiah Salim was introduced to a new world by an unusual father who saw brilliance in his little girl.

We realized that even bad circumstances can spawn young people who can weather life's brutal blows and take charge of their destiny. Claude Lamoureux didn't let his physical handicap keep him away from hockey. John Hammergren made his choice when he lost his father during high school. He stood tall and stands for values today.

These leaders, in their individual ways, faced up to their challenges to lead "against the grain." Perhaps "hard stuff" early on creates the "inner stuff" that Ron Greene believes is fundamental to all leaders in this category. When everyone is going in one direction, Greene says, "I want to be going in another. When everyone is getting on the bandwagon, I feel restless."

Some leaders, we discovered, derived their formative leadership experience through early trauma, a difficult childhood, or physical illness or injury. Such people often have great perseverance, determination, and courage. Sometimes, the early drive for success is all about compensating for those early difficulties—the abusive household, the lack of money, the war-torn country. The success that such leaders eventually earn gives their journey the flavor of a Horatio Alger story. Success may compensate for early deprivation, but it never seems to completely heal the suffering experienced at a young age. Those wounds can result in a difficult adult emotional life or an inability to slow down and enjoy the fruits of one's efforts. Getting past that pain, to whatever degree possible, can be enormously liberating. It can generate seemingly limitless energy and enthusiasm for one's fellow human beings.

Leading Against the Grain: The Story of Ron Greene and Renaissance Energy

Ron Greene has been recognized with many awards from the Canadian business community, and was named Natural Resources Entrepreneur of the Year in 1994. In 1974, he founded one of the most successful companies in the history of the Canadian energy industry, Renaissance Energy Ltd., and for a period of time, it rose to become the most active driller in North America. These accomplishments far exceeded the dreams of a boy born and raised on a farm in Western Canada.

What was it that helped Ron develop the skills, instincts, and ambitions to achieve these remarkable accomplishments? Ron said that he became a leader without consciously doing so. He noticed that good leaders didn't necessarily set themselves that goal. It was a product of who they were as people. He said that he didn't wake up one morning and say, "I want to be a leader." He said he was born with a personality that, for whatever reason, drove him to be independent. He craved independence, sought independence, and found independence.

He described how his innate need for independence evolved. It was the driving force that made his path clear. It was also clear to him that you need people to work with you along the way. He found it interesting that when you are young, there is a tendency to think that your feelings are the same as everyone else's. You might believe that your requirements for work and desires for independence are commonly held. It was an eye-opener for him, as he assembled his small team to find that not everyone wanted to lead and not everyone wanted to be independent. He defined independence as being responsible for one's own financial destiny.

Leading Against the Grain

Ron Greene explains one important element of his entrepreneurial style in simple but sharp terms: "When everyone is going in one direction, I want to go in another. When I see everyone getting on a bandwagon, I feel restless." As a leader, Greene relies on that instinct to uncover opportunities that everyone else missed. He's not a knee-jerk contrarian. Instead, he assesses the competitive landscape and lays out a rigorous strategy to make the most of his position. His leadership brings everyone else in his organization along, committed with enthusiasm to their "go it alone" direction.

That philosophy was never as starkly demonstrated as in 1986, when the Canadian oil and gas industry hit one of its lowest points. The price of oil had dropped below $10 per barrel. As president and CEO of Renaissance Energy, Ron Greene was on the executive committee of an industry organization, the Independent Petroleum Association of Canada (IPAC). The board of directors of IPAC was comprised of 15 CEOs from competing companies. In response to the crisis, they discussed how best to deal with this iceberg that they had rammed into so unexpectedly. Rivals now sharing the same lifeboat, they bemoaned their fate.

Was there anything that could be done? Some suggested going to the federal and provincial governments and asking for royalty or tax relief. Others considered cutting budgets, laying off staff, reducing capital, and lowering production numbers. These remedies were all variations on the same theme. The only question seemed to be: How far and how quickly should each of the companies retrench?

Greene listened and felt that familiar discomfort. Everyone around him was going in the same direction, a direction at odds with his own view. His instinctive response to the crisis was radically different. When asked to describe his company's strategy, he voiced his doubts.

"I think this adversity is creating big opportunities," Greene said. In the preceding months, Renaissance had not retreated. Instead, it was hiring more people, ramping up exploration, and had just finished its second equity financing in three months. The riskiest part of the business was buying land and exploring for oil and gas. With land and drilling equipment prices drastically reduced, he felt it was time to grow, not retrench.

Greene's answer floored the others, and the room was silent after he finished. Then the CEO sitting next to Greene, the chairman of IPAC, said what everyone else was thinking: "Greene, you're crazy!"

Greene was surprised by the intensity of their reaction. Still rattled after the meeting, he discussed it with his old partner and chief confidante, Bob Paget. Were they really crazy, or was everyone else in the industry blind to the opportunity? They took apart their strategy and tried to look at it from different angles. Renaissance took pride in having the lowest finding and operating costs in the industry. It was obvious to Greene and Paget that as long as there was an oil and gas industry, they could remain at the profitable end of it. What better way to lock in low finding costs and low operating costs for the future? They would buy land at historically low prices and develop it when drilling costs and service costs were also at historic lows. Where they wanted to take the company was 180 degrees different from the direction everyone else was headed, but they still felt good about it. It was not deliberately contrarian. It was, at least to their eyes, obviously the right way to go.

The analysis was solid. Greene's moment of anxiety passed. The next day, the two men got back to work and executed the strategy they believed in.

They would remember that industry crisis as a turning point for Renaissance Energy. From a junior oil and gas company, constantly scrambling to maintain its cash flow and pay back its debt, Renaissance emerged as the most active and growth-oriented player in the industry. Different ingredients went into that success: people, culture, and relentless focus. But this change in fortunes was swift for a simple reason: when everyone else in the business had gone one way, Renaissance went the other.

Getting Out

Ron Greene has a charm and a kindliness about him, which provides an amiable cover for a tenacious and driven personality. That he has been such a successful business leader surprises him somewhat. It's a strange fate for a guy who was so intent on going his own way that he made himself largely unemployable wherever he worked. But from his earliest days as an entrepreneur, he attracted others who were capable, intelligent, and hardworking—and willing to follow him anywhere. It took Greene years to recognize the effect he had on people.

Greene's overwhelming need for independence arose from his childhood on a farm near Vulcan, Alberta, with a population of around 1,000. Life in rural Alberta felt like life in the dust bowl of the 1930s. His father was a farmer struggling to make enough money to pay for his small farm and equipment. From a young age, Greene had responsibilities that kept him from playing with his friends. He came to see business as a way out. He bought a pig and sold the litter. He bought a cow and sold the calves. And then he bought a horse, which gave him some independence to move around. Later, he sold the horse and bought a motorcycle for more freedom and independence.

Greene attended the University of Calgary. In his second year, he joined a fraternity, partied hard, and studied less.

Luckily, the fraternity he joined gave him his first contacts in the oil and gas industry. It was a course to follow after he graduated.

When he entered the job market, it was in the land department at Sun Oil. It was a temporary position, as a hiring freeze was in effect due to a merger. Sun Oil was in the process of converting its land records into electronic data for mainframe computers. It was dull, methodical, and somewhat mindless work, but Greene applied himself diligently. His managers noticed effort and potential. The hiring freeze was still on, but the top boss offered to send Greene back to school to further his knowledge until Sun Oil was ready for him. To Greene, returning to school felt like moving backward, so he declined the offer and looked for other work.

With his computer experience, Greene was hired as the first employee at a firm that assisted oil and gas companies to computerize their land records. A year later, his job was done.

He was offered a part-time night shift position, but instead went to work on the end of a shovel in the construction industry. The hard labor of shoveling wet cement was a blow to his pride, but he became resolute that he would work in business. He'd read biographies of successful businesspeople and wondered how they did it. He had no great expectations for himself, but he was driven all the same. His main objective was financial independence—to control his own destiny.

In four jobs over five years, Greene learned a series of tough lessons in what *not* to do as a successful entrepreneurial leader. In one case, he went to work for a man named Syd Kahanoff, who'd launched Voyager Petroleum Ltd. Voyager was an upstart oil and gas company with about twenty employees. It was considered an emerging player. Kahanoff, however, had a volatile personality. He hurled abuse at employees, made tyrannical decisions, and wore his people down.

But Greene was eager to learn all he could about the business. He worked hard while taking what Kahanoff threw at him, and he fought back when it got to be too much. Despite a few yelling matches, Kahanoff showed Greene a grudging respect. Greene saw how Kahanoff used and even destroyed others, and he knew that was no way to motivate people. (Ironically, Kahanoff did provide one extremely positive model of leadership. After his unfortunate and early demise, his foundation made enormous contributions to the city of Calgary.)

Another "anti-mentor" for Greene was Larry Darling at Concept Resources. Darling taught Greene what *not* to do to run a business with integrity. Darling was an entrepreneur who had made and lost millions of dollars a couple of times before Greene went to work for him. At age 24, Greene left his position as land manager at Voyager Petroleum Ltd. to be a vice president and director at Concept Resources. Part of his job was to set up a joint venture drilling fund, which was a big step for him.

Greene knew that Darling's business practices had been questioned, but he didn't realize how bad things had gotten until he returned after three weeks off for surgery. On his first morning back, his phone rang about 8 a.m. It was the company's only "outside" director and he wanted to see Greene immediately. Ten minutes later, he walked into Greene's office with a stack of files under his arm. He sat the stack in front of Greene and pointed to them, saying "If you know anything about what is in here, you are going to jail." The files detailed transactions that had been done when Greene was in the hospital. He knew nothing about any of it.

That day, Greene decided to head out on his own. He tendered his resignation from Concept Resources, walked across the street, and purchased a do-it-yourself incorporation manual. Thus began Renaissance Resources Ltd. in April 1974.

Greene resolved to apply the lessons he had learned from his two anti-mentors: Treat people as you would like to be treated and always conduct business with honesty and integrity. These principles would be the foundation of his leadership philosophy as he took the next step forward.

Moving On

One of the most important principles at Renaissance was a deep commitment to treating people with integrity. Its hiring philosophy was to source competent people in every critical discipline and ensure that their compensation reflected their contributions. Renaissance was a leader in setting option- and stock ownership-based compensation policies in the energy industry. Many companies have modeled their compensation plans after Renaissance's. Respect and integrity were critical elements of their culture. Bob Paget, Greene's closest partner at Renaissance, played a key role as watchdog and critic, to ensure that their principles were upheld.

The contrarian moves of 1986 were not the first—or the last—for Renaissance Energy. The company successfully implemented brilliant strategies through the 1980s and early 1990s that were often contrarian or contra-cyclical to the strategies of other exploration and production companies.

The 1990s would become the decade of the junior oil and gas companies, and Renaissance led the way for years as the most active driller in North America. By the summer of 1990, Renaissance had established itself as the thirty-fifth-largest firm in market capitalization on the Toronto Stock Exchange. Attending executive meetings at a Calgary hotel, Greene and his management group walked by a rival company's empty meeting room and spotted copies of the Renaissance annual report on every table. It was a sign of the company's new position and reputation. The go-it-alone company had become the company everyone wanted to follow. Renaissance had raised the consciousness of the entire industry about what was possible.

Renaissance continued to double in size every two to three years. Its culture stayed strong. The company got big, while remaining small in terms of its family loyalty and level of commitment. Renaissance had always been a trailblazer in employee compensation. They provided everyone, including the rank and file, with equity stakes in the business. At the same time, its executives stayed on board despite lucrative offers from rival companies.

In 1995, Bob Paget was diagnosed with pancreatic cancer, which took his life. A year later, Ron Greene presented an annual report titled, "Our Strongest Position Ever," and he called for a moment of silence to honor Paget.

From nothing, Renaissance became a company with over $5 billion in market valuation and 350 employees. It produced over 80,000 barrels of oil and 430 million cubic feet of gas per day. Ron Greene was amazed by how many lives and how many families depended on the success of the company. It was a heavy burden to know that so many people were dependent on what he had created.

He realized that leadership was not about him, it was about them. He was reminded that their achievements were the result of the efforts of devoted employees, dedicating their hearts and souls to make the business succeed. Greene realized that leadership is about letting people realize their full potential. Other people make a good leader great. When an organization becomes successful, hubris can creep in if leadership and employees believe it is because of them. For success to continue, leaders must learn that it is not about them. They must remain humble and remember their beginnings, or hubris will prevail.

One of the most crucial aspects of Greene's job involved investor relations. Over the years, he had stepped increasingly back to let others take over critical operational roles. He ultimately stepped back completely, to become a non-executive chairman. The succession strategy worked smoothly until Renaissance finally got caught in a situation that it neither anticipated nor handled well.

Oil prices plummeted in 1997 with the "Asian Flu," when the economies of such East Asian countries as Thailand and Indonesia collapsed. Too focused on growth, Renaissance had to lower its production forecasts twice, and its share price took a devastating hit.

Ron Greene believes leadership is about responsibility. In an introspective moment, he says that he takes too much responsibility for anything he becomes involved in, so he has to be very careful in making commitments.

He talks about a difficult period at Renaissance, when he had to deal with the questionable business practices of a senior manager in the company. Greene felt responsibility for the breakdown in integrity. Someone needed to take responsibility, and he had no choice but to take on the challenge. In his opinion, if a leader does not have moral integrity, he or she is in no position to lead.

Fallout from the errors of 1997 and 1998 continued, and Renaissance faced missed production targets, as well as questions about its reserves and its ability to grow. This led to management changes and eventually to a merger with Husky Energy, Inc. Greene felt badly for his employees and their own sense of loss. The new organization would affect everyone: Some would keep their jobs and others would lose theirs. It would take the company a few years to get over that change. When he met with some of the old Renaissance people a few years later, a new perspective arose. They weren't so concerned about themselves. They wanted to know how he was doing and how his family was doing. They said they were honestly glad to see him. He felt guilty and disappointed because of the way this incredibly successful company had ended through a merger that looked more like a sale. But the employees who knew what was really going on felt very differently. They felt he had created a good opportunity in a difficult situation. That sentiment was meaningful to Greene and brought him joy. It left him feeling that his integrity had ultimately shone through.

This reinforced Greene's belief that the real meaning of leadership was in creating something with, and for the benefit of, others. At the time, Greene thought that Renaissance was the end of his business career, but it marked a new beginning. He became lead director of the phenomenally successful WestJet Airlines Ltd. and chairman of Denbury Resources Inc., which has become one of the most highly respected junior oil and gas companies on the New York Stock Exchange. Paget and Greene always said how lucky they'd been to be involved in a successful world-class company in the course of their lives. Now Greene has been a major figure in three.

The joyful and meaningful realization that comes from building a successful company is that, whether you realize it or not, you are serving or helping others. Ron Greene and Phil Swift have also spent time in India, participating in humanitarian activities for the needy and underprivileged. As Greene would sum it up, to serve others in need is one of the most noble and joyful things in life. Serving others is not always intentional and can occur in different ways. That service can occur through running a business with integrity and treating employees with dignity.

Business as Sport: The Story of Claude Lamoureux and the Ontario Teachers' Pension Plan

When Claude Lamoureux watches hockey on television, he enjoys the game, but relates more to the coaches than the players. From an early age, he learned the difficulties and satisfactions of directing others to perform and win.

He loved sports as a youth, but an illness left him unable to skate for a year. What would have been a crushing blow to most children became an opportunity to Lamoureux.

Hockey was his favorite sport, so at the age of 14, he became a coach. It was a big responsibility to direct players his own age, but he looks back on it now as a wonderful gift. And he was surprisingly good at it. He learned to make difficult decisions, such as pulling friends off the ice. It was never fun to take someone out of the play, particularly, when you'd need them to come back and work hard for you later.

This responsibility emotionally prepared Lamoureux for a lifetime of leadership. Forty years later, at the helm of one of the biggest pension funds in North America, Claude Lamoureux would need to make some tough decisions indeed.

Getting into the Game

Lamoureux thinks that in some ways, business should be run more like sports. In both fields, thousands of decisions need to be made. Many of the most difficult ones are based on people's performance and their ability to help the team. Picking the right people is hard, but letting the wrong people go can be even harder. You need to release people who don't fit the team's needs, and you need to make those decisions early.

In that regard, Lamoureux has been a success. Although a firing can be the most acrimonious encounter between boss and employee, it need not be a negative experience. Some people have thanked Lamoureux for letting them go. His sincerity and evenhandedness let them realize that his decision was fair. They might walk away saying, "Claude did me a favor." No matter how painful a decision it may be to cut someone, you can't postpone that decision in hopes that things will improve. A leader needs to think clearly and realistically, while remaining caring and genuine.

Lamoureux's first job out of school was with MetLife in New York. There were 10,000 people there, with 1,000 in the controller's department working on old Monroe calculators. The noise was deafening.

Lamoureux quickly learned a powerful lesson: It was important to have a good boss. His first boss was fabulous. He was open and he treated people the way he wanted to be treated. Lamoureux learned a lot about leading by watching him. He learned the importance of emulating the people who impressed him. His boss always thought the team could do better and was constantly pushing, but he treated people fairly and developed a solid organization. His boss said, "You work hard, get the best people, and then you get results." It was a viewpoint Lamoureux would adopt himself.

Lamoureux's boss saw talent in him and made him manager of his group. Claude questioned the decision, thinking the job was too big for him. But his boss wanted Lamoureux to give it a try because he wasn't getting the results he needed.

So, just as he had done as a young hockey coach, Lamoureux learned to lead a group of peers. He developed a team of talented people, and they all "worked like hell." His affinity for people was genuine, but he was also clear about his need to get the right people on his team. Again, he had to make tough personnel decisions right away to create the conditions for success.

Lamoureux was next asked to lead a small pension group for MetLife. It had 120 financial analysts, and the business was losing money. His boss said, "We're giving you a mess, but we think you can make it work." In three years, Claude turned it around, making it one of the most profitable groups in the company. He built the right team and culture, and focused everyone on the bottom line. Later he did the same thing with MetLife's marketing team. He took a group that was dispirited and losing money and reversed its fortunes.

Eventually, Lamoureux became head of MetLife's Canadian operation. By then, he had worked there for 24 years and had become one of the top five people in the company. He saw that the financial service industry was changing, and he developed a company plan for the next five years. He believed that the Canadian operation had to get larger, or it would be bought out. He also wanted to raise money in the Canadian market. Feeling confident of his strategy, Lamoureux made the pitch for his plan in New York, but senior executives saw things differently. They didn't like his idea of entering new growth areas. Being at odds with the head office was a career killer. Lamoureux said, "They wanted to move me to New York and put me in the penalty box."

He was forced to leave the company. For a leader who had seen great success for his entire career, it was a tough blow. Then, one year later, his best friend became the company president. If business is like sport, then sometimes the outcomes are not what you hoped for, no matter how much passion you poured into winning. For coach and player alike, it's not easy being on the losing team.

Avoiding the Iceberg

In 1990, the Ontario Teachers' Pension Plan (OTPP) was about to change. For 73 years, it had been administered by an agency of the Ontario provincial government. But its deficit was mounting and problems were starting to surface. A decision was made to establish the OTPP as an independent corporation.

Lamoureux was only moderately interested when he first interviewed there, as he was more focused on the insurance industry. He had lunch with Gerald Bouey, former governor of the Bank of Canada and OTPP chairman. The two men hit it off. Bouey made an offer to Lamoureux to lead the organization, and Lamoureux said he would give it serious thought—even though he was thinking of moving in a different direction.

He had always wanted a demanding board as a way of embracing excellence at the top. With people like Gerald Bouey, Ted Medland, Gail Cook Bennett, and Margaret Wilson, he would have just that. In part, it was his respect for those board members that intrigued him. Sold on the job, Lamoureux promised to transform the OTPP from an $18 billion portfolio of government bonds and indexed equity funds into a broad-based active-investment manager.

Hiring the right people was critical. One key hire was Bob Bertram, a passionate genius who would set things on the right track. Both men wanted to run the OTPP like a company focused on the bottom line, in contrast to its previous passive pension fund strategies. They worried about liabilities as much as assets. Their plan let the OTPP grow from $18 billion in passively managed assets to $80 billion in actively managed financial assets, outperforming key benchmarks. It is now one of the largest and most respected pension funds in Canada. It is also one of the largest private equity managers in the country—and in North America.

Getting there was an enormous task. Lamoureux and Bertram inherited a huge portfolio of nonmarketable and nonnegotiable securities. Bertram and another early hire, derivatives expert Neil Petroff, came up with a plan using derivatives that created a $1 billion swap of a portion of these assets into marketable securities. To convince the board to make such a radical change, they briefed them and sold them on the benefits. The OTPP became one of the first pension funds in Canada to use derivatives as a financial tool.

Hiring the right people was easy compared to the administrative challenges that they faced. They had over 100,000 pensions, and they needed to recalculate 55,000 of them. To do this, they had to improve their information technology. When Lamoureux was the controller at MetLife, he had the use of a $250 to $500 million information system. At the OTPP, they still relied on hand-entered information, microfiche, and data cards. But when they undertook a detailed pension analysis, Lamoureux and his team discovered something shocking. The historical and future overpayments were close to $150 million, and the retroactive and future increases in pensions were around $350 million.

In fact, the errors were systemic, complex, and pervasive. There was no one root cause—it was the accumulation of thousands of small mistakes over decades. Some pensioners had been getting less money than they were owed for years. Other pensioners were getting more money than they deserved. Once the leadership team saw the extent of the problem, they had to make a critical decision. They could pretend nothing had happened, or they could fix the problem for the future but not tell anyone what had gone wrong, or they could announce their findings and promise to remedy the problems. The last option was the most painful, and also the most likely to create panic and lack of confidence. Lamoureux knew that it was the only option truly available to him—legally, as well as in terms of leadership credibility.

The OTPP faced another critical decision. What to do about the miscalculations that affected individual pension holders?

Lamoureux decided that although it was not a legal ruling, it was critical to fulfilling the organization's mandate. First, the OTTP would not reduce the pensions of those who had been overpaid for years. It would continue the pensions at the same rate, since lowering a retired person's income might disrupt his or her lifestyle. Secondly, the OTTP would pay back all the money owed to those with reduced pensions.

The financial hit would be enormous. On December 4, 1995, Lamoureux stood before a conference of business leaders and news media to deliver the shocking news. Yet the crisis did not destroy the OTPP. In fact, it would turn out to be its finest hour.

Leadership by Example

Under Lamoureux's leadership, not only has the OTPP become an active manager, but it has also beaten key benchmarks in all asset classes each year. Lamoureux brought discipline and teamwork to the organization. With about 150 investment professionals working for him, he knows there is no way that he can supervise what each person is doing. Investing is a humbling business, since every investment number is there for the world to see. Lamoureux learned to be more patient and to let people make their own mistakes. He would first nurture and develop them, then trust them with a lot of money. As he put it, "Investment is a team sport, and we need to understand each other." Even young people can speak at the investment committee. The team is now more mature, and everyone works well together. They trust each other. Sometimes when you're young, you think it can be done in a year or two, but the secret of success is the long term.

Lamoureux believes that management by example (MBE) is more impactful than management by objectives (MBO). If an organization needs lots of work done, then its leaders have to work hard. They need to be smart, enthusiastic, committed, and excited about coming to work. The key is finding people who are eager to imitate their manager, and who put their heart and soul into it. One candidate stuttered throughout his interview, but wanted the job so badly that he was hired anyway. He turned out to be an outstanding performer. As David Ogilvy, founder of the large advertising firm Ogilvy & Mather, said, "If you like to grow roses and go home at 5 p.m., we like you but don't come here to work." Lamoureux knows the importance of finding people who love the work and have a passion, since passion will overcome many obstacles.

How does one become a leader? For Lamoureux, the answer goes back to thc illness that sidelined him from playing hockey. He could have watched from the stands, pining for his loss, but he chose to contribute. Sometimes, when an opportunity presents itself, one has to stand up and say, "I'll do it." Given the opportunity, you either choose to lead or you don't. Lamoureux gets one of his great satisfactions from developing people's leadership abilities. His people see him as a tireless leader with the qualities and characteristics of the best: humble, sincere, visionary, and motivating.

Lamoureux is fond of walking the hallways, even into the evening. He meets others who are still working late. He encourages them in their work. He knows the names of most of his employees. His personal touch is genuine and meaningful. In word and deed, he puts the needs of the organization above his own.

One of the leadership choices that Lamoureux has made in recent years is in corporate governance. He felt that there was great value in having a tough, honest board. He's seen the benefits of being straight with shareholders and customers when mistakes happen. Even before the financial scandals of

Enron, Tyco, and WorldCom, Lamoureux became an advocate for strong corporate governance. As the head of one of Canada's largest funds, he felt that it was not only his fiduciary duty but also his leadership duty to remedy a situation that worried him deeply.

As a powerful institutional shareholder, Teachers' became a strong voice demanding corporate governance reform. Opponents of reform characterized Lamoureux as a governance zealot, who restricted a corporation's ability to act according to its own best judgment. But in Lamoureux's view, good governance is good business. Making boards more demanding, and executive leadership more responsive, is a top-down means of improving performance. Picking his battles carefully, Lamoureux has been one of the key leaders of this charge in recent years. As scandals spread to many organizations in North America, his efforts gained growing support.

Leadership is sometimes about seeing what needs to be done and then doing it. It doesn't matter the arena or how successful you are. The important thing is to put your heart into it because you know it's a game worth playing.

Claude Lamoureux retired as president and CEO of the Ontario Teachers' Pension Plan Board on December 1, 2007.

Were It Not for Kindness: The Story of Henri Landwirth and Give Kids The World

Henri Landwirth divides his life into sections. The breadth of emotions and experiences embraced by those sections might seem unbelievable even in a Hollywood movie. But Landwirth's remarkable journey offers testimony to the best and the worst that humankind has wrought in this world. He was shaped by an idyllic European childhood in a loving family, as well as by his survival of Nazi death camps. A true Horatio Alger story, he rose from penniless immigrant to hotel mogul. Ultimately, his is a heart-wrenching story of philanthropy that has touched the lives of the most vulnerable and needy.

As is true of many of the people in this book, leadership for Henri Landwirth was never the goal. Leadership was the means by which he realized his dreams. Even so, Landwirth's approach to work, managing people, and giving of himself makes him an inspirational model of leadership. Were it not for the kindness of strangers, he never would have survived the tragedies of his youth. Were it not for the kindness that he showed to others, this world would be a lesser place.

Childhood

Until age 13, everything in Henri Landwirth's life was good. His parents were beautiful, successful, and loving. He was close to his twin sister Margot, whom he called "Doda." The Landwirths lived comfortably in Belgium and later Poland. But by 1939, Henri's father Max grew concerned about the tensions and conflicts surrounding the rise of the Nazis. Even so, his wife Fanny did not want to uproot their family and flee Europe, as long as they were together and had a home to live in.

Little did anyone realize how soon life would change. After the Nazis invaded Poland, Henri watched soldiers ransack his home for valuables while a gun was held to his father's head. That same year, Max Landwirth was arrested and taken from his family without cause. It was the start of the great sadness in Henri's life. His mother risked everything to win her husband's release, but without success. Later they learned that Max had been executed with a bullet to the back of the head and buried in a mass grave.

The family was driven from their home and into the walled Krakow ghetto. While pointless tragedy was commonplace, Henri witnessed many acts of bravery and kindness. When the Jews of Krakow were rounded up by the Nazis, healthy young men were separated from women, children, the old, and the sick. A young man, Landwirth was separated from his mother and sister Margot, and sent to a labor camp. Despite the cruelty he experienced at the labor camp, it was only after he had been sent to Auschwitz that he realized that the camps had been built to exterminate Jews.

At Auschwitz, the horrors were unimaginable. The sick, the old, and the infants were murdered first. Amid such grief, suffering, and humiliation, people's spirits withered and their existence became a struggle to attain life's most basic needs. The young Henri endured the pain of constant hunger and thirst for five years. He was sustained by the belief that someday he would find his sister and mother. His defiant determination to live grew stronger as the Nazis tried to hasten his death. Like everyone around him, he wondered where God could be in the midst of such pain and suffering.

Eventually, he realized that God was everywhere. He was in the spirit of each survivor and in the small acts of kindness that kept each person alive.

From Auschwitz, Henri was sent to a series of labor camps, each one more inhumane than the one before. Finally, he was interned in an underground camp where he did not see the sun for a year. He slept in his own fleas. When typhoid broke out, the sick were piled into a single room to die. Mysteriously, in the middle of the night, an unknown man walked over the bodies and roused Landwirth from a feverish sleep. The man gave him a pill and a drink of water. When Landwirth woke the next morning, the room was filled with corpses. He sensed that an angel had visited him, and it gave him a strange power—the will to go on.

Homeless

In 1944, Allied bombing raids had killed most of the people in the munitions camp. The survivors were rounded up and led off to be executed. Landwirth and two other prisoners were taken to the woods expecting to be killed. At the edge of the forest, a soldier—tired of killing—let them escape. He told them to run when he fired his gun.

Near death from starvation and plagued with festering wounds, Landwirth stole food and kept himself hidden as he moved from village to village. After weeks without human contact, he was found sleeping in an empty house by an old couple who took him in. They bathed him, fed him, and called a doctor, who saw that his leg was badly infected. The couple nursed him back to health and reacquainted him with human decency.

He learned that his mother's death had occurred only weeks before the war ended, but found that his sister was alive in a German town. After Landwirth walked 500 miles to reach it, no one there had heard of a girl named Margot. But when he called out her nickname, Doda, Margot heard his voice and came running to him.

The war had changed both of them greatly. Landwirth was 19 years old and filled with anger and hate. If he had encountered

a former Nazi guard, he would not have hesitated to kill him. He worked for the Allies translating for their interrogations. He took pleasure in seeing former Nazis arrested and punished. He formed a gang that smuggled medicine across the border for money, with no fear of getting caught. Later, he worked for the Jewish Underground to save the Jews who had survived the war but were unable to flee Europe. Still, hate and pain were eating him up.

Landwirth wondered why he survived when so many died. Did God have special intentions for him? He realized that he could not truly live again if he didn't transform his anger into love and caring.

This realization freed him to embark on a new path and leave his hatred behind. Released from that burden, he decided to seek success. By succeeding, he would help others too. It didn't matter how challenging that path might be. After Auschwitz, life's normal disappointments and difficulties were trivial.

New World

He traveled by ship to New York, unable to speak English and with only $20 in his pocket. He worked a series of jobs as a laborer. He did anything that came his way, but he did it to the best of his abilities to honor the memory of his parents. Eventually, he found himself in the hospitality industry because it did not require a college education. Willing to work harder than anyone else, he did every entry-level job in the hotel.

He soon learned that success in the hotel business meant pleasing people: Figure out what they need, give them what they want, and always provide the best service possible. It was a lasting lesson: Success in business comes from success with people. Listen carefully to them, and you'll find out what people want.

Landwirth got married and left New York for Miami in hopes of a better life. He continued working in hotels. His salary was miniscule, but he enjoyed the rewards of doing a job right. He assumed more responsibility and assembled a team of people who worked as hard as he did.

Whenever the hotel faced a problem, he asked himself what solution would be best for the customer. His ideas worked, and he discovered that he had a talent for business. One day, a customer needed a necktie, which was required to enter the dining room. Landwirth offered him his own. That customer was B. G. McNabb, manager of the Intercontinental Ballistic Missiles Division of General Dynamics, one of the companies that had been contracted to develop the U.S. space program. McNabb was in Florida to build a motel in Cocoa Beach to house workers for the space program. He named it the Starlight Motel and he asked Henri Landwirth to run it.

Blast Off

Landwirth worked tirelessly to refine the service and the facilities at the Starlight Motel—and its popular Starlight Lounge—until it offered a world-class atmosphere. Because of his emphasis on customer service, Landwirth was the first person many in the community turned to when they needed help. He became the unofficial host of Cocoa Beach, a close friend to the Mercury Seven astronauts and to journalists like Walter Cronkite.

Landwirth was young, energetic, friendly, and possessed a mischievous sense of humor. The astronauts lived hard and played hard, and would blow off steam by engaging Landwirth in practical jokes. Even though the space program was shrouded in strict military secrecy, Landwirth enthusiastically celebrated the young astronauts' successes. He threw lavish parties, twisted civic leaders' arms to hold a parade when President Kennedy visited, and even served a giant cake that looked like Gordon Cooper's space capsule to celebrate his successful flight.

Landwirth was successful enough to be lured away from the Starlight. He took over the Lakeland Holiday Inn, and quickly uncovered some challenges. Its manager refused lodging to African-Americans at the hotel. Landwirth fired him immediately.

Assuming the manager's job himself, he realized that the staff would never provide the kind of service necessary for success. Within three weeks he had fired all but two and replaced the rest, assembling a great team. The hotel soon prospered. And when Walter Cronkite broadcast a news report with the Holiday Inn sign in the background, it helped propel the franchise into national prominence.

In business, Landwirth always did what he thought was right, even when it put his career in jeopardy. His integrity was proven again and again. His staff appreciated his leadership because he had done every one of their jobs himself. He also knew each of them—and their families—personally. He treated everyone with respect and dignity, from the wealthiest guest to the poorest member of the cleaning staff. He embraced those who shared his values of diligence, service, and hard work.

Henri also focused on the needs of children, who he treated as special guests of his hotel. He believed that if the children were happy, the parents would be happy—and more inclined to return as customers. He was devoted to great service and attention to detail. He never allowed himself to worry about the competition. As a result, his hotels were always desirable places to stay, filled to capacity, and highly profitable.

Soon, his connections and capital allowed him to go into the hotel business as a developer. He became partners with the Mercury astronaut John Glenn. Glenn was the charming political front man and Landwirth the magician of hotel management. (John Quinn, a financial and real estate expert, also became a partner.)

When the Walt Disney Company decided to build its theme park in Orlando, Florida, Landwirth and his partners obtained the franchise for its first Holiday Inn. Landwirth's generosity to children was well suited to this new trend in family entertainment. All his years of hard work—doing the best job he could, caring for his people, seeing to the customer's needs, making sure that children were welcome—came together in an explosion of growth.

The Suffering of the Innocent

Landwirth now had wealth, business success, friendships, and accolades. Still, he felt that something was missing. There was a numbness inside. It affected his family. It returned whenever he let the commotion of his life ease up for a moment. When he slowed down to enjoy the fruits of his labor, he would find himself thinking about the suffering of the innocent. Of all the horrors and humiliations he had witnessed, he grieved for the children the most.

In 1986, a little girl with incurable cancer expressed a wish to visit Disney World. Landwirth wanted her to be a guest of his Holiday Inn. But the arrangements took weeks and the child died before she could make the trip. The pain Landwirth felt over this propelled him into action. It was not right for children who were dying or seriously ill to have their wishes thwarted. Something needed to be done. He knew that this need was tapping into the thing that had been missing in his life. Landwirth focused his urgency, energy, and vision to the dream that was forming inside him.

He approached Disney with a plan to bring foundations, corporations, and individuals together to help sick children and their families. He called it Give Kids The World.

Disney agreed on the spot. Sea World followed suit.

Landwirth asked the Mercury astronauts, Walter Cronkite, and newspaper columnist Art Buchwald to join in. He acquired office space, solicited donations, and arranged for 87 Orlando-area hotels to provide rooms.

That first year, Give Kids The World helped realize Landwirth's dream by bringing 380 families to Orlando. There were so many applicants that new housing had to be built for the visiting families. And so the Give Kids The World Village was born.

Landwirth began with 35 acres of land, where spectacular villas would replace swamps and burnt-out orange groves. He spoke to everyone about his vision. He generated excitement and momentum, recruiting thousands of volunteers and contributors. In the spirit of a great cause, corporate sponsors one-upped each other to provide resources, equipment, and man-hours for the project. Landwirth let no obstacle stop him, which wore him out physically. But every time he despaired that the project would fail or fall short, a miracle or coincidence answered his need.

Landwirth ultimately built a 16-villa complex spread over 61 acres. It featured swimming pools, a water park, game rooms, a "Castle of Miracles," a restaurant, and rooms for thousands of children and their families. The project had been completed without debt and with no written contracts, except to purchase the land. Despite its corporate donors, the complex was also logo-free.

Over the years, the Village has expanded. Landwirth runs it like a service business with extra heart. About 3,000 volunteers work on-site and 67,000 families have visited. A network of relationships with over 250 wish-granting organizations worldwide ensures that seriously ill children who want to visit Disney World can do so with little delay.

When families arrive in Orlando, they're greeted at the airport by a volunteer and brought to the Village. The children's faces light up when they see where they are going to stay. The parents, weary from their everyday struggles, may take a bit more time to relax.

On the first day, the parents are often reserved and formal. By the second day, their tension dissipates and they seem more peaceful. No one can totally lift their burden, but the joy of seeing their sick child enjoy special pleasures certainly eases their load. There was one child who doctors worried would not survive the plane flight. But she hopped out of her wheelchair on arrival at the Village and ran toward the topiary garden to look at the funny animals clipped out of hedges. Her mother was so astonished that she called the doctor, but the doctor simply told her to let her child enjoy herself. That little girl lived another six months, which was far longer than anyone had expected.

The relief on those parents' faces shows the power of spiritual healing. Medical realities are unavoidable and most of the children who visit the Village will never recover. But Landwirth knows that those children are given a gift of happiness, and each day parents can spend watching their children play is precious.

Giving More

Landwirth sees the connection between his youth, his business success, and his philanthropy. He believes that he survived the death camps of Nazi Germany to offer a hand to people in need, especially children. He believes in life's deeper meaning and a higher power. He recognizes that each of us has a responsibility to take action in our own corner of the world. He is compelled to make a difference in the lives of the most vulnerable. The more he can do for others, the more fulfilled he feels. The rewards are plentiful.

His great joy can be seen on his face. He is a private man, but one filled with energy and love. There's a lot of hugging and laughing in his world.

Amazingly, he transformed the hate that devastated his youth into love. He became a success despite so many disadvantages: poverty, loss of his family, lack of a formal education, and the challenge of learning his adopted country's language. But Landwirth learned that it's important to make the most of what you have inside. The path a person's life takes is ultimately determined by that person's spiritual values and beliefs. Landwirth understands that he might never have succeeded if he hadn't gone through so much agony to learn the importance of caring and love. He also knows that as a leader, he couldn't give so much of himself if it wasn't for his feelings of fulfillment from serving others.

We asked him about knowing when enough was *enough.* His reaction was telling. As a businessman, it had been relatively easy for him to discover his own limits, although he had seen how difficult it could be for others. When Landwirth had amassed a certain amount of wealth, it meant less and less to him. He turned to something more fulfilling.

One day he realized that he would have to leave Give Kids The World. It was a tough challenge for him to reduce his involvement in his philanthropic efforts. It would have been emotionally fulfilling to remain in charge of operations, but his health was not robust enough for its intense demands. He turned the leadership role over to others.

At age 72, Henri Landwirth tried to retire from philanthropy. He anticipated that it would be tough to stay away from the office, so he moved to another part of Florida. But he soon became bored. An emptiness had set in and he knew he needed another cause. Within six weeks he'd found one.

He had always felt a bond with homeless people. Their plight reminded him of his life after the war: wandering around in rags, starving, racked with festering wounds, foraging for food, stealing clothes. He and his daughter visited a homeless shelter to see what he could do. He talked with residents there about what they needed most. It became clear that homeless people needed clothes as much as food and shelter.

Landwirth got right to work phoning his old contacts. Soon he had started Dignity U Wear, which would donate clothes and food to homeless people around the country.

It's no surprise that Henri Landwirth keeps so active. Leaders who have been shaped by tragic circumstances at a formative age often find it difficult to deny their life's mission. Giving to others helped make Henri Landwirth whole. Through service to others, he knows he is ultimately serving himself.

Life-Altering Events: The Story of John Hammergren and the McKesson Corporation

John Hammergren became CEO of McKesson Corporation in 2001. The next year, at only 46, he also became the chairman, making him one of the youngest people ever to run a Fortune 50 company. In the first three years of Hammergren's ascent, McKesson had a run rate of over $80 billion in annual revenue. That was twice the revenue it had when he assumed the top role. Under Hammergren's leadership, profits tripled and the company advanced to No. 15 on the Fortune 500. At the same time, McKesson emerged as the leading provider of supplies, information, and care management solutions to the health care industry.

John Hammergren may not be a household name like Jack Welch of GE or Andy Grove of Intel, but he has risen faster than either of those men by his age. After a successful career in the health care field, Hammergren now takes pride at the helm of the world's largest health care services company. Despite its lack of visibility, the McKesson Corporation is a venerable company. It traces its roots back to 1833, when John McKesson and Chester Olcott opened a drug import wholesale company in New York City's financial district. Their partnership thrived by providing customers with botanical drugs like herbs, leaves, bark, and vegetable extracts. The company expanded its business with ventures into alcoholic beverage distribution, milk-based products, and processed water.

The company was renamed McKesson Corporation in 1984, and divested itself of its nonperipheral businesses. Instead, it focused on research and development and strategic acquisitions, particularly in technology. It entered the twenty-first century—its third century in business—merging its health care information and supply management businesses to establish itself as the world's largest health care services company.

John Hammergren is coming of age as a global executive with a growing reputation as an exceptional leader. Warren Bennis recognized Hammergren for excellence in leadership at the 2004 conference of the Global Institute for Leadership Development. We spoke with Hammergren then about his life and leadership journey.

Hammergren projects a distinct air of sincerity that conveys trust, wisdom, and caring. In discussion, he finds a way to touch on values and beliefs. He is crystal clear that leadership is about: a) core values; b) committing to continuous improvement within the leader's sphere of influence; and c) seeing collaborative approaches to serving customers. In an age where the ethics and integrity of big companies are called into question, no question marks surround John Hammergren. His leadership is set into the bedrock of enduring principles.

Life-Altering Events

(*Hammergren made these remarks about his leadership journey when he accepted the Warren Bennis Award.*)

> When I was 16 years old, I woke up one morning and my father was gone. He had been diagnosed with pancreatic cancer and died within 12 months. This left my mother and me alone to fend for ourselves economically, socially, and emotionally. My mother hadn't worked in 30 years. She had been a housewife, raising a family, and was nearing retirement with my father when that tragedy befell us. Neither one of us were sure of the way forward.

My mother didn't have the economic ability to survive on her own, and I was still struggling to figure out how I would grow up.

This experience reflects how I became who I am. I was raised in a small town in Minnesota, about 140 miles northwest of Minneapolis. I had a great childhood. My middle-class family was hard-working. I was an Eagle Scout with mostly straight A grades in high school. Everything in my life was going well, until I woke up one day without a father.

Deeply shocked by this sudden change, I looked around my rural high school of about 600 students and started to think about the other students who didn't have two parents. Most of us were farm kids, bused to school from long distances. Quite a few of us were missing a mother, a father, or a brother from some tragedy, death, divorce, alcoholism, or abuse. Among my friends and my teammates on the football and hockey teams, those who were missing a parent seemed to lack an internal compass. The tragic, life-altering event that had visited their lives failed to galvanize them to do something positive. Instead, they lost their way and were influenced by people who guided them down the wrong path.

The loss of my father scared me for those reasons. As a result, I began to think about principles for living my life. I knew that I needed to keep myself centered. I did not want to find myself heading down the wrong path, like so many other kids. Naturally, as a young man, I frequently tested boundaries and limits; but now I began to think more about what I valued. I knew that I needed to deal deliberately with this new life. If I didn't, I feared that I could be lost.

Many of us have experienced such moments in our lives, or read about those who have. Clearly, trauma can help galvanize a person's conviction and confidence—even their personality and ambition. Most great leaders and organizations experience life-altering events. Periods of tremendous challenge always create tremendous choices and opportunities. Facing such difficulties, we are forced to make decisions about where we want to go, how we wish to travel, and what we ultimately stand for.

Of course, a young person experiencing a life-altering event might not always have clarity at that moment about what he or she ultimately wants in life. You might not know what leadership capacity you want to develop or how you want to spend your career. Nevertheless, you are aware that the decisions you make can set your destiny. In my life—from the death of my father, to my early working life, through the time when I was building my career—that awareness continued to frame my point of view.

Home for Dinner

Along the way, I had help from others who reinforced those beliefs. For instance, when I finished at the University of Minnesota, I was hired right away by American Hospital Supply. There, I was awestruck when the 80-year-old chairman emeritus came to one of our first sales meetings and introduced himself to me. He said, 'Young man, you were hired because I would be proud to have you to my home for dinner. You would be welcome at my home any time. So if you come to Chicago, I want you to give me a call and join me and my family for dinner.'

At the time, American Hospital Supply was a company of 30,000 employees and a leader in its industry. I was impressed that the chairman would reach out to a young sales rep and say, 'I hire people not for what they are doing today, but for what they can be. I make that judgment of their potential based on whether or not I would be proud to bring them home with me to have dinner with my family.'

That perception acted as a filter for bringing people into the organization's family, and it has stayed with me during my career. As a result, I've also tried to surround myself with people I would be proud to bring home and introduce to my family. I enjoy spending both work and personal time with them because I trust and like them.

When leaders get together and talk about the job, they often discuss the importance of execution, focus, and being oriented toward results. These concerns go in and out of fashion. Right now, some people argue that execution beats strategy every day. But I believe that culture beats execution every day. In fact, culture is the foundation of execution, and people are the foundation of culture.

My chairman at American Hospital Supply was right to evaluate people the way he did. Having pride in inviting someone home to dinner is a strong indication that you have selected the right person. In order to gather the people you want to have by your side in whatever daily battles arise, you need to feel as good about those people spending time in your home as you do about them representing your company in the marketplace.

The Importance of Culture

Beyond selecting the right people, a leader also must set a cultural climate. As an organization, McKesson has experienced tremendous growth over its 170-year history. But in 1999, we went through a period of turmoil during which I was named CEO. We had gone awry and were following the wrong path. In a world of ever-increasing stock prices and short-term Wall Street goals, we became highly focused on one metric in our business and lost a balanced approach to the evaluation of culture. Hitting the numbers, executing the strategy, focusing relentlessly on business goals—those concerns became the single measurement by which we evaluated ourselves. We no longer focused on our ability to hire the right people, develop them, and lead and inspire.

Our stock price trailed off. The dot-coms began picking us apart. We were a broken organization. But this turmoil gave us a chance to retrench, reevaluate our culture, and think about the values of our company. We looked at what factors were important to us from a retention perspective and launched a new set of shared principles as a team.

We called the shared principles 'I CARE.' This stands for 'Integrity, Customer-first, Accountability, Respect, and Excellence.' We now talk about those shared principles in our hiring process as well as in our mentoring and on-boarding processes. We talk about them with our customers and with all the constituents that we serve. Our shared principles have also become the most important factors in our performance evaluations. If someone violates the principles, regardless of that person's financial contributions, they won't be elevated to the next level. In other words, if you are an excellent performer on the financial side of the ledger but a poor performer on the cultural side, you may not be allowed to stay with the organization.

During turmoil, opportunities arise to assess and set principles that determine the way forward. Having the right culture, the right values, and the right strategy executed with excellence has allowed us to win in the marketplace and create a world-class team.

The Leader's Role

Culture is formed by a leader's ability to build trust. In turn, the ability to build trust is based on your ability to understand the people that you are required to lead. A leader needs to know what those needs are, while also being aware of the organization's needs. And a leader must recognize that the organization's needs and the individual's needs may not always be aligned. Even though the leader is responsible for the organization as a whole, that leader must also influence or set the direction of each individual in order to maximize their performance. It's not an easy task. This capability comes down to the balancing of 'I' and 'we.' Some leaders talk on the 'I' side, for themselves and many individuals in their organizations. Others have a more collaborative approach to management that focuses on execution as it contributes to the 'we.'

The key for future leaders, as you grow and expand your responsibilities, is to develop a capacity to move between the 'I' and 'we' perspectives. You will never encounter a black-and-white situation, in which one viewpoint clearly trumps the other. If you find yourself in a situation where somebody is looking to you for help making a decision, you need to make that decision and move on. If your people have the ability and desire to lead on their own, you must fall back and allow them to lead in a more team-oriented way.

In the book *Everybody Wins* (Wiley, 2004) there is a chapter about bicycle racing. The sport of cycling, as exemplified by Lance Armstrong and his team of cyclists at the Tour de France, is a combination of individual and team performance. A cyclist will draft along with his team for a while, pulled along by their momentum, then move to the front and take his turn leading the fight up the next hill.

In my view, winning business teams know how to function by putting different people in the lead at different times to carry different legs of the race. The team optimizes its performance at all times by allowing some to pull the load for a while, as others draft along, waiting for their turn.

World-class organizations function this way. The success of a great organization is not about Jack Welch as CEO, but about having an organization filled with individuals with the ability to be the leader when the need arises. When executing a particular strategy or development effort, someone is always in charge, leading the pack with other members of the team surrounding them to make sure that they are successful.

It is not easy for a leader to handle that dynamic. You can't lose control of the enterprise and see it turn to chaos. At the same time, you can't usurp the power and responsibilities of the people around you. You need to allow a winning leader to emerge from the pack and lead the team while also creating other winning leaders. The key is having a good sense of perception on the balance between 'I' and 'we.'

I've spent the last 25 years of my life trying to determine how to effectively lead. It's a constant process of internal reflection and review. As a leader, you experience frequent criticism and doubt about your ability to do what you need to do in the next phase. If you have the right instincts, put the interests of your people at the forefront of your decision making, and put your customers' best interests in the balance as well, you will create a winning culture and a winning organization.

Her Father's Table: The Story of Rafiah Salim and The International Center For Leadership In Finance

Rafiah Salim is representative of a new class of women leaders in Asia. A leadership pioneer for the past 50 years, she carved new territory for women in Malaysia by becoming a lawyer, then the first dean of a university law school. She also became a senior human resources (HR) officer for Malayan Banking Berhad, an assistant governor with Bank Negara Malaysia, and the senior HR leader at the United Nations. Today she is living her dream by developing the next generation of top leaders in her country at the International Center For Leadership In Finance (ICLIF), where she serves as executive director.

When we met Rafiah, we were struck by her focus, her passion for excellence, and her ability to speak directly with grace and ease. It is clear that Rafiah is comfortable with herself and feels no pressure to impress others. She discusses issues and challenges candidly.

Rafiah Salim was born to parents without means in a small village in Malaysia, which would not become an independent state until 1957. Malaysia borders Thailand, Indonesia and Singapore. Malaysia's history was shaped by Indian, Chinese, and later, British colonial influences and a mix of Muslim, Buddhist, Hindu, and Christian religions. It embraces multiple faiths, languages, and cultures, with a population that's 50 percent Malay, 33 percent Chinese, and 9 percent Indian, with an assortment of indigenous peoples making up the rest.

When Salim was a girl, there were fewer than 15 million people in Malaysia. There were no super-cities. Today, the population has doubled; and its capital Kuala Lumpur has emerged as an international city, whose twin towers are the world's tallest. Although the country retains its rural character, it has become an important economic engine in the region, with an open and adaptable culture.

Rafiah Salim was educated in a British-modeled school system, but was also shaped by strong ethnic and religious traditions. She was impressed with the legal traditions inherited from the British. She admired the sense of fairness and order of their bicameral parliament, a true house of representatives.

Central to her character was a sense of doing the right thing in the right way for the right reasons. Yet how far could a Muslim woman of modest means go in the twentieth century?

This question is answered by a statement issued by the spokesman for United Nations Secretary-General Kofi Annan on August 27, 1997: "The Secretary-General has decided to appoint Rafiah Salim, a national of Malaysia, as Assistant Secretary-General for Human Resources Management. Mrs. Salim's appointment will be effective on 15 October 1997. She will succeed Denis Halliday, who is taking up his appointment as Humanitarian Coordinator of the Oil-for-Food Program on 1 September 1997."

Such are the mysteries of the leadership journey. We never know where or how far the drive to lead can carry us.

From Village to School

Rafiah Salim started her leadership journey at her father's table. In Malaysia, girls were relegated to domestic chores, serving the men and boys. Rafiah's mother served her husband and ate separately from him. But Rafiah's father called her to his table. He liked her questions and enjoyed her ability to understand complexity. Did he see a leader in her? Did he understand her potential?

When Rafiah speaks of her father, her face shines. Her eyes well up when she recalls how he recognized her character and abilities. Repeatedly, he told her that she could—and should—strive for achievement in her life. He framed her perspective by treating her with the respect of a leader and giving her the belief that for her anything was possible. He did this in a Muslim family that was devout in its daily spirituality and deeply faithful to Islam.

It must have been difficult for this reverent man to encourage his 10-year-old daughter, his favorite child, to attend boarding school. But he wanted more for her. At the time, Malaysia was a country with a deep social divide. There were only two social classes: the few with means and access and the less fortunate living in villages.

Many children might have been intimidated by boarding school; but Salim had courage, passion, and purpose. She wanted to be something and to make a difference. She needed to pass a test to win a scholarship, since there was no other way to pay for her schooling. With her father's guidance, Rafiah won the scholarship.

At age 11, Rafiah left her village for a journey that would transform her. She didn't know what was ahead of her or even where she was going. "When I got on the train," she said, "I was disoriented. I knew I was going to a school in Kuala Lumpur, a big city. My father could only hope that I would find my way when the train arrived. I befriended a man on the train and told him where I needed to go. That man was the brother of one of the secretaries of the government, and he helped me find my way."

School was a great experience for Rafiah Salim. Her ease with schoolwork brought her popularity. She loved to debate social issues. The stimulation of ideas spurred her impulse to do something special in the world.

She applied for another scholarship—this time, to go to college abroad. She decided to study law and become a policy maker who could improve social conditions. As she put it, "I was looking for schools in England, but a friend advised me that the Irish were friendlier, so I decided to go to Ireland. In retrospect, I found that the Irish were just what was promised. I fell in love with the law and the adventure of studying, and I read everything I could."

In Ireland, Rafiah's life changed even more as she met her future husband, another Malay who, like her, was studying finance on a scholarship at Queen's University Belfast. True to her rebellious nature, she decided not to sit for the bar exam in the United Kingdom when she finished her law degree. Rafiah and her husband returned to Malaysia. She was determined to use her education to make a difference. She also vowed to work only for managers who would allow her to be an advocate and leader for change. She kept this promise.

While raising her family, she joined the University of Malaya as a law professor, and ultimately became its dean. This prepared her for great things.

It was 1988 and the world was changing. Kuala Lumpur was becoming an international business center. She got a call from the managing director of Malayan Banking Berhad, also known as Maybank. He told her that she had the perfect background to join as head of human resources.

Excited and apprehensive, she went home and weighed the pros and cons with her husband. Stepping into the commercial world would require her to give up a lot. She told the managing director, "I will do the job under one condition: I want undivided support from you. Without that commitment, I won't take this job." The managing director promised her his total support.

Rafiah never imagined herself in a business hierarchy, yet she was quickly promoted. It was a satisfying and rewarding feeling. She realized that she could make a difference through her leadership goals. As a senior executive and policy maker, she could bridge social divides. It bothered her that the low earners at the bank did not have adequate medical facilities for themselves and their families. So she raised money to build a medical facility for them. She went to the executive committee and proposed her plan, but was met by puzzled faces. However, Rafiah never gave up. Within months, she had changed the executive committee's minds and developed an elegant solution for the problem.

During her tenure at the bank, Rafiah accomplished a great deal and developed a new kind of leadership. She combined tough-mindedness with a personal quest for improving conditions for everyone. Her altruism was never confused with weakness. She had low tolerance for mediocrity and no tolerance for poor performers. Her steadfastness and high standards proved that a little girl from a village could enter business and build a reputation around the question *How can I help you?* Although those in power were sometimes disturbed by her bold and audacious style, they often reacted by making her a valued member of the team. She became a colleague trusted for her leadership acumen and capabilities.

Global Leadership

After 10 years at Maybank, Rafiah needed a new challenge and a larger playing field. She had never been afraid of change and always followed her heart. Some leaders speak of their good fortune, but Rafiah seemed to make her own luck. Again she was recruited for a different challenge: the United Nations. The organization was looking for a leader of human resources. It needed someone who was not afraid of change, who could navigate through a complex multicultural organization, and who could get things done. The job also required her to move to New York City.

Rafiah agreed to meet with Kofi Annan, who had been the head of HR before her. As she had with other positions, her primary concern was how much freedom she'd be given to make her own decisions and how much support she would get. When she visited the United Nations in New York, her first thought was, "Oh, my God. What a bureaucracy!"

Kofi Annan responded, "God created bureaucracy for the United Nations." After meeting with her husband, weighing her decision's effect on her now grown children and her extended family, she signed on for five years.

She reminded herself that she was there to change paradigms. Her new assistant, Kevin, sent her countless e-mails on her first day, even though he sat only a few feet away. She told Kevin, "I am from the Third World, so you must talk with me, because we don't read or write there." Kevin was dumbfounded. She laughed, grasped his hand, and said, "I love direct contact, and we must become great friends." They did, and their friendship remains strong today.

As her first interaction with Kevin illustrates, Rafiah Salim is comfortable in her own skin, capable of connecting directly and honestly with others. She doesn't mind ruffling feathers or stepping on toes. She does so with humor and charm, having perfected the art of getting what she wants gracefully, because it's always for the right reason. In every respect, Rafiah Salim cuts through complexity and gets things done. Perhaps the discussion skills she learned at her father's table had a lifelong impact.

Today, Rafiah is running a nonprofit association in Malaysia, the International Centre For Leadership In Finance (ICLIF). In a way, she has gone back to teaching, outside the confines of a university. There she can oversee the development of leaders by providing traditional and nontraditional education opportunities.

It has been more than half a century since her train ride to a city that has become one of the most modern in the world. Rafiah set out that day on a mission to lead and make a difference. She never forgets that mission, because she keeps her father's memory alive in her heart. He was a true leader, because he knew that leadership must be developed and nourished. Rafiah looks for this in others with an evident passion when she tells you about the leaders she is working with at ICLIF. Echoing the impact her father had on her, she says that being a grandmother is leadership, too: "My role is simply to love them so that they can love others."

Chapter 5
A Personal Mission

There are leaders who were forced to lead because they couldn't follow. Such people are misfits, but in the most positive sense. They don't fit easily into the fabric of organizations or sometimes even social institutions. They have an overarching need to differentiate themselves from the rest. They often sense their personal destiny, feeling that they are unique or are meant for special achievements. Most are motivated early on by a desire for wealth, success, or accomplishments. Sometimes they transcend those needs and gain satisfaction from helping others reach the same kinds of objectives.

Each one of the leaders in this chapter—Mac Van Wielingen, Jim Lewis, John Lloyd, Hans Zulliger, and John Coleman—sensed a deep personal mission. Some followed an illuminated path before others did. All of them experienced the dream and drafted a blueprint for how to get there.

Their stories illustrate how each one reached a point of near paralysis after striking obstacles. They had to ask themselves *Why am I leading?* or variations on the question, such as: *Can I do it? Is it worth it?* or *What will I do?*

These leaders differ in many ways, but each faced adversity with innate, God-given talents. Yet common traits unite them: a deep fear of failure and an absolute, nearly paranoid hatred of losing. They love playing the game, and they have to win.

These leaders come from different parts of the world and gained insight into their competitive nature in different ways. Mac Van Wielingen is an intuitive, charismatic Canadian with roots in Europe. Jim Lewis is a Bostonian basketball player who grew up in a tenement and moved to Saudi Arabia. John Lloyd rose from humble beginnings and personal loss to achieve great things. Hans Zulliger was a Swiss Boy Scout and shoemaker's son who became a highly successful businessman. And John Coleman is a driven man from Maine who overcame dyslexia to become an engineer.

A Human Enterprise: The Story of Mac Van Wielingen and ARC Financial

Launching ARC Financial Corporation was a kind of experiment. It was a deliberate attempt to create a supportive corporate culture in which everyone was respected. This was unheard of in the investment and private equity industry, where the bottom line was everything. Its founders—Mac Van Wielingen, Phil Swift, and John Stewart—were successful energy analysts who had thrived in the competitive world of finance. They shared a belief that a bold vision and a disciplined yet open culture could achieve extraordinary things. Each of them had technical strengths that shaped the firm's strategy and operations; but Van Wielingen was the caring, empathetic steward of its culture. The role of president and CEO fell to him, and with it came people problems.

When the young firm was growing fast and struggling to succeed, these people problems caused great anxiety for Van Wielingen. Transitions in strategy created upheavals that upset everyone. To keep this talented group of employees committed, Van Wielingen had to listen to every concern, parse out every problem, and work through the emotional challenges. At the same time, his focus was on bringing in business, forging deals, ensuring deliverables, accomplishing transactions, and keeping productivity high. The three founders had a million different ideas they wanted to enact. Every day there were opportunities to be seized.

But the personnel issues refused to go away. A steady stream of people came to Van Wielingen's office each week. Some were having problems with coworkers. Others were trying to find some clarity about their careers. There were also issues of compensation and ownership, questions about the company's vision, and countless clarifications of its message.

Van Wielingen drove into the underground parking area one morning and felt exhausted from managing his projects and people issues. He tried to keep a lid on the people problems by jamming in 15-minute meetings here and there. The approach satisfied no one, however. He was feeling pulled in too many directions and stretched too thin to make the deals that were the lifeblood of the firm. He was worried that his preoccupation with people matters was impeding his ability to create value for the firm. He was feeling overwhelmed by his responsibility for the ever-present needs of others.

A minute ticked by, then two. He wondered if he was having a nervous breakdown. He thought about his dreams for the company and how exhausted he was from the reality of leading. He realized that being a leader had much more to do with people than he had ever imagined. And that's when a light flicked on.

He realized that a leader has to understand needs. The organization has needs, and people have needs. And those needs change over time. The leader must be resilient and adaptable to change in order to meet those needs. That's what leadership was about: not just the deals, the numbers, and the growth, but people's needs, too.

That moment, he felt reconnected to the firm's original vision. His emotional burden was lifted. He got out of the car and was buoyed by the insight that he had received.

Painful but Positive Lessons

His renewed appreciation for the people side of the business came to him through a degree of personal pain. Yet he didn't see pain as a necessarily bad thing. Pain had marked his family life since before he was born.

His parents were Dutch. His mother had been raised in Indonesia. After the Japanese invasion of World War II, she was interned in a concentration camp with other Europeans. Van Wielingen felt a lifelong sadness at the suffering she must have endured. At the vulnerable and tender age of 14, she lived for four years under the most brutal conditions. That experience shaped her character.

The war had been just as painful for his father. As a young man, he had been a Dutch freedom fighter and witnessed horrors that he could not speak about to his family. At 85 years of age, he was only beginning to discuss those years.

Growing up in an otherwise happy home against a backdrop of pain and suffering, Van Wielingen developed a nuanced understanding of a person's emotional tone. He could read people and groups quickly, with an intuitive grasp of the feelings that lurked below the surface. He also had a natural ability to bring those emotions to the surface by articulating them for people.

He became a leader through his recognition of others' concerns. He understood what people were thinking and expressed their needs with remarkable clarity. He could then help improve the situation.

Even in primary school, his teachers observed his tendency to sit back, stay quiet, listen intently, and then present a summary of the discussion. Even today, when complex issues are being discussed, he always feels a need to pull together what is said and to provide clarity.

As an undergraduate student at the University of Calgary and the University of Western Ontario, Van Wielingen became interested in economics because inflation had become a staggering problem. He figured that he would play some sort of leadership role in research or politics.

After doing postgraduate work at Harvard, Van Wielingen left the ivory tower of academia and started a small construction company in Vancouver. Then he took his background in economics and policy to a government agency. But by the late 1970s, he returned to Calgary and joined his father in an energy business he had started. After working in economics and planning for a few years at his father's company, Mac joined the investment industry as an energy securities analyst. Starting with a small firm in 1980, he quickly established a national reputation for his rigorous and insightful analysis.

He brought on his partner Phil Swift in 1983, and they were soon ranked as the Canadian energy industry's top securities analyst team. Van Wielingen also proved expert at providing corporate advisory work on mergers and acquisitions.

Van Wielingen, Swift, and their new partner, John Stewart, then switched firms. The team excelled; but by 1989 a new dream had become irresistible. They wanted to start a boutique investment firm and invest as principals in the energy industry. It wasn't just about the money, though. They envisioned a unique company that based its business, strategy, and operations on a set of clear values.

Each of the partners had experiences with negative cultures that bred distrust, hypocrisy, and every-man-for-himself attitudes. Van Wielingen had known leaders who were autocratic and dictatorial. But with business so competitive and challenges so complex, leaders need a team rich in creativity, commitment, and the passion to win. Van Wielingen believed that creating a respectful and supportive work environment was necessary not only for success, but for survival as well.

Their timing was good. The energy industry was on a strong upswing, and Van Wielingen was the president in those early growth years. He was also the partner who was most intently focused on the culture and the people. He began to see how much his emotional intelligence influenced his leadership style. People who worked or met with him could feel how well attuned he was to their anxieties or needs. He exuded an air of understanding that brought working relationships to a deeper, more productive level. People in finance and private equity are accustomed to managers and senior executives who foster conflict, manipulate fears, and punish those who do not exceed expectations. Van Wielingen was able to channel anxiety and vulnerability toward positive outcomes.

Hiring was one area where this ability proved itself invaluable. Many who were recruited or drawn to the company had incredible depth and intelligence. In the interview process, Van Wielingen would probe areas that might be considered sensitive. Once the standard questions had been asked and answered, he would go over his notes and circle back through the conversation to dig deeper at these emotional places. This fostered trust, allowing the interviewee to open up. Then it became possible for mutual understanding.

Sometimes friendly and well-loved employees had to be let go because they weren't contributing at a high enough level. Van Wielingen could deliver that news so that people might appreciate how the situation was not good for them either. He wasn't simply going through the motions to ease someone's discomfort. He genuinely connected in a way that made their dismissal less distressing. Van Wielingen treated employees not as objects or assets, but as human beings. The company appreciated his approach.

His ability to connect emotionally became an asset in the firm's business dealings. Merger-and-acquisition deals in particular were fraught with complex issues and entangled with sharp emotions. Van Wielingen's knack for establishing trust and rapport with the senior parties proved itself a crucial factor in many deals. He would often sit quietly during the emotional negotiations that took place in group settings, listening carefully and taking notes. At a lull in the discussion, he would voice his interpretation of the issues at play. His analysis would make everyone nod their heads in agreement. They were relieved and uplifted by his clarity and ability to connect. The firm became the first one to be called upon when deals were in the works and counsel was needed.

The firm's strategy was refined and evolving. Sometimes this required transitions and reorganizations. When the three founders decided that they wanted to leave the mergers-and-acquisitions business or to produce research, many people's jobs and ambitions would be affected. Van Wielingen understood this emotional toll and worked hard to manage expectations, get people on board, and deal respectfully with dissonance and resistance.

This gift for listening to people and involving them in the process of change consumed much time and energy. Mac had become so focused on the deal side of the business that each people issue stretched him thinner. The fatigue and stress took a toll on his health and well-being. As his doubts grew, he wondered if he really wanted to lead.

Its culmination came that morning when he couldn't get out of his car. In hindsight, he recognized that what felt like the trap of leadership—the never-ending needs of people and the organization—turned out to be his salvation. It was all a matter of perspective. He had always seen leadership as an instrument for achieving his ends in the context of a group or team. Overwhelmed by what leadership demanded of him personally, he realized that he could no longer work hard just for himself. He needed leadership to be about serving others. This was an insight that seemed to lead to more personal and organizational success than he ever could have imagined.

Playing to Win

His parents taught him lasting lessons about pain and suffering, but they'd also shown him how to survive and succeed. He would reflect on that as the firm began to flourish. Starting with the three partners, it grew to 300 employees. Its well-honed strategy produced an income trust of more than $5 billion and another $2 billion in private equity. Just as importantly, the firm stayed true to its values. Its culture has remained supportive and open, despite its size and the fact that a new generation of leaders is now in place. Van Wielingen believes that the firm's success didn't preserve its culture. Instead, the culture of the firm made its success more likely.

Van Wielingen was never very good at celebrating his triumphs. Like the other partners, he was always focused on the next milestone. But he also has an affinity for pranks. It was an aspect of his leadership style that created memorable moments of humor and relaxation.

Once when his partner Phil Swift was giving a nationally-broadcast radio interview, Van Wielingen attempted to duct-tape him to his chair. Listeners complimented Swift on his knowledgeable answers but wondered why he paused for so long before he spoke.

Another time, partner John Stewart was subjected to a prank. His habitual punctuality created some tension between him and Van Wielingen, who was chronically tardy. When the two men were scheduled to meet an important client, Stewart called Van Wielingen's hotel room to confirm that he was dressed and ready to leave. Stewart came by his room a few minutes later, only to have Van Wielingen answer the door naked—except for shaving cream on his face. Stewart stormed off to the sound of Van Wielingen's laughter.

In a way, Van Wielingen's habitual lateness, his understanding of human emotions, his air of being totally present when someone is talking and his love of pranks all combine to produce a calmness and connection. In a high-pressure, hard-driving environment, he would provide comfort and security, as well as a sense of fun and meaning. The joy that Van Wielingen feels about leadership stems from smaller things like personal memories and trivial incidents as much as the satisfaction of seeing individuals change and grow. He believes wholeheartedly in what leadership expert Warren Bennis said: "Leadership, in essence, is about personal growth." One paradox of leadership is that you help yourself grow by helping others grow. This principle is scary for many in leadership positions, because it means moving beyond your own needs and narrow self-interest. A leader must develop a capacity for love and compassion. Those are not words that many associate with leadership success in the private equity or energy industries.

Effective leaders need a deep understanding of the strategic interests of an organization. Their challenge is to detach themselves from their own interests and view matters objectively and dispassionately. Such an ability must also incorporate sensitivity, openness, and an orientation toward others needs. Being objective about business and personal needs, while remaining compassionate, caring, and mindful of others is a delicate balance. It is also a leader's foremost responsibility.

Leaders might let success distort their view of themselves and their place in the world. To stay grounded and humble, it helps to reflect back on the human incidents that happened along the way. For Van Wielingen, a dual understanding of suffering and playfulness keeps him well centered.

Years ago, he was making an important presentation before two potential clients in an office boardroom. The room had gotten warm by midafternoon and both men had eaten heavy lunches. As Van Wielingen made his points, he noticed with growing unease that the others were nodding off. He didn't know what to do. Should he just drop his business card on the table and leave? Instead, he rushed toward his conclusion as though nothing had happened. The men woke before Van Wielingen was finished, to some embarrassment. Mortified, Van Wielingen left the office and tried to figure out how he could have made such a dull presentation. He asked a colleague who was there at the meeting, "What went wrong?"

The colleague's response was, "Why, what happened?"

The hilarity of the situation delighted Van Wielingen. His colleague had also dozed off. But a truth also occurred to him. "Don't take yourself so seriously," he said out loud. "I probably would have fallen asleep myself had I been listening instead of talking."

People are the challenge, the complication, and the reward of human endeavor. Forming deep connections with people and remaining grounded are necessary conditions of successful leadership.

I Did It for You: The Story of Jim Lewis and the List

In the early morning hours, Jim Lewis's car meandered through the traffic in Taketavooz, a residential section of Tehran, Iran. Sensing that he was getting nowhere fast, he asked Farmarz, his driver, how long it would be before they arrived at the U.S. consulate. Farmarz replied with an uncertain "Who could tell?"

It had been a hectic week, and the call he received the day before from the senior officer at the embassy was disquieting. "Mr. Lewis," said the caller, "we're asking a few American businessmen to come to a private meeting on Wednesday morning. It's in your very best interests to be there."

Lewis heard the seriousness in the man's tone and asked, "Can you tell me about the nature of the meeting?" There was a long pause.

"It's not a matter we prefer to discuss over the phone. We would prefer that you come in person," the officer replied.

It must be important, thought Jim. He looked at the traffic around him in frustration but realized there was nothing he could do. He was going to be a few minutes late. That was life in Tehran in 1974.

Thirty years before, Tehran had been a city of a few hundred thousand people. By 1970, its population approached five million, making it one of the ten largest cities in the world. Sitting in terrible traffic jams was something you had to get used to as an American doing business in Iran. Normally, Lewis made good use of the time to think, but today concerns about the mysterious meeting pushed everything else aside.

When they got nearer the consulate, Lewis got out of the car to walk the rest of the way. A big man, his long legs needed to unwind. When he stood up straight, he cut an imposing figure above the crowd.

The streets were bustling. He studied the scene, as he had been trained to do. Then he headed toward the blue-tiled, mosque-like consulate building, its turrets reaching into a pure blue sky. The weather in Tehran was similar to that in Scottsdale, Arizona. It was a spring day, but the temperature had already hit 80 degrees. As he neared the entrance—a grand, ten-foot-high sculpted wooden door—he noticed that guards from the Savak stood out front with automatic weapons, alongside the usual detachment of US. Marines.

The Savak were the often-feared Iranian secret military police. Foreigners viewed them as an Iranian CIA or KGB, but some experts considered them among the most highly respected security agents in the world.

When Lewis had first arrived in Tehran, there had been no need for extra security; but these were changing times in the Middle East. Just two weeks before, three American businessmen from the defense contractor Rockwell International had been slain while driving to work. More than 500 bullets had been fired into their car. Their cold-blooded murder was a clear warning to the American community, particularly defense contractors. Lewis had become a well-known figure as the senior executive for the defense firm Raytheon in Iran. After this brazen terrorist attack on American civilians, the city shut down. When their television broadcasts stopped, people turned to BBC radio reports. Soldiers were stationed throughout the city. This new military presence transformed Tehran's crowded streets. More than 30,000 American civilians worked in Tehran. They were advised to stay at home, hunker down, and await official word.

When things had quieted down, Lewis hoped for a return to better days. Yet he knew that Iran was still a tinderbox. Joseph Stalin once said that the only thing needed to start trouble in Iran was for someone to drop a book of matches. In 1974, the potential for violence seemed dishearteningly real.

As Lewis entered the consulate, he was greeted by a young American man with the air of an Ivy Leaguer. He escorted Lewis into a large room with 20 chairs set up behind a projector. Other American business leaders were congregating around some tea and coffee. He recognized three friends, including a senior manager at Rockwell and Bell Helicopter, a subsidiary of Textron. His friend, like many Western business leaders in Tehran, was a retired military officer.

After the Americans were seated, a polished, British-accented Iranian introduced himself as a Savak officer. The forty-ish man was solidly built, dressed in a western business suit, and had slick black hair combed back from his forehead. He said, "Gentlemen, I am very happy to report to you today that Iranian security forces have joined together and eradicated the anti-Iranian element that executed our brethren and friends two weeks ago. I wish to inform you and warn you of some special circumstances that we have learned about through our interrogations of these evil terrorists."

The projector was turned on and the Savak officer proceeded to show them 30 slides of young Middle Eastern men and women who had been executed. Their bodies were lined up in the rubble before a shattered house and next to a burned car. Lewis fixed his eyes on a slender young woman who lay on the ground. Were it not for the bullets wounds in her body, she seemed to be asleep. He thought of his own children, some of whom were the same age as these young men and women.

No words were spoken for some time. Then the Iranian agent said, "I regret that I have one more slide I must show you, since each of you was identified as a target in our investigation of this safe house." On the screen in front of them, a list of names appeared. Jim shuddered when his own name appeared.

What in the world am I doing here? he thought. The meeting would forever change his perspective on his place in the world.

Where It All Began

As a youngster, there was nothing unusual about Jim Lewis, who loved to play basketball. In Lawrence, Massachusetts, basketball was the only game in town. He spent every minute of his free time shooting hoops, and practiced going into the key just like "the big men," although he was barely five-foot-eight. A lot of the Italian-American boys in his neighborhood had already reached that height, and Lewis was envious of anyone taller.

He lived in an inner city tenement house with his mom and dad. He had already lost both of his brothers. One died as a youth and the other was killed in a car accident while serving in the military. Lewis felt he had something to prove, a burning ambition to be the best. Everyone knew that he was competitive. He had a short temper and hated to lose. In the schoolyard, even when he lost a pickup game, he would stay and shoot baskets until dark. In the winter, he would scrape the snow and the ice off the court so he could keep shooting. There were no indoor gyms for kids. Basketball was played outdoors. There, kids shot into rims with no nets and against steel backboards. Lewis learned how to get the good bounce. He was all about winning.

In the eighth grade, he wrote down five important things he wanted to become. He decided to keep the list of those five goals in his wallet, so he'd never forget them. That said it all about Jim Lewis: He set goals and met them. Every day he looked at the list in his wallet and prayed for the strength to see his goals through.

During the summer after World War II ended, his life was changing. He grew six inches in six months. As he looked at his list, he circled the first goal: "Be a great basketball player and lead a winning team." It was time to pursue this one. He worked on his own skills, but understood that his friends and fellow players would also have to become great if they were going to win it all. He wanted the state championship for his school Central Catholic. His relentless drive for this objective overwhelmed some of those around him. His friend Bucky Poole found himself engaged in nonstop basketball with anybody who would play. It was never for money, always for pride.

Lewis's dad would search the neighborhood courts to find him. His mom used a whistle to call him when it was time to come home. Whenever he heard the shrill sound of the whistle, he'd say to his friends, "five more minutes." Then those five minutes would turn into ten—or twenty.

But, this group of boys from Central Catholic dominated high school basketball in the state. They were all shooters, but they could also dribble. When they were inside, they gave the ball to Jim Lewis. The other team would have no chance. The record books were rewritten around Jim Lewis and the team Lewis built at Central Catholic.

One of His Biggest Lessons

Three things were said about Jim Lewis's leadership of his basketball team: He hated to lose, he hated to lose, and he hated to lose. The negative side of that passion led to Jim's most memorable life lesson.

It was the final game of the state tournament. Lewis's dream was to be there. He had scored almost 20 points in the first half and his team was ahead. The state title was within his sights. He could taste it. And then, after what he thought was a horrendous call by the referee, his temper flared. He went right at the ref, nose to nose. The referee called a technical foul. Lewis swore as he walked to the sidelines.

His coach, Brother Leo, called a timeout. He looked at Jim Lewis, who was his star, the best player in the state, and one of the top players in the nation. Brother Leo told him, "Take a seat."

Lewis couldn't believe his ears. It wasn't possible. How could he sit down in the state tournament? But Brother Leo said, "Just sit down, Jim." Then he added, "Not another word."

Lewis's heart broke as his team began to lose. He couldn't even look at the court. Tears ran down his face as his anger swelled. With just a few minutes left in his last game of high school basketball, he realized it was hopeless. They were so far behind it would be impossible to catch up. Brother Leo looked at him again and said, "Jim, go in for number nine." Lewis went into the game at the next break, but it was too late. They had lost. His dream to be state champion was over, and it had ended not because he hated losing, but because he couldn't control himself in winning. It took him a long time to thank Brother Leo for that lesson. But every year thereafter, he made a point of sending a note to his coach to say, "Thanks for teaching me that leadership is about character."

Several colleges wanted Jim to play basketball for them. Lewis would have had his choice. One night he sat in his room and took the list out of his wallet. He circled goal two: "Go to a great school to play basketball." He decided on the College of the Holy Cross in Worcester, Massachusetts. There, he could follow such basketball stars as Tom Heinsohn and Bob Couzy, who were busy winning the national championship. Holy Cross was a basketball powerhouse, and no one appreciated that more than Jim. They said he could shoot the eyes out of the basket. He played so much that by the end of his junior year, he knew that it soon would be time to move further down his list.

He took out his wallet and circled goal three: "Find a beautiful woman to marry." That year he stood at a bus stop with a young woman who took his breath away. He went back to his roommate and said, "I've found the girl I'm going to marry. Her name is Jacqui." He repeated her name, *Jacqui* three times. His roommate said, "I heard you the first time." Lewis made a concentrated effort to win her, and win her he did.

After Jim Lewis and Jacqui were married, he moved on to goal four: "Have a big family." Their babies were born in short order, but Lewis's career progressed much more slowly. The family business he had joined was too small and felt confining. Eventually he found himself at Raytheon in the purchasing department. It was a major company with more than 80,000 employees that was focused on engineering. Jim began to plan his way to the top. *It won't be easy*, he thought, *but it can be done.*

Then came a big break: a chance to go to Saudi Arabia to run purchasing on the HAWK missile system. When he explained it to Jacqui, she smiled and said, "We're going to take our seven children to the Middle East? Where are they going to go to school?" He told Jacqui about the benefits package, which included good schools and the opportunity for their kids to study in Europe. Before long, they were on their way to Saudi Arabia.

They lived in an American compound on the Red Sea. It was on the edge of Jeddah, a seaport city of about 200,000 people. There were many adjustments to be made. There was no television and the older children had to be sent away to school. But it was a chance of a lifetime.

From day one, Lewis took full advantage of the opportunity to learn Saudi Arabian customs and to speak Arabic. Within a few years, he had become a senior manager. His management skills were growing every day. For him, his work was like pickup basketball—a competitive match with a game plan. With his playbook and his strategy, he had become a master at execution.

He loved Arab culture, and the Arab people he worked with admired him. He stood six-feet-six inches tall, and his blond hair and radiant face seemed to reflect his ability to solve complex problems. Lewis made everybody a winner and every meeting a win-win proposition. He didn't seem to mind the business traditions of the Middle East that include interruptions throughout the day for tea, prayer, and idle conversation. He worked hard and drove his teams to perform impossible tasks. Lewis had become the unofficial mayor of the compound-like city where he lived and worked.

Then he got the call to go to Iran to head up one of Raytheon's largest-ever contracts. There, he and his family would live in a city, not a compound. After discussing it with Jacqui, they were off again with their seven children.

Before Tehran, they first needed to go to Beirut, Lebanon. It was a tumultuous time. Trouble had broken out in the Middle East, and Beirut was a battleground. The Lewises had to close off the front room of their apartment and live in the back for fear of stray of bullets coming through the window. Still, they were undeterred. The bustling city of Tehran would be a much safer place. After all, the U.S. government was an ally of Iran, and its Shah had American support. Nothing bad could happen.

Lewis wondered when he could cross off goal five on his list: "Be the boss." He would look at that last goal and remember the 14-year-old boy who had written it. Even at that age, he had wanted to lead and make his mark. Now, he had finally done it.

Raytheon had set up a separate company in Iran; and he was its chief, with responsibility for thousands of lives. His years in the Middle East had made him a different kind of leader, one who always put his team first. Every individual was important. That's how it had to be for Jim Lewis.

In the beginning, things went smoothly. The fixed-price contract that Jim inherited was on target and on plan. The delivery of equipment and the training of Iranian technicians were going well. Morale was high. Then three Rockwell employees were executed by militants from the People's Mujahedin of Iran.

Becoming a Leader

When he left the meeting at the American consulate, Jim could not stop thinking about how things had changed. As he got back into his car, he realized that his days of managing were over. It was time to lead.

He reflected on Beirut and remembered what had happened in Saudi Arabia during his last assignment. He realized that the Middle East would never be the same again in his lifetime. He had to think of safety before business. He focused on the security of the thousands who came from all over the world to work for him. He had to do all he could to preserve their well-being and spirit. He felt the weight of this responsibility.

What would he tell Jacqui? How could he explain this to his managers? He knew that things would get worse. Inside, he asked himself questions posed by many leaders: *Why am I doing this? Have I finally had enough?* Then he remembered why he was doing it: because of the people around him. He needed to calm them down, help them adjust, and regain their sense of fun and competition. He got things back on track.

Three years later, Iran was rocked by revolution. By that time, Jim Lewis had returned to Saudi Arabia, where he was running all Middle East operations for Raytheon. It amounted to billions of dollars and thousands of employees. He was among the top 15 leaders in the company. He had risen from lowly beginnings as an individual purchaser to someone responsible for a significant percentage of Raytheon's profits. Lewis spent his last years on the job as a man marked for terrorist assassination, who was also an inspiration to his employees.

Despite those treacherous times, none of Lewis's employees or executives quit. One measurement of great leaders is the commitment and dedication of their followers. Everyone wanted to work for Lewis, from one assignment to the next. One young manager said, "I'd follow Jim anywhere. If I couldn't work for him, I'd come and watch. It's that much fun."

In the early 1990s, when the first Gulf War broke out, Lewis found himself a confidante to princes, kings, and presidents. Jim Lewis had earned their trust. He always came through. He never let you down. His leadership had become prudent, global, influential, and powerful. He was an expert in Middle Eastern business and governmental affairs when such counsel was in high demand.

In 1994, he had finally had enough. He had reached his goals. He wanted to spend the rest of his life being with his family and working at his church.

Today

Jim Lewis's life story is more than "local boy makes good." From early days, even before Lewis knew what the word *leadership* meant, he had wanted to become a leader. He wrote it down on his list as "be the boss," and followed through on that goal. He did it with panache, charm,and a passion for building and leading teams.

What about that fateful day in Tehran when the world changed for him? Did that make him aware of his leadership needs? Did it make him more of a leader?

Lewis listened closely to our questions and nodded. Even though his memory tends to escape him these days, his radiant smile is ever present. We wondered about the importance of the list he still carried, and asked, "Why did you keep leading even when you had achieved your goals?"

Lewis's eyes were clear and bright. He said, "Once you make your goals, you learn that there is more. I did it for you and for the team. It was never about me. I did it for you."

Jim Lewis was Phil Harkins' first boss in business many years ago. Like the others, Harkins would have followed Lewis anywhere, and he did. He did so because Lewis made leadership about others, never about himself. He met his own goals but made you feel like it was about you. And it was.

Beautifully Focused: The Story of John Lloyd and Meridian Health

Many leaders must rise to the occasion because they are up against incredible odds. The sense of urgency that propels them to leadership seems stamped into their character by some formative event in their lives. Such men and women follow a trajectory of accomplishment worthy of Shakespearean drama. They seem to have larger-than-life virtue, as well as destructive faults. It's easy to get caught up in their stories and consider leadership to be a quirk of fate or personality rather than as a deliberate choice.

For those reasons, John Lloyd might not belong in this book. He is a decent man. He grew up in a military family, the second of two children. His parents loved each other and provided a secure home environment. His family had strong, no-nonsense values that could be expressed as "work hard and don't make excuses." That defines him today in his belief that leaders need to talk about results, not about how hard they worked or how much time they put in.

In Paulo Coehlo's inspirational work *The Alchemist* (HarperOne, 1993) he notes that the secret of life is "falling seven times and getting up eight." What John Lloyd didn't know at age 17 was that his life would change and his family would take a big fall. His father's sudden death left him, his mother, and his brother alone. He had been a consummate leader of people in uniform, as well as John's role model and guardian.

He had to make a choice, one that most boys don't have to consider. He had been an athlete and scholar. But should he stay in school and stick to his educational course? Or should he step out, perhaps to play more and study less?

His mom, a secretary, didn't equivocate. She stood tall and demanded he remain strong. He explained her belief as "put

are so high in hospitals. He didn't believe in failure anyway, so he was certain that things would just work out for him.

His confidence was boosted—and his capacity was tested—by a series of promotions. He was undeterred in his mission to change health care. Rather than think like a charity, health care had to become a well run, entrepreneurial system that could produce better results. He envisioned health care for patients and their families that was greater, safer, faster and more accessible for everyone.

His reputation grew in nearby New Jersey, and while he was still in his thirties, he had the unusual opportunity of leading a major teaching hospital, the Jersey Shore University Medical Center. He accepted the challenge.

He set in place an inclusive strategy, built a team, worked collaboratively with his Meridian staff, and for the next decade and a half, gained the hospital national recognition for quality and patient care.

Today that hospital is part of Meridian Health, a system which he was elected to run. It was comprised of multiple hospitals and many businesses that support the health care industry. It is a leading health care provider in New Jersey and the United States. People in the health care field recognize John Lloyd as a leader with a passion for excellence.

One such passion is nursing.

The Magnet Recognition Program was developed by the American Nurses Credentialing Center (ANCC), the nation's largest and foremost nursing accrediting and credentialing organization, to recognize health care organizations that provide nursing excellence through quality patient care, nursing excellence, and innovations in professional nursing practice. The Magnet Recognition Program is based on quality indicators and standards of nursing practice as defined by the American Nurses Association. Less than 3 percent of the nation's hospitals achieve Magnet designation, which is bestowed to honor the nursing staffs of the hospitals that meet the highest professional standards.

In 1998, Meridian Health was the first health care system in the nation to achieve the prestigious Magnet nursing designation at each of its member medical centers. Meridian has continually maintained its Magnet nursing status at each of its medical centers.

In addition to extensive scholarship and career development programs, Meridian has pioneered an innovative approach to nursing. Meridian's Model of Care Nursing Units offer a high nurse-to-patient ratio, which allows nurses to have more time at each patient's bedside. In addition, Meridian nurses are empowered to make operational decisions with physicians, and are offered robust professional development and education programs with dedicated educators just for nurses.

As a result, Meridian has one of the lowest nurse vacancy rates in the nation. Also, over 40 percent of Meridian nurses are nationally certified in their areas of clinical expertise, compared with the national average of only 11 percent to 13 percent. Meridian nurses also are extremely well published in national professional journals and regularly present Meridian's nursing approaches nationally and internationally. Meridian's nursing excellence is something of which John Lloyd is most proud.

In John Lloyd's presence, one feels his confidence. It is distinctive. He speaks easily and laughs a lot. He plays down his accomplishments with a charismatic charm. He loves being the leader and it shows.

At the same time, he loves to win. Taking second place doesn't fit his profile. He wants to see better results for the health care system he leads. His vision for health care is like the children's poem: "Good, better, best. Never let it rest. 'Til your good is better and your better is best."

Some leaders make their goals clear and command others to reach theirs. John Lloyd made early choices and found an important field in which to lead. Today, he is certain of his legacy. He learned so much from a mother who got it right. She believed in her relationships with her family, friends, and community. She always helped others. She was confident in what she stood for, believed she had enough, and let others understand that they too had enough. Perhaps the lesson is that when "enough" is clearly understood from the start, leaders somehow discover more.

The Business of Sustainability: The Story of Hans Zulliger and the Love of Sustainability

Dr. Hans Zulliger doesn't know why he finds himself in a leadership position so often. All his life, he has been blessed—and cursed—with an inventive mind that combines a compulsion to make things better with an inability to remain in the background. He has used his incredible curiosity to solve complex problems in many different realms over a 60-year period. This led him to acquire a Swiss subsidiary of a U.S. company and to turn it into a highly successful venture by putting into practice his own business sustainability concepts.

These impulses are deeply rooted in Zulliger's life. His father was a shoemaker employed by others for a third of a century, but one day he could no longer stand doing things someone else's way. Switzerland's social structure was a caste-like system at that time. Striking out on your own would be difficult. Nevertheless, Zulliger's father felt oppressed by the way his work was structured, so he opened his own shop. That decision burdened his father with heavy responsibilities. This caused Hans Zulliger—and his brother and sister—to vow never to become businesses leaders.

All of the children were given tasks in their father's new business. Hans was responsible for washing the shoes in the basement. It was tiresome, routine work to carefully wash every shoe. What he hated most about it was the way that it robbed him of his creativity. Not only was it wasting his energy, but it was also wasting precious water.

One day, young Hans took a break from his work and dealt with his frustrations by sketching out a way to wash the shoes that would save time and make more efficient use of water and cleaning materials. He showed his father his drawing and the old man understood immediately. It was a water wheel, with the shoes set on each shelf. The force of the water powered the wheel, automatically washing the shoes.

Hans Zulliger may not have known it at the time, but he had begun a lifelong love affair with sustainability. He wanted to develop systems that would give more back to the environment than they took away. In the end, his company would exemplify these principals, operating from a Zulliger-designed building that served as a model of sustainability at work.

Boy Scouts of Switzerland

Nothing about Hans Zulliger's early years would have led one to predict that he would leave Switzerland, obtain a Ph.D. at Stanford University, and return one day to run a successful business venture. His family was lower middle-class and traditionally-minded. Punctuality and doing the right thing were very important.

Zulliger wasn't in the top ten percent of his class in school. He only paid attention to subjects he liked. If something didn't catch his interest, he daydreamed about new designs. It might seem obvious in retrospect that Zulliger would become an engineer and scientist, but as a young boy, he had no such aims. He only knew he didn't want to inherit his father's business. There had never been any scientists or business leaders he could look to as role models. Only a so-so student, he had no way to distinguish himself from others who were clamoring to get out of the working class.

His one love outside of his family was the Boy Scouts. Boy Scouts in Switzerland were organized differently than in the United States. In the United States, adults do most of the leading, but in Europe, young people do the active work while adults stay in the background. Given that leadership opportunity, Zulliger shined. He enjoyed team activities and was asked to lead expeditions.

At a recent reunion, one of Zulliger's fellow Boy Scouts told him how much his leadership meant to the others, saying, "You were a great example to us, and we all admired you. You helped us win the contests, and you were an inspiration in how you dug in and did the work."

To Zulliger, "digging in" was the real lure of leadership. He was reluctant at first to take the lead, but he felt that somebody had to. And having someone tell him what to do was unappealing. Over the course of his life, this dynamic played itself out again and again. He knows that the responsibility of leading is a burden that he would be more comfortable without, but he found it impossible to hang back.

Zulliger also discovered a great love of nature in Boy Scouts. Going into the woods took on a spiritual dimension. Where some boys threw rocks at frogs or killed insects, Zulliger saw the woods as a haven, life as precious, and nature as an interconnected force. All living things were part of the cycle of life, with their own purpose for being.

By the time he was 17, Zulliger was tall for his age and strong from his work in the shop, as well as his expeditions in the woods and mountains. He had developed a vitality and an excitement for life. He loved taking the lead as the planner and organizer. He didn't mind the energy required to be up in the morning, make sure that everyone was safe, and plot routes through the Swiss mountains. He loved to find the one special ledge where the troops could look out over the best vistas.

A friend of the family saw that Zulliger had tremendous potential and encouraged him to apply to school in the United States. Zulliger had no plans to study, because he'd always wanted simply to work. But the friend gave him a list of top schools, including Stanford, MIT, and Harvard. He encouraged Zulliger to apply to them.

The natural beauty of the Stanford campus, as depicted in their brochures, appealed to Zulliger. He applied and was accepted. When he arrived that fall, he discovered that he owed a great deal in tuition. He thought he had paid for a full year's tuition up front, but learned that it was only for a quarter.

In a panic, Zulliger had to find a job. A schoolmate suggested that he ask for work from one of the professors, the Nobel Prize-winning physicist Dr. Robert Hofstadter. A desperate Zulliger knocked on the professor's door. Despite the fact that he was a foreign student who knew no one and had little experience, Hofstadter hired Zulliger to work in his lab at an engineering-level salary. (As an employee of the university, Zulliger got a 30 percent discount in his tuition.) If he had known what obstacles lay ahead of him, Zulliger might never have gone to Stanford in the first place; but it turned out for the best. His confidence in his own resourcefulness told him that everything would be all right.

Return from America

Zulliger got his Ph.D. in nuclear instrumentation and became a successful businessman in the United States. He launched a start-up company, had a good run, and sold it profitably. Then he returned to Switzerland.

Back home, Zulliger started working for Ciba-Geigy, a U.S.-based company. As part of the management team, he would help turn around the business. The organization's prospects were not good. It was losing money, the customer base was eroding, and sales had dropped 30 percent. In short order, Zulliger and two colleagues were handed the opportunity to buy the business for next to nothing.

The three men borrowed start-up money and drew collateral from the organization's real estate to keep things going. Becoming business owners, with all of the challenges of managing and leading, was overwhelming for these young men. Zulliger's greatest challenge came from his partners. The three men had different personalities, each with something unique to contribute, but that did not always mean that their relationship ran smoothly. The banks were hounding them and threatening to sue. The business remained flat in a terrible economy. The stress was mounting.

By Christmas Eve, it had come down to the wire. They weren't sure if they could meet their payroll. One colleague agreed to keep things afloat by mortgaging some of his patents. Zulliger went to a notary to get the documents signed, but they closed before he got there. Another notary was miles away and the road was blocked because of a nearby house fire. On his third attempt, Zulliger found a notary who was still open on Christmas Eve and would sign the paperwork.

The next day, while shopping with his wife, Zulliger felt suddenly sick. He was experiencing strong pressure on his heart. He had to sit down. It was all too much, he felt. He questioned whether he could keep going at all.

A few weeks later, Zulliger still had a terrible feeling that everything was falling apart. He would admit that he was scared in his bones. He didn't want to fail. People trusted him. If he didn't put the last ounce of his energy into keeping the company alive, he couldn't face himself. Talking through his worst fears with his wife allowed him to get a grip on things. "We're so close," he told her. "If we have some more time, I know we can make it."

He started working out strategies for keeping the banks happy. He came up with a list of promises to satisfy their loans, and every month he met with the banks to check more items off the list. Zulliger had only promised the bank things that the company had already accomplished, but the impression that they were sticking to a plan rekindled the banks' confidence. With the banks off their backs for a time, they had breathing space for the next round. Five years later, Zulliger and his partners had a moneymaking venture on their hands, and brought two parts of the company public.

Sustainability

The lessons of pushing so hard and driving to the brink of failure were not lost on Zulliger. His company's rise rekindled his interest in sustainability. He put together programs that met ISO 9000 standards for quality management systems and renewed the company's research and development operations. This practice became part of his leadership philosophy.

It started with the evolution in his thinking about corporate mission statements. The first mission statement was the ultimate goal to become number one—a familiar objective for anyone in business. But Zulliger believed that this goal was outmoded. "Dinosaurs were quite successful for a while—on top of the world—and all of the other animals were the losers. I don't think that's a good strategy, because once you've reached the pinnacle, you find yourself in a lonely position. Everybody envies you. You become arrogant and complacent, and you view others as losers because they are not number one."

In place of the hierarchical dinosaur strategy, Zulliger proposed a pyramid, where the ultimate goal is sustainability for yourself and the world. "Your organization is part of the global system—biologically, economically, and socially," he said. "It needs to find sustainability in that system." In Zulliger's view, most successful leaders see themselves as servants of society, unwilling to exploit their success. Zulliger has made that attitude intrinsic to his mission, systems, and corporate strategy.

His company's headquarters building puts that belief into action. Zulliger dreamed of a building that would be kind to the environment while allowing for maximum productivity and better health for the people inside. This goal would be met by an economic model that might be expensive in the short run, but would provide a good return in the long run.

"There are three ways you can build a building," Zulliger said, "You can build it as a monument to the architect or build it to obtain the highest economic return. Or you could build it for sustainability by creating a comfortable place for people to work that is economically acceptable and sustainable in its use of resources. When we chose this third option, everybody told us it would be expensive and unaffordable. I said, 'Let's do it anyway.'"

It wasn't easy to stick to this goal. He was met with a lot of resistance. After the first plans were made, the designers told Zulliger that the building would be too expensive to build—about 10 percent more than a traditional structure. Knowing that was just the building cost, Zulliger told them to recalculate their estimates by considering what would be saved in maintenance and lower energy use. The new numbers showed that the returns would be adequate.

The next fight Zulliger had with the designers was over the interior. Classrooms in the building made heavy use of computers and server stations, which generated so much heat that huge air conditioners were needed. Once again, the designers wanted to kill the idea, but Zulliger discovered that some of their assumptions were wrong. But there was still a serious problem with the available cooling system. "Okay," Zulliger said, "we'll invent something better."

Eventually, his team patented a system of small copper tubes that ran cool liquid through the ceiling to absorb the heat from the computers. Zulliger is especially proud of this system. "It's dynamically sensitive, because it uses a small mass and you can draw the heat out of the room quickly. Then, the moment they turn the computers off, the cooling system turns off, too." The system was perfected and incorporated into the building's design. This time, his planners returned with a pleasant surprise. Because the system was so much smaller, they were able to save half of one floor's space in the building. Zulliger turned that extra room into rental space that compensated for any of the building's short-term cost deficits.

He ultimately achieved his dream of creating a building that was a monument to sustainability—wonderful to work in and efficient in economy and energy use. Getting there, however, was not easy. Zulliger needed to be tenacious, technically knowledgeable, and convinced that he was doing the right thing. Yet he was willing to pay the penalty if he failed. To Zulliger, the risk of that leadership was worth it. His building became the legacy of his own dedication to sustainable business practices.

A Sustainable Life

Today, Dr. Hans Zulliger is retired from his business and his board. He has not given up on leadership, however. He is strong, vibrant, and always on the move. He has established organizations—like his Foundation for the Third Millennium—to focus on projects that raise consciousness for life and humanity.

Perhaps the greatest leadership lesson of Hans Zulliger's life is in the area of personal happiness. When he was a graduate student at Stanford, he wanted to find a life partner. A dashing young European, Zulliger had several opportunities. But instead of dating women randomly, he defined the traits and characteristics or "core makeup" of the woman who would be the ideal life partner for him. She had to be someone who shared his values and principles, and who believed in sustainability. After he wrote up this profile, he began his search. As soon as he met a woman named Ann, he knew he had found who he was looking for.

Almost 40 years later, Ann and Hans met with us in a small dining room in Zurich. They spoke openly and honestly about how they still work hard together today. They've built a sustainable life for themselves and their families. The evidence of their success was plainly visible in the love they share.

Tenacity: The Story of John Coleman and the VIA Group

John Coleman's mother and father had never seen him like this. It was a crisp Maine day. The leaves were turning early. He sat in his parents' living room unable to look them in the eye as he explained how difficult things had become.

This is not John, his parents must have thought. The extroverted, driven, happy guy who loved everyone was torn apart inside. He wasn't sure that he could carry on, even though he was a consummate optimist who loved what he did and loved new challenges. But the changes wrought in the market by the burst Internet bubble and a depressed post-9/11 business climate had destroyed the business base of VIA, the company he founded in 1993.

Coleman's six-foot-three-inch frame took up a lot of room in the chair, and his dark mood enveloped his parents' house. "John, are you okay?" his concerned mother asked. He looked up at her and his father, saw their love and compassion, and gave them a wry grin. At that moment, he knew he would find a way. He renewed his belief in the dream that he had built. "I can figure this out," he said.

"You can figure out anything," his father said. "You can make this happen."

John Coleman left the house with a new resolve. He knew that this had been one of those moments in life where you simply have to make the future happen. He went home to tell his wife. Coleman's life had always been about persistence and fortitude. Hard things don't come easy, so he would just have to dig deeper. He thought it was funny for a grown man to go to his parents first before talking with his wife, but something about the depth of the challenges drew him to them.

Driving home, he realized his revived optimism did not dispel the sick feeling in his stomach. Failure was not an option. He had a responsibility to feed his family and pay for his children's education, but he also had to help the people at VIA who had trusted his leadership. He had always enjoyed being a leader when times were good, but circumstances could turn brutal. On a day like this, it was just awful. Strategy and brilliant ideas were not enough. Sometimes only tenacity can keep you going. He was certain he would pull everyone through.

In the end, he did. But the sick feeling in his stomach stayed with him for months.

Early Days

John Coleman is the leader of a highly successful start-up company, but his personality doesn't fit the profile of a typical entrepreneur. We wanted to know: *What makes a lucky, successful, easygoing, extroverted man take on the burdens of leadership? How does a leader show the tenacity it takes to win in hard times?*

Coleman had an idyllic childhood in a small city in Maine. He was the middle child among three brothers and three sisters. His mother was a highly creative person who was a great writer, dedicated reader, and passionate lover of life. She stayed home to look after the children, and was a powerful force in their lives. Coleman's father was more intense. He was an engineer who ran the Department of Transportation for the state of Maine with 600 other engineers under him.

Coleman is the combination of an analytical father and a creative mother. He was a starry-eyed boy with his head in the clouds until he realized that he had a learning disability. Unlike the other students, Coleman couldn't read when the teacher asked him to. Even though he was judged not as smart as the other students, his fun loving, friendly ways made him popular. Then a doctor diagnosed him with a form of dyslexia.

It wasn't a debilitating handicap, but it made Coleman become more conscientious and deliberate. He realized that there was much to learn in school, so he started using his brain more.

He ended up among a group of students who faced many challenges. Some were dyslexic, some had attention deficit disorder, and others had come from difficult home lives. Among that group of castoffs, Coleman enjoyed some of his best and most formative learning experiences.

He learned how to push relationships deeper to form real connections. He worked hard at everything he did, even if he wasn't particularly gifted at it. He loved getting to know everyone in his small high school. He realized how precious that experience was when he met people later in life who felt lost and isolated in their own, larger communities.

By the time he finished high school, Coleman had been involved in everything. He played basketball, was a member of the student council, acted in the theater, excelled in math and science, and rose to the top of his class. He still wasn't as strong as others in English and reading, but he continued to develop those skills.

In college, Coleman became even more serious about his studies. He enrolled in a rigorous program at engineering school. True to his balance of analytical and creative sides, he also studied philosophy and music. (He was also serious in his dedication to the viola.) When he met his future wife, Linda, he knew almost immediately that he'd found his soul mate. In high school, he would have been voted the last guy to ever settle down. When Linda and John got married before finishing college, his friends were shocked.

The Dream

In his early twenties, Coleman thought about starting his own company. He was an engineer with a great job at a great company. He made substantial money, but he loved creatively solving business challenges. An idea began to take shape.

He wanted to build a company that would tackle challenges in the advertising industry. He wanted it to be no ordinary ad firm, but a multidisciplinary company that could provide a spectrum of business solutions all in one: PR firm, identity shop, Internet services company, strategy house, and design boutique. Coleman saw it as a powerful concept that could bring a customer's products, services, and brand together with a unified strategy for a singular market impact.

It may seem remarkable that a dyslexic man with an engineering background would be drawn to the creative business of advertising with no experience in the field. But Coleman's launch of an advertising company wasn't a task he took on to overcompensate for any deficiencies. He did it to combine his analytical and creative sides, and to seize an incredible business opportunity. He had a special ability to solve complex problems from both analytic and creative angles. It was a different way of perceiving and engaging with the world, and Coleman saw an outlet for it in advertising.

Despite his excitement, the dream felt distant and intangible. It was a daunting goal that seemed out of reach. Yet it wouldn't let him go. One day, he told Linda that he wanted to quit his job. Although they had a large mortgage and three children, she could see how euphoric her husband was whenever he sketched out an idea. She knew it would be risky to abandon the stability of his engineering career, but she gave him her support without hesitation. Security, material belongings, and a luxurious lifestyle weren't as important as living a dream. "You absolutely have to do this," she said.

Coleman's desire to build a company did not come from a longing to assume a leadership role. Rather, he was excited to use his skills on something challenging. He anticipated the pleasure of looking at a blank piece of paper and deciding how to fill its blankness with a great story or a beautiful painting. He felt an exhilaration to try something new, an intense energy he'd feel when speaking to a crowd of people or stepping onto the basketball court for a big game. Quitting his job was easy, judging by how he felt. In his bones, he knew that his highest motivation was to create something original or meet an enormous challenge.

He wrote out a business plan, even though his reasoned engineering side couldn't do justice to the vivid, full-color picture he envisioned. The pieces quickly fell into place. With his friend Rich Rico, he launched a company called VIA, an acronym for Vision, Instinct, Action. Using that motto as a touchstone, Coleman and Rico put their heads down and went for it.

Advertising is a business built on credentials and past success, and VIA had nothing to show its customers: Coleman and Rico hadn't gone to the right schools, didn't have a portfolio of work, and weren't located in a big city. They were based in Maine. But they won their first customers on pure passion combined with a refreshing way of tackling challenges. They solved problems, created big ideas that transformed their clients, and always delivered. Their reputation grew.

As their company expanded, they set out to hire the best people and lure them to Maine. Coleman had to convince people that he and Rico could succeed, even though they didn't have the experience or the track record. He also needed to convince them that it could all be done from Maine. That location was a big stumbling block. But looking back, Coleman recognizes that it brought him more talented people with greater passion and ideas. Those people who came on board wanted to be part of something exciting with a spirit of purpose and fun, and enough risk attached for its rewards to be that much greater.

Coleman realized that the rewards were not always financial. Most people looked for great work experiences. Accordingly, Coleman focused his message on people he wanted to hire, as well as those already on board. He could not promise the big money with 100 percent certainty, but he could promise an incredible ride. "You'll do things you've never done before," he told people. "You'll be confronted with challenges that make you weak in the knees, but you'll gain enormous satisfaction testing yourself."

The people who were drawn to VIA were also drawn to its culture. Coleman and Rico stressed the values of the company: curiosity, integrity, respect, and doing the right thing. They also stressed seeking out incredible challenges, taking big risks, striving with determination, and celebrating success.

Many people choose a path that is safe and sure. They willingly put up with bureaucratic organizations where values are not important. The people who joined VIA enjoyed taking risks to gain personal satisfaction from their work. They are gifted and talented people who would be successful at any advertising firm, but they want something different. At VIA they got the chance to do interesting things and to gain attention for their work while winning advocates and converts. Coleman wasn't just blowing smoke. People could feel the difference when he spoke about his dream, and the people who joined VIA helped make it real.

The Challenge

Leadership is easy when times are good, hard when times are hard, and difficult even when things are going phenomenally well. In the middle to late 1990s, the growth of VIA brought moments of strain that tested Coleman's leadership. Not everyone who came on board in that rush had the same priorities. Money was threatening their values and integrity. How could Coleman keep the fast-growing company steady, committed, and focused when dot-coms were exceeding GM and GE in value?

Then, in 2000, the first blow struck. The Nasdaq plummeted and the Internet bubble burst. Over half of VIA's business was in Silicon Valley. The company was left highly exposed with an extensive roster of venture capital dot-com clients. Over the next year and a half VIA started to regain its footing. Then the terrorist attacks of September 11, 2001 struck a second blow.

The paralysis after 9/11 and the recession impacted all industries. Advertising budgets were slashed and the industry hollowed out almost overnight. As VIA struggled to stay afloat, it experienced a 100 percent turnover in revenue, meaning that it lost as much revenue as it managed to gain. Many of VIA's competitors were going out of business, and some days Coleman thought his company would too. One day he and his team visited a potential client whose seven-figure contract Coleman had expected to close on. The moment the meeting started, the client told Coleman and his group that the project was cancelled.

Over lunch, Coleman and his five colleagues struggled to keep their desperation in check. Coleman tried to be calm and clearheaded about it. "That certainly was unexpected," he said. Privately, he told himself, "There's no way we can recover from this."

Still, they were meeting with another client after lunch, so they put their game faces back on. The client's project was in its early stages, and the meeting felt like a hollow formality given VIA's sudden problems. To everyone's shock, the client decided to sign a major contract that afternoon. VIA lived to fight another day.

There were many such up-and-down moments. For Coleman, the worst aspect of that difficult time was his inability to relax. As an obsessed problem solver, he couldn't stop thinking about ways to rescue his company from its difficulties. It didn't matter that many of his challenges were economic and geopolitical—outside the realm of any company, let alone any individual, to solve. Coleman simply didn't want to look his employees in the eye and say, "We can't make it." Too many of those people believed in the dream and were relying on Coleman to keep it alive.

When Coleman's spirits were lowest, he went to his parents' house and told them how bad things had gotten. They listened, but their faith in his abilities remained unbroken. He'd always done it before, they believed, and he would do it again. His wife, Linda, despite her fears, believed the same thing.

That night, Coleman went online and found himself looking at VIA's home page. He remembered the acronym: Vision, Intuition, Action. He clicked on a link to their philosophy and values: "Be curious. Do work that makes you proud. Be on budget. Create respect. Honor the process. Be on time. Figure it out. Find the magic. Think like the audience. Believe." These values made VIA a special place. "We are passionate about meeting every challenge," the slogan went on. "There is nothing we love more than a tough challenge. The harder the better."

Coleman went to bed feeling better that night. A new day would bring new opportunities to solve the biggest business challenge of all.

The Reward

Four years later, on April 26, 2005, the VIA Group was ranked as one of the top 50 U.S. business-to-business agencies in *B2B Magazine.* Agencies on the list have to provide full marketing communications services with an emphasis on advertising. These companies range from multinationals to large conglomerates. Flying under the radar—and based in Maine—VIA had emerged triumphant.

From the depths of the post-Internet bubble and 9/11 difficulties, VIA had reinvented itself. This renewal reenergized the organization and helped it overcome difficult economic times. Many competitors were exhausted by the formidable challenges and went out of business. VIA, because of its culture, people, and leaders, survived—and then thrived.

John Coleman created his dream job by building his dream company. He found a way to thrive in a challenging industry. To Coleman, creativity is about unconventional thinking and meeting challenges with unique approaches. Unconventional thinking allowed VIA to survive harsh economic challenges.

Coleman's upbringing and education—and his need to compensate for his dyslexia—may have been perfect training for leading an unconventional company through tough times. Coleman knows that a business leader needs the stomach to handle those tough times. Effective leaders must remain calm when things are changing dramatically, but must also drive people for new approaches and outstanding results. In a dynamic industry like advertising, nothing formulaic or predictable will succeed for long.

Coleman's ability to connect deeply with a wide range of people helped him immeasurably as a leader. He needed to attract and manage extraordinarily creative people as well as people whose talents are analytical and detail-oriented. Coleman created a sense of trust, respect, and encouragement by respecting people's talents and letting them contribute fully. He learned when to push and when to back off.

Some of his greatest satisfaction as CEO comes from his love for people and his ability to tap into their unique strengths. A leadership role at VIA is not defined by job title. Leadership there is defined by what inspires and excites people so much that they seize the reins and pursue their passion. In the end, Coleman knows that the dream of VIA is not about him. It's about seeing customers and employees succeed.

Had John Coleman, a leader now in his early forties, ever grappled with the concept of *enough?* There were days, he told us, when things were difficult and he wondered how much longer he could go on. But most days, Coleman still brims with the excitement and the thrill that led him to quit his job and found VIA in the first place. He believes that because there is so much more to learn and do, the feeling will stay with him for a long time. "When I stop thinking that a new day holds the excitement of a new beginning, then I'll know that I've finally had enough and walk away without looking back."

If that happens, he'll most likely find something else to do. He's driven to be creative. That's what presses him to keep making his company better.

Chapter 6

The Quest

The quest is a combination of a "never give up" attitude with an inventive spirit. We created this category for those destined to create or build something that outlasts them. Such leaders believe that their life needs to be about accomplishment. You will find in these leaders—Larry Strecker, Paul Brainerd, Anthony von Mandl, John Keane, and Mary Robinson—a boundless passion and energy that focuses on making things happen. They never let themselves get backed into a corner. Some of the businesses that they created were a means to get what they wanted: distinctiveness, contribution, branding, or just a name on the door.

Mary Robinson found out early on that she truly was needed. When tapped to be president of Ireland, she found her answer to the leadership question. The word was *justice.*

Three people in this category, each in a different field, started businesses from nothing when no one thought they had a chance. Two still have their names on the door: John Keane and Anthony von Mandl. They've put in a combined 75 years of service to their businesses. Their leadership has made them exceptional in their respective fields and given them a major position in the marketplace. Paul Brainerd and Larry Strecker have refocused and rebranded themselves. They are now focused on service to others.

Seeker of Answers: The Story of Larry Strecker, Payless ShoeSource, and the Burning Desire to Learn

Larry Strecker is the prototypical leader-manager. When you talk to people around him, they say that he is the most focused and driven person they've ever known. His discipline goes hand in hand with his structured and process-oriented work ethic. As a result, he's an extraordinarily clear thinker who sorts and sifts through complex issues until he discovers their essence. Then he sorts and sifts some more.

On any given day, Strecker will send out 150 e-mails and receive another 150. He follows up on every detail, big or small. He outworks, outthinks, and outperforms everyone around him. His meetings with employees, colleagues, and supply partners are legendary for the way he seeks information until he reaches the heart of a problem. His solutions are often bold, courageous, and transformative. They can launch a team, a division, or an entire organization onto a better way of doing business. Strecker is a caring, outgoing, and compassionate man with strong family values, a spiritual side, and a generous capacity for friendship. Those who know him appreciate and tolerate him as an intense, determined, relentless seeker of truth.

Unsurprisingly, Strecker has obtained extraordinary results as a leader and a manager wherever he has worked. Groups, divisions, and companies have sought out his leadership. He rose rapidly to the top ranks of corporate America. While in his thirties, he was promoted to senior vice president of worldwide sourcing for Payless, an organization with over 4,500 stores and 26,000 associates around the world. He then became senior vice president of retail operations and finally, of international and supply chain.

At the age of 44, he quit—and not because of his health or job performance or personal difficulty. He had never been so successful at work and at home. His chairman begged him to stay. Friends assumed he was leaving for a more glorious business opportunity. But Larry Strecker had something else in mind. Armed with many questions, he was looking for an entirely different set of answers.

Come Work with Us

Strecker was born and raised in western Kansas, in a stable, secure, and strong Catholic family. He wanted to join the Air Force Academy and become a pilot; but because he wore glasses, he was disqualified from flying for them. He learned that the Air Force Academy and West Point accepted engineers, so he decided to study engineering. Rather than an academy, he attended Kansas State University, where he graduated summa cum laude with a Bachelor of Science degree in industrial engineering.

Even in college he was unusual. Most students are comfortable to drift along without getting to know their teachers or digging too deeply into their studies. As a student, Strecker met with his teachers whenever they had office hours, to ask just one more question. His burning desire to learn made him a challenge for those teachers, but it also endeared him to them. He remains close friends with some of them today.

His family didn't have a lot of money. During the summer, he worked as a janitor in a factory. There he would listen to other people's problems and learn what made their work frustrating or difficult.

After college, he went to work as a plant engineer at John Deere, setting up factories. He spent most of his time on the factory floor with the workers. He found himself listening to them describe their challenges while he tried to explain to them the seemingly irrational behaviors of management. He decided that industrial engineering wasn't exactly what he was best at. He wanted to work on the nuts and bolts of making companies run better.

His next job was at PepsiCo, in the Frito-Lay division. He soon realized that if he wanted a leadership role within the company, he needed to broaden his experience. He sought advice from various people. The salespeople thought sales was the way to go. Production people believed that their department was the right place to get experience. Everyone who knew Larry was united in a desire to bring Strecker on board. "Come work for us," was the refrain.

Strecker distilled all of the advice he received and determined the right path. To develop leadership experience, he needed to take on a group with as many people as possible of different backgrounds, personalities, and job functions.

He chose to work in Frito-Lay's logistics center in Topeka, Kansas. It was the largest distribution center in the country, mostly comprised of truck drivers and office clerks. It was also two steps lower in the hierarchy, resulting in a change of title from director to manager. Most people couldn't understand why he had made that decision, but he was there to learn. Since he came from a staff position, he wasn't expected to enjoy his new role. Indeed, a major cause of career derailment is a shift from line to staff—or vice versa. Most executives fit better in one world than in another. Strecker found that he was good at both, but he loved working on the line.

Still, he made many mistakes. He grew impatient working with 125 truck drivers, each of whom had a different agenda. He was quick to make his mark, and he moved too fast. But he learned that winning was not a battle. You could be absolutely right, but still not be successful if you didn't bring the right people with you. A leader was someone who may not always be 100 percent right, but would bring more people along.

Over the next 10 years, his people skills developed even further. One difficult issue was worker safety. Strecker addressed the problem to make the company more responsive. After some probing and analysis, he realized that the best way to make a trucker safe was to reward his family if the driver didn't get injured. In creating that program, he made a big difference in the morale of the culture.

The senior executives at Frito-Lay gave him practical problems that they couldn't solve. His need to understand and his knack for asking the question behind the question helped him uncover more effective approaches. All problems took shape as a diagram in his mind, like an engineering schematic. He was such a clear systems thinker that he revolutionized whatever he touched. His innovations were rooted in the most basic problem of how to organize work more efficiently.

Going Global

His boss wanted to move him to the head office in Dallas, but Strecker didn't want to go. He had had a less than amicable relationship with that manager.

Strecker was content at Frito-Lay, but had been called five times by a head hunter to recruit him for Payless ShoeSource. Payless was founded in Topeka, Kansas in 1956 by two cousins who wanted to sell shoes in a self-service environment. It grew to a few hundred stores before it was bought by May Department Stores in 1979. Payless then became an independent, publicly held company when it was spun off to shareholders. It had 3,600 stores globally, but kept its head office in Topeka.

The sixth time the headhunter called Strecker about the job he finally agreed to learn more about it. Strecker was hired for the sourcing group, which spent $1 billion a year sourcing shoes. Virtually all the shoes they sold in North America were made in China, where hundreds of agents worked to identify products. At the time, most Payless purchases were made through agents rather than direct buys.

Strecker brought his trademark discipline to the group. He asked question after question about what troubled him or didn't seem right. He decided that the purchasing strategy wasn't as effective as it could be. Strecker was instrumental in moving from a system heavily reliant on agents to one that predominantly involved direct purchases.

He also consolidated the Payless factories. The company had been buying from hundreds of factories in 15 countries, but there were 15 to 20 large factories that were consistently top performers. Strecker decided to focus the buying on these "core" factories. This reduced the company's dependence on agents and consolidated factory buying.

It was a revolutionary shift for the shoe industry, and Payless asked Strecker to move to Asia to expedite the strategy. He lived in Taiwan for the next three years. There, he got deeply involved in the line and worked closely with the subcontractor manufacturers to learn everything he could about how shoes were made.

He also worked tirelessly to improve conditions in Payless factories in China, Indonesia, and Brazil. He wanted to ensure that work was done right and workers were treated fairly. In the process, he learned about the cultures of China and elsewhere in Asia. This broadened his perspective and kindled some of his closest friendships.

After returning to Kansas, Strecker told the chairman that Payless was a wonderful place to work, but he wanted to do something different. The chairman refused to accept his resignation and asked him to run the retail side of the business. There were 26,000 people working in Payless stores, and the chairman knew that Strecker couldn't resist the opportunity to learn more about the people side of the business—and gain that leadership experience.

He was right. Strecker agreed to devote himself to retail for the next two to three years. Once again, he loved being in the field. He focused on worker safety, and sought strategies to reduce the number of robberies in Payless stores. He increased the number of stores across North America and significantly raised their level of success.

When Strecker made his impact on the company's retail side, the chairman asked him to help reorganize the business side. Strecker agreed to take charge on one condition: He needed to start at the top.

Strecker's clear systems-oriented thinking and probing questions resulted in innovative and bold ideas for reorganization. The chairman was pleased. In return, all Strecker wanted was to be let go. Something was telling him that he'd had enough, but his responsibilities made it hard for him to stop and figure out why. Again, the chairman convinced him to stay on. He would run the growth side of the business while the reorganization was being implemented. Strecker only committed himself to seeing the company through the change. During that time, he was senior vice president of international and supply chain, where he was responsible for international retail operations in 11 countries and for Payless's supply chain.

After successfully implementing the reorganization, Strecker finally resigned. The chairman asked Strecker to work with Payless for up to 15 days a year and he agreed. Strecker set his retirement date for May 23 because that was the day his daughter would be graduating from school.

What does he think about leadership, now that he has stepped off the fast track? The discoveries are simple but resonate powerfully. The most joy that Strecker ever achieved in business came from seeing people do what they thought they couldn't do.

He remembers a part-time worker in her first job at Payless. She was from a low-income neighborhood and had few viable options in life. To see her gain confidence in helping customers and become successful was heartwarming. Another memory is of a young mainland Chinese technician who was trained to become a supervisor in Taiwan. The Taiwanese employees were resistant to anyone from China taking on a supervisory role; but the technician won them over. He grew in confidence as his skills developed. He was the first Chinese employee to rise to that position.

Strecker believes that as a leader, you have greater leverage to make a difference in people's lives. A leader's command over resources is aimed at making a company more successful, but it can be equally powerful in creating meaningful experiences for people. That's where the joy comes in. And it's just as important to create meaningful experiences for someone who fails.

For instance, whenever people are fired from a company, they often go on to do better somewhere else. Typically, this is because they discover a position more in line with their skills. Larry always hated firing people, but he learned to turn that difficult experience into a positive one by helping them refocus and by staying in touch with them.

People asked him, "When will you come back to work?" knowing that he has so much to offer. But Strecker says he isn't coming back. He feels that he has more time now to touch people in meaningful ways.

If Strecker does return to an active leadership role, perhaps he will do so outside of business—through a nonprofit organization, a school, or a church. Indeed, the spiritual dimension of life holds great fascination for Strecker. He even formed his own personal board of spiritual advisors to help him in that quest. Nevertheless, the drive for *more* makes it difficult for any successful young person to resist the call to get back in the game. And we are as surprised as Strecker's friends that he has resisted thus far.

To Larry Strecker, the reasons are easy to grasp. Life is a journey, not a destination. The journey shouldn't be focused just on work, but also on health, friends, family, and spirituality. Trying to fulfill this new role in his life, Strecker may not be able to convince others, but he believes he can serve as a model. In fact, that's the most challenging leadership role he has ever assumed. After all, in order to be a successful model for others, you need to truly live by your own principles. Few things in life are simpler—or more difficult.

Between a Handshake and a Bear Hug: The Story of Paul Brainerd, Aldus Publishing, and the Social Venture Network

Perhaps all revolutionaries are idealists at heart, but few seem to live up to the purity of the vision they promise the world. Paul Brainerd has proven to be an exception to that rule in two disparate leadership endeavors.

In the area of software applications, Brainerd revolutionized desktop publishing by giving ordinary individuals the power that was once exclusive to media organizations and large corporations.

And in the area of philanthropy, Brainerd revolutionized the concept of giving back by showing people of wealth how to leverage their skills, experiences, and passions to amplify the impact of their charitable donations.

Although his career is divided in two, his leadership path connects them. Like a pattern of concentric circles, old ideas are revisited from a fresh perspective, even as new ideas continue to spiral upward.

From Reporter to High Tech Publisher

As a student in the late 1960s and early 1970s, Paul Brainerd had a passion for journalism. While studying for his undergraduate business degree at the University of Oregon and his journalism master's at the University of Minnesota, Brainerd edited campus newspapers. Reporting on the wave of antiwar protests during the U.S. involvement in Vietnam, Brainerd became a believer in activism. He embraced the idea that individuals can influence government or business if they have the right tools at their disposal.

He also learned some lessons about leadership. As an undergraduate, he participated in a sociology experiment in which a group of people needed to solve a problem together. It was necessary for someone to take a leadership role and focus the direction of the others. Brainerd also recognized that trust was needed within the group. For years after this experiment, he continued to develop his leadership and trust-building skills. He found within himself an ability to take risks, make decisions, and help people move in the same direction.

After completing his journalism degree, Brainerd went to work for the *Minneapolis Star Tribune.* He learned some tough but valuable lessons on the job. Although he had no mentor, he observed some key people around him and recognized what he was *not* cut out to do.

The editor was a respected journalist. Brainerd could see that he would never be successful in that role because he lacked the political savvy that was critical to providing editorial direction. This awareness gave him a sense of freedom. It let him see his own skills more clearly and taught him how to better apply his energy.

He liked technology and he understood what it took to publish a newspaper. He also had a strong drive to get things done. These interests were eventually united in a single dream. While that dream was developing, Brainerd moved from Minnesota.

He left journalism to become an executive at a high tech company. When the division he was managing was closed down, he was eager to give his own ideas a try, so he left the company and started the first leg of a great adventure.

The vision he had for publishing, although highly technical, was radical at its heart. Brainerd wanted to develop software that would serve as productivity tools for laying out newspaper pages. Seeking seed money, he worked the venture capital circuit and pitched his idea 48 times before getting two investment groups to back him. Even then, much of his own money went toward the launch of his prototype.

In 1984, Brainerd named the company Aldus. He refined his business plan and his pitch to high tech companies while his four engineers worked on coding in a Seattle studio apartment. Initially, Brainerd and his team were going to sell their product to publishing companies for several hundred thousand dollars. One day, he had a face-to-face meeting with Steve Jobs, the CEO of Apple Computer. Jobs flipped Brainerd's business model upside down. He told Brainerd that Aldus ought to be in the business of "democratic publishing" and that the software product PageMaker should be sold for $99 and bundled with Apple's Macintosh computers.

Brainerd found the meeting with Jobs to be frustrating, but something about his idea resonated with Brainerd's own values. He did the numbers. If he radically altered the Aldus business model for a low-cost, high-volume approach, could he price PageMaker at under $100?

The numbers didn't work. The lowest price he could manage and remain profitable was $495. But the vision of a broad market appealed to Brainerd, so he decided to take a risk. Tied to Macintosh's exciting marketing campaign, PageMaker was sold to 60,000 customers in the first year. Brainerd was able to secure the revenue he needed to allow Aldus to survive—and flourish.

What he didn't anticipate was how PageMaker and Aldus's suite of desktop publishing products would revolutionize communication. With the advent of the personal computer, the power of professional publishing was put into the hands of individuals, small businesses, nonprofits, and anyone else with a message to convey. Artists, entrepreneurs, and graphic designers gained more creative freedom.

Paul Brainerd changed the nature of publishing and gave desktop computer users a critical platform. In 1994, he was awarded the prestigious Gutenberg Prize for his contribution to the art and craft of printing.

Leading Aldus

Brainerd never saw himself as a tycoon in the model of Bill Gates, Steve Jobs, or Larry Ellison. He did not want to be linked to the life of his company. He intended to hand over the reins at a suitable time and move on. But after launching Aldus in 1984, Brainerd felt a moral obligation to lead his firm through its critical early years.

He faced many entrepreneurial challenges in expanding that small, five-person studio to a business that had 1,000 employees operating in 50 countries. As he steered Aldus through that growth phase, Brainerd focused on finding good leaders to help run the company. His goal was to hire people who were more skilled or capable than he was.

His philosophy of leadership separated skills from abilities. Leadership skills included team building, hiring, setting objectives, resolving conflict, and articulating the vision publicly. Leaders would use these skills like a tool kit, adding to them or refining them as circumstances required.

To Brainerd, a leader's abilities were more a way of being. These included listening, empathy, healing, awareness, persuasion, conceptualization, foresight, stewardship, and commitment to individual and community growth. Leaders who developed these abilities were special assets.

Brainerd cultivated a cadre of senior executives who shared his view and advocated the key principles of the Aldus culture. Within its culture, they would pursue collaborative problem-solving efforts in small groups. The company actively embraced their customers' core values and listened carefully to their needs. Everyone worked hard at creating a sense of community in an organization where values really mattered.

Aldus went public in 1987. Brainerd was already beginning to miss the days of creative product development and customer relations. As CEO, he needed to stay focused on the numbers, but he knew that he would eventually want to move on to other interests. In 1991, he told his board that he wanted to find a successor before the company's 10-year anniversary.

It was more difficult to replace the founder than he would have expected. By 1994, he actively sought a partner to buy or merge with the company. In the industry, Brainerd was considered a gentleman—someone with the personal and professional respect of his rivals. This made it relatively easy to initiate merger talks. He drew up a list of potential partners and started discussions.

John Warnock, CEO of Adobe Systems, was one of those potential partners. Since the inception of Aldus, Adobe had been an admired competitor. Despite the fact that Adobe and Aldus fought for the same customers, some of their product offerings did not overlap. Conceivably, they could be great partners.

Brainerd and Warnock worked hard to communicate the merger to the employees of both companies in such a way that it would feel like the marriage of equals. For Adobe, the merger came at a critical time. It was ready to scale up its desktop publishing capabilities. For Paul Brainerd, the merger gave him the capital and the freedom to engage in a new adventure in philanthropy.

Entrepreneurial Philanthropy

If philanthropy was a tool to reach an outcome, how should it be used for maximum impact? Brainerd brought his leadership skills, abilities, and experiences to bear on this question. With one-third of the money from his deal with Adobe ($40 million), he created the Brainerd Foundation. Then he tried to figure out how best to devote his time and resources to it.

He used his journalistic skills to investigate the situation. For three months, he traveled the West Coast to interview activists, researchers, and politicians to determine what his philanthropic philosophy should be. Traditionally, most wealthy people "gave back" at the end of their lives, to leave a legacy. There was a new generation of idealistic, successful young people who were also eager to give back. But these younger philanthropists didn't want simply to write checks to charities; they needed to feel actively engaged. Brainerd saw untapped possibilities, and he was eager to explore them.

Most of those young idealists made their money in the high tech sector by obtaining venture capital and realizing their entrepreneurial visions. Brainerd had traveled the same path. Building successful entrepreneurial ventures involved the rigors of honing an idea, pitching it to experienced investors, and receiving not just their money, but their business advice and partnership. Brainerd realized that the venture capital model offered a radical but compelling new approach to philanthropy that could forever change the way people give back.

In 1997, Brainerd formed Social Venture Partners. From a core group of 30 friends in the Seattle area, the organization expanded to include hundreds of partners in 24 cities throughout North America.

The approach is simple but effective: Each member of the Social Venture fund must commit a minimum of $5,000 a year for two years. In return, members participate in the fund's management and select grant recipients. They may also directly contribute their time and expertise as volunteer advisors for the recipient nonprofit organizations.

Compared to traditional giving approaches, Social Venture Partners works to develop a longer-term relationship with its network of nonprofit companies—much like a venture capitalist's long term perspective on investments. Venture volunteers work side by side with the leaders of the organizations they are funding, and use their skills to assess needs, set objectives, and fulfill strategic plans.

Brainerd has found important differences between the business and nonprofit sectors. By principle, Social Venture Partners approaches nonprofits in a learning mode. It listens closely to each nonprofit's concerns, goals, and needs before making any recommendations.

Some nonprofits are surprised by this, since they are used to making a pitch and receiving a check without the donor seeking involvement. But Brainerd and his partners establish a level of trust with those organizations. They learn first, and after a time make suggestions, but never give directions.

In turn, Social Venture volunteers learn about leadership. Nonprofit leaders connect passionately with their causes. They communicate a depth of emotion and feeling from the heart that holds peoples' attention and motivates them to support their causes. From them, Brainerd learned to be more collaborative and less directive in his leadership style. In the volunteer world, it is critical to show respect for the feelings and interests of others. Brainerd feels that such abilities will be critically important with the emerging leaders of tomorrow.

The Difference

Through Social Venture Partners and the Brainerd Foundation, Paul Brainerd made an impact in many areas of the world. He takes great joy in founding new philanthropic ventures and developing leaders to head these nonprofit organizations.

Brainerd stepped back from board chairman to director and moved on to the next challenge. It was an incredible experience to see an idea grow, mature, and flourish, and to see the team become confident in their direction. Brainerd knew that feeling very well during his years in business, but that feeling was more profound for his philanthropic works. They imparted a deeper sense of satisfaction and meaning.

Brainerd tells a story to illustrate that feeling. He and his wife Debbi recently established a facility called IslandWood. Built on 225 acres of Bainbridge Island in the Pacific Northwest, it provides inner-city youths a pastoral setting where they can learn about science, art, and technology. Brainerd likes to visit and have dinner with the children, as well as watch their programs and interact with its faculty.

One evening, he asked a fifth-grade girl how she was enjoying her experience. She walked away without answering. Taken aback, Brainerd asked an instructor about the young girl. He learned that she was from a troubled family. In fact, she'd only spoken about 10 words all year in school.

The next day, the little girl was out in the woods and saw a deer. She excitedly ran back to the rest of the group to show them what she had seen. She was so moved that it unlocked something in her soul. According to the instructors, the girl began to talk openly—and hasn't stopped since.

That's the distinction, Brainerd said, between his work in business and philanthropy. It's the difference between a handshake and a bear hug.

Climbing Mission Hill: The Story of Anthony von Mandl and the Wine of the Okanagan Valley

Leaders must endure many low moments in the struggle to reach a lifelong dream. Sometimes the climb is lonely, and no one in the leader's life can bolster the passion and effort required. Sometimes the leader lands on plateaus of difficulty, where unforeseen setbacks make the vision seem distant. How, despite these struggles, do some leaders not only keep going for it, but define their leadership through it?

In the fall of 1972, Anthony von Mandl was a slight 22-year-old who'd grown up in Europe and Canada. Despite his age, he already possessed an unusual dream: to create his own wine business. Nine years later, after a great deal of entrepreneurial hardship, he bought a run-down winery in the dry, sun-soaked interior of British Columbia known as the Okanagan Valley.

The move would have astonished any expert in the wine industry. No one in the world had ever heard of Okanagan Valley wine. The region was famous for its apples, cherries, and peaches, but not its grapes. The few wines produced there were of the cheap, screw-top variety. It would have been easier for von Mandl to have purchased a similar property in California's Sonoma County or Napa Valley, but he took the road less traveled.

In fact, he believed that the extraordinary microclimate of the Okanagan Valley had everything necessary to make great wine. Also, he had been born in British Columbia and wanted to build a world caliber wine business for the province. He would create a legacy of lasting significance and turn the region he loved into a destination.

Achieving his dream would require building a world-class winery from scratch, confronting the prejudices of the international wine community, weathering the heavy-handed tactics of established competitors, and overcoming Byzantine government restrictions to private commerce in alcohol. (And within a year, interest rates would hit 25 percent.) Still, on that June day when von Mandl took over the old winery outside Kelowna, British Columbia, all of those obstacles were made small by the excitement of the moment.

When von Mandl opened the doors of the winery, his heart sank. It was in disrepair and infested with fruit flies. It was just another setback. He gathered his information and went to work. He renamed the winery Mission Hill.

Standing Apart

Anthony von Mandl carries himself with the bearing of a trained actor or skilled politician. Articulate and intelligent, he conveys an air of worldly sophistication perfectly balanced by his relaxed informality. He gives a likable and trusting impression. He puts people at ease by directing all his attention to them, as if he has all the time in the world. It's not apparent how hard he has worked all his life and how much he takes on each day.

His family fled Vienna, Austria for Canada just ahead of Hitler's army. They had to leave their fortune behind. Both his parents were sophisticated and educated. His father was a doctor of law and a classical scholar and historian. His mother was a fashion designer with a love of music and art. Neither showed any predilection for business, but they gave their son his aesthetic sense and an artist's eye.

When he was nine years old, his parents returned to Vienna to reclaim their lives and belongings. Tearing him from the familiarity of Vancouver had a major impact on von Mandl. Back in Austria, he had no language skills or cultural knowledge. He had to adjust quickly as a foreigner. The next five years in

Vienna may have been difficult, but they helped him build inner strength.

At 14, he returned to Canada to attend high school. After studying economics at the University of British Columbia, his interest in finance and banking brought him to the Bank of Montreal as an associate. Three months into the training program, his instructors had grown frustrated with him. As a trainee, von Mandl was always asking "Why?" The program was not looking for people who asked questions, it wanted people who executed efficiently. A distraught von Mandl knew he didn't fit in and left the bank.

But he did have another passion. As a student, his love of wine led to a partnership with an Austrian family friend to distribute it in North America. He thought he could make that side business his main focus and build a wine company.

Filled with excitement by this new idea, he talked with his father about his future. His father was not a businessman and had no sense of what starting up a business entails, but he gave von Mandl all the emotional support he needed and let him live at home while he got on his feet. "Whatever you need," he said.

So, at 22 and without financing or personal capital, Anthony von Mandl started his wine business from a room in his parent's house.

Never Make a Decision When You're Backed into a Corner

Next, he spent some time in Europe. He met small high-end wine producers in Germany's Moselle Valley and formed a marketing company. He was advanced $1,000, to be repaid from sales commissions. With that, he set up a modest office in Toronto and went to work. No one he worked with in Europe spoke English, but he fortunately spoke some German. He was good at selling, but it took time to execute orders.

Another challenge was Canadian liquor regulations. Sales were controlled through a bureaucracy of provincial liquor control boards. Restaurants, for example, were required to buy their wines through the control boards. The only domestic Canadian markets open to von Mandl were airlines. His wines had high quality and low prices, so he did well at first. He expanded quickly to all three national airlines; but the market was small and it was a difficult time to be in the private wine-marketing business.

Frustrated with the restrictions, von Mandl wrote to the liquor control board with a modest proposal. He challenged the experts there to taste his wines. If they concluded that he offered better value than the wines currently sold by the control board, he deserved to sell his wines in their stores.

Unfortunately, that private message went public. One night, over dinner with some of his restaurateur friends in Vancouver, von Mandl told them of his struggles in the wine business. A business writer in attendance wrote an article about von Mandl's proposal. The story resulted in von Mandl being blacklisted by the liquor control board.

His business was squeezed by this lack of access, but he learned a valuable lesson. With one revenue door closed, he needed to think laterally to keep others open.

He moved to California just as a white wine boom was happening in the United States. He obtained a California wine importing license and rented a bankrupt oriental carpet store in an unsafe part of Los Angeles to serve as his warehouse, office, and bedroom. Von Mandl ran an ad in the local paper, drove around in his station wagon selling his wine during the day and then delivered the wine at night. Then he would return to the carpet store and sleep on an army surplus cot.

Nothing worked. Ordering from distributors, he thought he could sell 50 to 100 cases of wine at a time, but few buyers were interested in quantity. He finally received an order from a liquor store for 90 cases. On the day he went to pick up his check, a sign on the door said that the company was in receivership.

He felt there was no point in going on. Even though his experiences selling on the street would help him later, he felt like a failure when he decided to abandon his Los Angeles operations. The sun was setting as he drove to the airport. He was planning to fly to Miami to attend a wine convention; but when he tried to use his credit card, he was informed that it was tapped out. To add insult to injury, she kept his card.

Despite those blows, von Mandl was soon thinking about business again. He instinctively sensed that there had to be a silver lining to his misfortune. Over time, his faith was reinforced. Some of his most important lessons came from his mistakes. In this case, what could he do differently or better? He knew that if he could just crack open the fortress, he could push all the way in. He had failed because he had been naïve about people and strategy. He needed to make better long-term decisions and keep his ultimate goals in mind. Restless, eager and driven, he pondered those lessons and concluded that he needed to diversify his supply.

He looked for suppliers in Europe and in California and discovered that no one would give over their marketing rights to a 24-year-old. To compound the problem, he needed to offer better-quality wines at lower prices just to get in the door with Canadian customers. He canvassed wineries that were not yet selling in Canada, but most didn't care to go there. Finally, he got a break with Sebastian, a well-known California winery. He then gained a listing at the British Columbia Liquor Control Board.

His business soon began to grow. He offered better value, added other great wines to his list, and gained a bigger share of the wine-import business. Soon, larger distillers started to take notice. As von Mandl made a new wine successful, large distillers like Seagram would move in for the kill, convincing the suppliers to switch over to them. There were no long-term contracts in the business then. The large firms' sales force outnumbered von Mandl's ten to one, and quickly scooped up the market he had so painstakingly built. After four years, he wondered if it was finally time to quit.

He was frustrated. Every move he'd made had been the right one. Single-handedly he was creating excitement in several wonderful new wines. But he couldn't compete against a behemoth like Seagram. He called his father to tell him it was all over.

His father—who knew little about business but a lot about life—told him to think through the options and alternatives. "Never make a decision when you're backed into a corner," he said. He also suggested that his son return to Vancouver and live at home until he worked things out from a position of clarity.

These words of support gave von Mandl a sense of calm, and the importance of his dream came rushing back to him. As he reflected on how he could make his business invulnerable to competitors, the answer came to him: If he owned his own labels and brands, no one could take them away.

Own the Brand

In Bordeaux, much of the wine is either insipidly dry and characterless—or very sweet. Von Mandl created his own blend, mixing several Bordeaux varieties to shape a wine with more character and color. He created a brand-name upscale label to go with the wine and called it St. Jovian. The wine was a huge success. Almost overnight, his fortunes as a wine marketer were transformed.

After that, the major brands came to von Mandl. This time, he drew up long-term contracts. He was unnerved to be so businesslike with suppliers who were decades older than he was, but he put on a brave face and held his ground. The suppliers agreed to his terms, and taught him important lessons. He had taken out the middleman, gone to the source, established a world-class brand with his blends, and secured long-term contracts to buy in bulk. This made him invulnerable to any moves by his competitors.

When he purchased his own winery near Kelowna in British Columbia, the strategy grew out of his determination to own the brand. Still, the early years were difficult. Interest rates shot up to 25 percent, which crippled growth.

To create cash flow and to finance his dream, von Mandl had to think laterally again. First, he attracted Corona beer to the Canadian market, just in time for the Expo '86 world's fair in Vancouver. And second, he started the Okanagan Cider Company and created the world's first line of flavored ciders.

He marketed his cider in Canadian beer bottles. At the time, there was only one standard bottle size in Canada. It was a wide, stubby-necked bottle that could be reused up to 40 times. It was cheaper to recycle them than to make new ones, so von Mandl became part of the recycling float. He was presented with a multimillion dollar bill for his share, just as the float system collapsed.

It was a devastating burden for a cash-strapped company. He was left with an enormous inventory of used, beat-up beer bottles. At the time, there was no cider business in the United States, so von Mandl came up with a new marketing concept. He would sell Clark's Great Canadian Cider in genuine rugged

Canadian bottles. Eventually, he managed to sell all the cider at cost and get his money back. His employees were amazed by the maneuver, but von Mandl had remembered his father's words: "When you're in a corner, there's always a solution." Thinking creatively was a vital aspect of leadership.

The strong Canadian sales of Okanagan Cider helped to keep his business running. Von Mandl next introduced California Cooler to British Columbia, further diversifying his portfolio. But his heart was in wine. After ten years of trying to get the winery on a stronger foundation, it was time to begin his next quest. He needed an experienced wine maker who could turn the grapes of the Okanagan Valley into extraordinary wine.

He looked all over the world. In New Zealand, he met John Simes, who had turned around the wine industry in his home country. Von Mandl convinced him to do the same thing at the Mission Hill winery in British Columbia.

Two years later, they brought Mission Hill's first vintage, the 1992 Grand Reserve Chardonnay, to the International Wine and Spirit Competition in London. There were 300 tasters and thousands of wines for blind tasting. When the judges selected the top Chardonnay, they announced that it was Mission Hill, from the Okanagan Valley. There was a perceptible shock in the room. No one had ever heard of such a place.

Fearing that it must have been a mistake, the chairman asked for a second blind tasting. Mission Hill won again. John Simes received his award in front of the Lord Mayor of London and 650 of the world's greatest wine connoisseurs.

Building a Legacy

Winning the award for best Chardonnay marked a new leg in the journey. With Simes, von Mandl made an enormous investment in the Okanagan Valley. They used the latest scientific technology to gather data on climate and soil conditions, exploring the area's great potential. On the business side, von Mandl launched a new product, Mike's Hard Lemonade. It sold like crazy and yielded immense cash flow.

Then von Mandl returned to his long-term dream of turning the estate—and the Okanagan Valley—into a destination. He told his handpicked crew of architects and construction workers that they would be working on something significant, not just for themselves but for their children and grandchildren. They created buildings and a bell tower in a distinct European style, plus an amphitheater for an annual summer Shakespeare festival. The valley began to draw attention from all over the world.

It was an achievement 23 years in the making, and it had required more effort and creativity than he'd ever imagined. Although his own passion and drive was vital in achieving that dream, along the way he recognized that he needed to be a leader, too. In that sense, leadership grew out of pursuing his dream; although it was not his initial goal. He needed people and resources to get where he wanted to go, and that meant becoming a leader.

In the winery's first year, he needed to rebuild the facilities extensively. The beautiful wine cellars were hewn from volcanic rock, but the stone was unstable. Geological engineers told him that he would have to spray the rock with a concrete coating, but von Mandl didn't want to destroy the aesthetic character of the cellars. An employee, with no expertise in that area, discovered an approach that preserved the look of the rock.

It was a revelation to von Mandl that he now had people who shared his dream. In fact, while he only had 11 employees at first and no sales for months, he discovered that his team was united in a common vision. He began to involve them in every aspect of his business. He needed their expertise to secure his firm's existence. This was a symbiotic relationship since it was clear his people relied on him, too. He had been an entrepreneur for so long that relying on others was a switch for him. He found new leaders among his people and gave them opportunities to grow.

This was an awkward position for someone so used to being independent. He often found that it was harder to explain problems to the team—to build their confidence—than it was to come up with the solutions on his own. As a result, he often surrounded himself with other entrepreneurs. But such people usually left him at some point to pursue their own dreams. He recognized a need for diversity and came to appreciate different points of view. His staff solutions and approaches enriched the winery and the business in surprising ways. As their leader, von Mandl had to overcome the feeling that he needed to know everything. Instead, he let others go forward on their own. From his early struggles, he believed in treating people with respect and dignity. So he became receptive to new ideas and felt a deeper satisfaction from seeing people succeed at things that were too difficult at first.

Over the next two decades, his success mounted and his approach to leadership gradually changed. Initially, he felt only responsible for himself. If the business failed, he might lose his house, but he could always pick himself up and begin again. Today, he feels a strong sense of obligation and accountability to his employees and their families. He finds it deeply rewarding to meet with the children of his employees, many of whom he has known since they were born. He sees the business as an extended family and might lose sleep over a tough decision, since so many people's futures hang in the balance.

He has learned that an individual's vision can make a difference in the world. He thinks of his business as a European-style family company, which is focused more on the long view than quarterly earnings. He knows that success is not about money but about leaving behind a legacy—that the organization will continue to grow because young leaders contribute to the vision. In that sense, leadership is never about the leader. A service orientation—the opposite of narcissism—is necessary for long-term success.

Anthony von Mandl achieved everything he's ever dreamed about in his business. In addition to the winery, his firm, Mark Anthony Wine Merchants, became the largest spirits importing business in Canada. He aims to continue that legacy by fostering the next generation of leaders. A perfectionist like von Mandl can rapidly become absorbed in his passion to create, or in his drive to be first or best. But the connections he's forged with the people around him are real and deep. He gives everything to everyone, every day. Now he is reckoning with his own sense of *enough* and is looking for other areas of his life for fulfillment. He says, "It's not accidental. This is the time to move onward in life. After all, coincidence is God's way of remaining anonymous."

The Optimist: The Story of John Keane and Keane Inc.

John Keane is a septuagenarian who has faced severe medical issues and survived, yet he conveys a magnetic presence. He claims that he never set out to be a leader, but everyone who has ever worked with John Keane knows he is one. He has an artist's eye and an engineer's mind. He is visionary, process oriented, and detail minded. He knows what needs to be done and the importance of doing it right.

When Keane greets people, they become comfortable with him so quickly that they can imagine themselves heading out to a ball game with him or getting their families together to enjoy a picnic. At the same time, people want to follow Keane because he has vision and a unique way of making sense of complex strategies. "Genius," he once said, "is to put things into simple words that everyone can understand."

A determined optimist, Keane never gave up on his dream of turning his software development company into one of the premier companies in the world. Today, Keane Inc., which he founded in 1965 above a donut store in Boston, has grown from one person to 10,000, with offices on three continents.

Keane would never claim that those 40 years have been a straight line to success. But the greatness of his story rests on the fact that he founded his company in an industry that didn't exist. Software services were not considered something anyone could build a company around. Amazingly, Keane saw the future, created the dream, and built it on the prophetic premise that hardware would become secondary to software and that the greatest industry opportunities would come to those who could design ways to bind and connect businesses with each other and with customers.

This flew in the face of prevailing orthodoxies. But that is what leadership can accomplish. Even when the world seemed set in stone—or ruled by an iron fist, as IBM seemed to rule the computer world at the time—visionary leaders see a different future and make it happen. It takes a special person to carry that vision all the way and perhaps relentless optimism is the most important attitude to take.

Entrepreneurial Beginnings

John Keane grew up on New York's Long Island when it was still farmland and families sent their children to small schoolhouses. His father took the train every day into Manhattan, where he worked in the financial industry. Keane's family was competitive, and that became his way of living and working. His passion was never about beating the other guy, but about setting clear goals, going for them, and surpassing his own expectations. Along the way he learned to play tennis and excel in school while developing a sailor's love for the sea.

Keane attended Harvard, and after graduating in 1954, joined the U.S. Navy. When his service was over, he joined IBM in the early 1960s, heading up sales of their state-of-the-art mainframe computer. IBM was not providing any modification or support at the time, even though they promised service to get the sale. In this gap, Keane saw an opportunity he could exploit.

He had no sense of the risk he was about to take, but he quit his secure job at IBM and went out on his own. He obtained his first computer services contract for $9,000 a year. He saw great opportunity in the emerging computer industry for people with the technical knowledge and the wherewithal to obtain contracts to supply that service.

Initially, Keane had no idea how that new service industry would take shape. In his office above the donut shop, he drew up plans to convince companies that he could run their businesses better through better software solutions. Keane had to be the manager, salesman, and project manager on every account.

He convinced his wife, Marilyn, that everything would be okay. They would have to work hard for a long time, but some day Keane Inc. would be a formidable company. His wife's only worry was about imbalance in their lives, so they made an agreement. Every Friday night they would have a date together, and weekends would be reserved for spending time with their three children. During the week, John Keane was free to work at his own incredible pace.

Boston Gas, one of Keane's important clients, had a project for which he would be perfect. But Arthur Andersen was bidding on the project, too. The CEO of Boston Gas told Keane that his board would have a hard time approving Keane's bid because he had such a small company. After all, if something happened to John Keane, who would do the work?

Keane learned his first important lesson from that setback. He had to grow. After 90 days, he hired his first employee, and after 120 days, he hired his second. By the end of the year, he had 12 people, then 30, then 50.

Keane put a lot of thought into hiring. Who should be part of his company? He needed people to buy into his vision and leadership, not just his money. He decided that when he hired someone, he would not pay them more than they were getting in their current job. Therefore, he said, "I had to sell them, and they had to buy into the vision. If they didn't come, then they weren't the right people to help build my company." This was the theme he communicated to his people over the first seven years.

The business started to take shape. He was actively hiring staff and holding his customers' hands while determining their needs. He kept doing more work as his client base grew, and the clients became more appreciative and reliant on his assistance. During those early years, Keane never thought of what he was doing as leadership. He was helping to close deals, getting his hands into marketing and sales—whatever it took. He would take coffee breaks with the young people and help them understand where the company was headed, what its principles were, and what work processes it valued. As the company grew, everyone got so busy that face time with him became rare. So each month they had a team meeting at the Harvard Club.

"Leadership happened," Keane said. "We were too busy doing it to think about it." Leadership, he says, is not about managing people, but rather getting them to look at their job in a way that empowers them to increase their potential and have an impact.

The vision of Keane as a company was clear from the beginning, but they never considered it as a vision. They were trying to make their clients become more effective with computers. Standardizing work on projects was a significant challenge in the early 1970s, and Keane's company was no exception. At one point, Keane returned from a vacation to find that they were over budget on all seven of their projects. Therein lay the origins of Keane's principles of productivity management, an approach to systems thinking that is legendary in the information systems field. Keane's protocols allowed his people to work efficiently on various projects at various companies while ensuring quality control across all projects.

Seeing the Rocks

Today, Keane Inc. has nearly 10,000 employees in the United States, Canada, and the United Kingdom, plus an additional 2,000 outsourced employees in India. Although a large company, people operate in smaller groups. Keane found that small teams are a valuable way of handling workflow while maintaining and spreading the culture.

Keane can't have coffee and trade stories with every employee anymore. Those stories need to be told by others. But the executives of Keane all know the stories.

In the early 1990s, the computer industry was in a slump; and the Fortune 10 companies like IBM, GE, and AT&T were laying off thousands. For Keane, client budget cuts hurt the bottom line badly. For the first time in the company's history, there was an exodus of talent, and the numbers looked bleak. Everyone wondered, "How are we going to get out of this?"

Keane gathered his top managers, looked at each haggard face, and said: "We'll get through this, I promise." Keane used a sailing metaphor to explain his positive outlook: When the tide is in and the water is high, every boat looks good. Now the tide was out, and everyone was floundering. But Keane knew how to navigate at such a time. Sailing, after all, was in his blood. "When the tide is out," he said, "you can see the rocks. When the wind picks up again, we'll be the first to catch it. Be strong. Stay strong. We'll win. We have the right team and the right boat."

Keane knew how to make the best of a tough situation. "Sometimes your hard luck is your good luck," he said. His energy was unabated. If you went to John Keane with a challenge, he wouldn't see it as a problem. Rather, he loved finding solutions. He had a gift for teaching others, a belief in discipline, and an unshakable faith that things work out when everyone pulls together.

Despite his zeal, Keane is not a blind optimist. He knows that optimism alone will not get you to the top. He says that real entrepreneurs are not natural risk takers, but they do take calculated risks. The difference between being a real entrepreneur and a daredevil is that entrepreneurs carefully measure how far they will go with risk, and not beyond it.

"Imagine you are to receive $1,000 for every foot away from a bucket that you can throw a silver dollar into. How far does the entrepreneur step away from the bucket?" he chuckles. The real entrepreneur only steps as far back as he knows for sure he can throw the silver dollar in. The daredevil is a gambler and will take a long shot.

In information technology (IT) in the 1990s, there were many risk takers and few entrepreneurs. That's why Keane flourished where others failed. Leadership in an entrepreneurial culture is about making sure that the gamblers are kept in check; and the real entrepreneurs are able to move nimbly, innovate rapidly, and drive change.

Keane possesses another important characteristic for a leader of a new venture: He almost never exhibits stress. In turn, this calmness rubs off on others. Keane has an overbearing personality and an obsessive need for perfection and results. Yet he makes all of that palatable with his love of laughter, his ability to listen and connect with others, and the passion of his vision. He sees the role of a leader as making whole cloth: taking the many pieces of an organization and carefully weaving them into a fabric with the strength to withstand the pressure that would naturally pull threads apart.

Still Going for It

John Keane always believed that optimists do better. He was recognized as a master at harnessing his own energy around that enthusiasm. In his seventies, he practiced optimism in a new way after suffering a massive stroke. His family was told that there was no hope. But as Keane lay in Massachusetts General Hospital with no prognosis for recovery, somewhere deep inside him, optimism kept him alive. In fact, it allowed him to recover and return to the job, something that was well beyond the medical experts' expectations. Those who knew him best were not surprised. They'd heard him say many times that you need to stay positive in the worst situations.

What keeps John Keane going? He still shows up for work. In fact, six months after his stroke, he walked three miles to his office when it was closed because of a hurricane, just so he could be there in case anyone needed him. A few months later, he took a 27-hour flight to Australia to sign the biggest deal in his company's history and returned home two days later.

The truth is, John Keane loves to compete, and he has always seen business as a game, with all the requisite fun and disappointment. That business is a competitive and dynamic world keeps things interesting. When we asked Keane *Why lead?* he said, "If you don't, someone else will."

He has never felt completely satisfied with the many awards and rewards of leadership. Keane feels that the joy and meaning of leadership comes from the fact that "you never finally arrive as a leader—you always have to keep growing."

He feels great satisfaction at having built his company; but he continues to feel satisfaction playing the game, setting the vision, and watching it happen all around him. That's why he started leading in the first place, and that's why he continues to play the game today.

Believe in Justice, Pay the Price: The Story of Mary Robinson and the Presidency of Ireland

Most leaders have difficulty describing why they initially became leaders. Not so with Mary Robinson. She was born into leadership with a "judge's rectitude, a campaigner's zeal, the warmth of an old friend, and an acute sense of how to focus the global spotlight on a cause," said author J.F.O. McAllister.

Robinson has been a hero of twentieth century political leadership. She has been a barrister, a senator, the first woman to become president of Ireland, and United Nations High Commissioner for Human Rights. Today, in the age of terrorism, she took her leadership zeal to a new level with the Ethical Globalization Initiative in New York, which focuses on long-lasting security.

Robinson's concern for justice has been foremost at every stage of her remarkable career. Her beginnings may explain why justice is a primary issue for her and how her leadership has helped make the world a better place.

An Impoverished Land

Mary Robinson was born Mary Bourke on May 21, 1944, in County Mayo, Ireland. The history of County Mayo goes back thousands of years. When the Normans settled there in the eleventh century, they put in place a feudal system of large estates that created a dependency culture in land ownership and use. This system was at least in part to blame for Ireland's Great Potato Famine of 1845-49, which dramatically changed the nation. And County Mayo was one of its hardest hit regions.

Mary Rourke was the daughter of medical doctors. Her family had lived in County Mayo for generations. Her ancestors included Roman Catholic nuns and priests, as well as some adherents to the Anglican Church of Ireland. The poverty and the starvation of the Potato Famine drove many families out of Ireland, if they could afford to emigrate. That the Bourke family could have left, but stayed, had an impact on Mary Robinson. Instead of leaving like millions of others, the Bourke family endured and educated their children about the importance of justice. A dedication to making things right became part of the family code. As a young child Mary Bourke watched her parents struggle, even though, as medical doctors, they could have moved anywhere in the world.

When Mary was just reaching womanhood, she lost her mother. Mary's mother had instilled in her some important beliefs. She taught Mary that despite terrible hardships, doing the right thing and staying the course were crucial.

"When I was growing up, most people in County Mayo were poor," Robinson says. "I guess that's how I developed my interest in human rights. I don't mean to say that we were poor. In fact, I always considered myself quite rich. In addition, I had four brothers, two older and two younger. Being in the middle, I had to be interested in my own human rights!"

Robinson's parents viewed education as the best thing they could provide their children and sent Mary to a Catholic boarding school. She was a tomboy in a strict environment, who shied away from nothing and questioned everything. When she finished high school, she scored high enough on her examinations to enter Trinity College. There, she became involved in many leadership roles. This would hone her sense of right and wrong and stretch her intellect. Her successes at Trinity brought her to Harvard Law School.

"At Harvard Law, I was encouraged to think about wider issues," she said. "It was during the Vietnam War, when everyone was questioning the morality and injustices in the world. I was fortunate to spend that time at Harvard, when both faculty and students were taking on the issues of society."

Robinson also found herself among confident young people. Never a shy person, she found this atmosphere energizing. The experience gave her even more strength when she returned to Ireland to practice and teach law.

She had to decide what to focus on. It was a propitious moment in Irish history. Parliamentary elections were being held in both the lower chamber and the senate. No woman had ever been a senator in a legislative body that tended to favor such better known male professionals as professors and barristers. Robinson was only 25 years old, but a colleague suggested she fight for a seat, saying, "Why don't you put yourself forward and see if you can get elected."

She thought deeply about it, reviewing its disadvantages. She was young and a woman. She resolved that disadvantages could sometimes give one an edge, perhaps even let a new voice be heard. With great pluck, she campaigned and was elected to the Irish senate in August 1969.

Robinson now had a platform to advance the liberal agenda she believed in. In a country dominated by conservative Catholic doctrine, she fought for family planning and the right to divorce. As a spokesperson for women's rights, Robinson took on constitutional cases that had seemed hopeless. She represented women whose inability to afford a lawyer blocked their access to justice. She represented one particular woman who wanted a legal separation from a husband who beat her regularly. She took that case all the way to the high court and learned a valuable lesson: One has to stand tall and persevere when human rights are at stake.

The Presidency

Mary Robinson was an Irish Labor Party member of the senate for 20 years and was reelected six times. She effectively harnessed popular support for important causes and brought long-needed change to the system by working from the grass roots.

In 1985, Britain and Ireland were deeply embroiled in the long-running political struggle over Northern Ireland. Robinson's personal positions were not popular, and she was forced to resign from the Irish Labor Party. But she returned as an independent. It was a difficult change, but one made to stay true to her beliefs. As an independent, she rejoined the senate.

She also worked toward bringing Ireland into the European Union with her legal work for Irish business, trade union movements, and agriculture issues. It was a challenging and exciting time as Ireland transformed itself from a small, isolated country to one with access to all of Europe.

Then came a juncture that forced her to make a choice. In August 1989, she retired from the senate to focus the rest of her life on human rights and European Union law. She wanted to work from the political center as a lawyer and activist, and cut down on her teaching. It was an exciting change.

On Valentine's Day in 1990, she received a phone call from her old friend John Rogers, the former attorney general of the Irish Labor Party. Rogers asked if she could come see him in the morning. He had something important he needed to discuss with her. When she met him the next day, the subject could not have surprised her more. Rogers asked her to consider seeking the Irish Labor Party nomination for president in the upcoming election.

Robinson was completely taken aback. She had never considered the possibility. It was an incredible honor to be asked, especially since she was no longer a member of the Irish Labor Party. Nevertheless, her first impulse was to say no. The presidency was not a post for an activist. But how could she refuse?

She took a weekend to consider it, flying to London to mull over the idea with a distinguished colleague. The seed had been planted in her mind, and she couldn't root it out. She thought about the Irish constitution. Could there be a more influential position? She considered the constitutional responsibilities that would be hers.

On Monday, she told John Rogers that she was prepared to accept the nomination, but only if she could serve as an independent.

"I would not be rejoining the Labor Party," she explained. "Instead, I would go forward and gather a wide constituency and carve out a unique position for the modern Ireland that could emerge." The Labor Party agreed and nominated her as an independent. She was one of 300 to receive such a nomination, so the odds of her winning were slim indeed.

Campaigning was sheer drudgery for her, but she also found that it brought remarkable changes to her life. She connected with people of all backgrounds. The experience enriched her spirit and stiffened her resolve to elevate the cause of human rights to the highest level.

She wasn't prepared for the intrusions that would be made on her personal life, however. Her private life had always remained private. Now, it became public knowledge that her husband was Protestant and she was Catholic, which was considered a mixed marriage by many Irish. (Even her parents had frowned on their marriage.) "I had to be more public about who I was and what I was doing," Robinson says. "Initially this was difficult. But I found that the more I gave of myself, the more I gained the hearts and minds of others. And the people responded."

From these connections, she became the leader she is today. To establish trust with the people she wanted to represent, she had to become personally vulnerable. People needed to know who she was and why she deserved the privilege of leading them. She spoke from her heart about her passion for justice, how she would reconcile the disputes over Northern Ireland, and a host of other age-old troubles.

She gave speech after speech, each one a testament to her sense of justice. Her point of view emerged and strengthened. The support behind her began to swell, but in ways that had never been a factor in traditional politics before. She won the presidency with the support of Ireland's women, minorities, and socially downtrodden. An independent candidate, working from the grassroots, had stunned the powerbrokers. As Robinson put it, "I was elected by the women of Ireland, who instead of rocking the cradle rocked the system."

She used her inaugural address to discuss law and morality in Irish life. She looked around the house of parliament and remembered the December day in 1970 when she married and changed her name. She made the name change because her husband was her rock. They were both activists. In every election, there had been terrible criticism of her, and she felt that without his support, she never would have made it to the Irish Parliament. Still a tomboy at heart, she loved sports and competitive games; but rejection and criticism were always hard to take. As the newly elected president, she said, "I found that if you really believe in something, you must be prepared to pay a price to know what you are doing and feel confident about it. I was strengthened by having to pay that price early on."

Today, when she talks to young people, and even her own children, Robinson stresses the importance of taking a stand for worthwhile causes. Doing that will build an inner strength to support you in tough times. Being a leader, she believes, is full of tough choices. All leaders seek approval and want to be appreciated, even liked. Doing the right thing, however, is always more important.

Human Rights

After seven years as Irish president, Mary Robinson resigned. She had accomplished a great deal, particularly in the area of women's rights. When she began her tenure, birth control and family planning were illegal in Ireland. Today, they are available. Robinson transformed the position of president from a largely ceremonial role to one of true constitutional power. In the process, she was often stung by criticism and made to feel like an outcast in her own society. Nevertheless, the people of Ireland gave her a 93 percent job approval rating!

She resigned the presidency not to step back from the responsibilities of leadership, but rather to expand her focus to human rights on the world stage. In 1997, she was appointed the United Nations High Commissioner for Human Rights. Over the following five years, she fought many battles for people at the grassroots all over the world.

Today, Mary Robinson continues to lead human rights causes through her organization, the Ethical Globalization Initiative. "I have always had a strong sense of trying to break up imbalances, inequalities, and inequities," she says. Robinson is driven to make sure that the fundamental rights of all people are protected.

People have a right to avoid poverty and to have access to clean water and food. This is a long-term fight, for Robinson believes that the world will still be plagued by tyranny and terrorism as long as there is injustice and inequality. She works with some of Africa's poorest nations and brings the lens of human rights to issues of trade, development, and national debt.

Perhaps these unshakeable beliefs go back to Robinson's upbringing in a land forever scarred by economic and political injustices. But Robinson's search for solutions makes her a leader, even more than her sensitivity to injustice and her awareness of popular needs.

In her own words: "The aim of human rights is to move beyond the design and drawing-board phase, to move beyond thinking and talking about the foundation stones to laying those foundation stones, inch by inch, together."

Leaders are not pie-in-the-sky dreamers. They know how to get their hands dirty in the real work of achieving a goal. It is in this work that Mary Robinson—an activist, barrister, politician, and global advocate—has spent a lifetime.

Chapter 7
Someone Had to Do It

Ted Turner has a sign on his desk: "Lead, follow, or get out of the way." It's apropos to a category of leaders who stepped up because someone had to. Whether by chance or because they were born into it, Rajaa Khuzai, Mikhail Gorbachev, Hal Kvisle, Benazir Bhutto, and Ara Hovnanian became leaders because they had to.

Sometimes the right leader comes along at the right time and in the right place. Each of the leaders in this chapter, for monumentally different reasons, chose leadership. What was in their minds? Although such a question may not be answerable, you can read between the lines and reach your own conclusions.

Leaders lead, and rarely second guess themselves. You will find this to be movingly true when you read Mikhail Gorbachev's story.

You will also see that remarkable leaders arrive at the right time and do what has to be done, as Rajaa Khuzai and Benazir Bhutto did at dramatically different periods of their lives. The common thread? They had to do it despite the physical risks. And Benazir Bhutto made the ultimate sacrifice.

Then, there are leaders like Ara Hovnanian, who is a prime example of leading within a family as a second-generation leader. We know that family leaders are different from other leaders. After all, there is more at stake. Although leaders of family businesses are frequently not forced to take the role, subtle pressures to do so sometimes start with birth and continue every day at the supper table. It's not easy to fill your father's shoes. That becomes clear in Ara Hovnanian's story.

Hal Kvisle had always gotten the nod. Even when he was a youngster, he felt that he had to grasp the leadership baton. Isn't that what leaders do anyway? Many women leaders fall into this camp because they find it difficult to say no when others ask them to solve problems. Such leadership is almost always about making hard choices and personal sacrifices for the benefit of others. While it can be deeply stressful, draining, risky, and even dangerous, it can also be joyful. At times of crisis or war, it is said that leadership can be forged under fire.

As you will see from these stories, such fires can occur in many different situations. When a crisis arises and a leadership vacuum exists, someone must lead. Having become a leader, the burden of leadership becomes indelibly stamped on that person, and other leadership opportunities will emerge.

Leadership by Candlelight: The Story of Dr. Rajaa Khuzai and the Iraqi Governing Council

The intentions of the 11 armed men were clear. They had walked into the Women's Health Centre, a hospital in Diwaniyah, south of Baghdad, in order to loot it. The hospital director, Dr. Rajaa Khuzai, confronted them in her office. She was as frightened as she had ever been in her life, but she had no choice but to try and stop them. The hospital had 260 beds, half for obstetrics and gynecology patients and half for newborns and infants in pediatric care. For the hospital to lose any of their precious medical supplies would be devastating.

It was the spring of 1991. When the Gulf War began that January, the allies bombed post offices, gas stations, military bases, power stations, and bridges, but not hospitals or schools. The Iraqi Republican Guard had been quickly routed, and the allied troops were only 200 miles from Baghdad. There was no longer any Iraqi government to speak of and no sign of Saddam Hussein. Wild with freedom, the people brought down all of Saddam's statues and posters. The streets were in chaos, and looters ransacked buildings and houses openly. Indeed, other maternity hospitals in the region had already been looted and burned.

In her own hospital, Dr. Khuzai was the last doctor on staff. Everyone else had disappeared. Now, she was working day and night, acting as obstetrician, gynecologist, pediatrician, and administrator. Food, power, and medicine were in severe shortage; and she was struggling to conserve those supplies wherever possible. She discharged patients quickly so that their families could feed them. She changed the way she performed operations in order to save sutures for emergencies. She sent porters to the river a mile away for buckets of water to scrub the operating theater. She did 22 cesarean sections by candlelight.

She knew she could perform a cesarean with her eyes closed if she had to, but she prayed each time that her patients avoided severe bleeding. Now 11 men with guns had come to take what supplies she had left.

She was scared and alone, but stood her ground as though she felt no fear. Her indignation saved her. She told them that this wasn't her hospital—it was theirs. The hospital existed for their mothers, wives, and sisters, and for the babies of those women. If the men still wanted to loot, she was powerless to stop them; but she wanted them to know whom they were harming. Speaking to them in such a way put her own life in great danger. But the men with guns listened and went home. Amazed, she gave herself a moment to contemplate what had happened. She didn't know where that strength and determination had come from, but she sensed that it had more to do with her patients than with herself. There was no time to consider it more deeply. She got back to work.

Mother, Doctor, Leader

More than 14 years later, Dr. Rajaa Khuzai has become a political force in the creation of a new Iraq. Nevertheless, she views herself as an unlikely leader. Her journey illustrates the strength of an individual during a long period of hardship and the power of leadership as a beacon for others.

In her own mind, Dr. Khuzai is first a mother. She and her husband raised seven children in Iraq during 20 years of sanctions and intermittent war. Despite these circumstances, they have managed to create a strong, caring home life. Their children have survived wars, food shortages, political tyranny, death threats, and car bombs. They have learned to do their homework by candlelight. Yet they support their mother's political leadership efforts because of these hardships, not in spite of them.

While Rajaa Khuzai was busy studying and working, she was also busy having babies. Her nanny, a woman from New Zealand, had never even heard of Iraq. In those prewar days, Iraq wasn't yet making the news, but the Khuzais knew that much had changed in their country since their departure. The Baath Party, whose operatives sported mustaches like the one worn by Saddam Hussein, now controlled the government. Nevertheless, despite all the trappings of the good life in England, Rajaa Khuzai was an Iraqi patriot. She wanted to serve her country and raise her children there. Her husband realized that she would not be dissuaded. Together, they agreed to return to Iraq and be of service to their people.

In May 1977, they bought a new Mercedes-Benz in Stuttgart, intending to drive home in style. They traveled through Europe and Turkey before entering Iraq. At the border, the police told them that they were under arrest for spending too long outside the country. The Khuzais protested that they were now returning to Iraq as qualified specialists, fulfilling a great need. But the police insisted that their names were on a blacklist. It was only through the intercession of a friend from London—now a high-ranking Iraqi military doctor—that they were freed after several days and allowed to travel home to Diwanyiah. Even so, they were forced to travel with a soldier in the back seat and their children in tears throughout the journey.

Later that year, Rajaa Khuzai was appointed head of the Department of Obstetrics and Gynecology at the maternity hospital. The medical staff was well trained, and the hospital had excellent facilities. Still, Dr. Khuzai could impart a lot of knowledge and technical skill she learned from her advanced studies in England. The other doctors were afraid of her strong personality and associated with her only hesitantly. But Dr. Khuzai took the time to teach, showing the others what she knew. Soon, those colleagues began to feel close to her. They began to view her almost as a mother figure and turned to her for answers.

Twelve years later she was asked to be director of the hospital. The previous director had been dismissed amid accusations of corruption. Corruption was found everywhere in Iraq, a climate promoted by the Baathists. Few people could be trusted with authority. Many of Khuzai's colleagues and friends feared that she would fail, given the situation; but she accepted the responsibility and her new role as a leader.

Within four months, her challenges and responsibilities multiplied exponentially. Hussein invaded neighboring Kuwait. The United Nations punished his government with sanctions, but Saddam passed those hardships on to his own people. Basic necessities had grown scarce, making the operation of the hospital even more difficult. With a staff of 21 doctors and modern facilities, the hospital had once prided itself on providing the best care. Now Dr. Khuzai had to teach those doctors how to stretch their supplies and work under increasingly primitive conditions. When war broke out, bombing devastated the infrastructure of the country. Her colleagues fled in fear for their lives and the safety of their families. Dr. Khuzai stayed because the hospital needed her.

A ceasefire in the Gulf War was finally announced in 1991, but their relief was short-lived. Saddam Hussein was still in power and reasserted control over most of the country. The Republican Guard hit Diwanyiah with ground-to-ground missiles, indiscriminately blowing up houses, schools, and even hospitals.

Dr. Khuzai was in the middle of a cesarean section when her own hospital was hit. She had to evacuate everyone, workers and patients alike. They worked fast. She applied a dressing to her patient, put her on a trolley, and wheeled the woman to her husband in the waiting room. "Take your wife home," she said. "If we're all still alive in 10 days, bring her back so that I can remove the sutures." The man nodded, and started off hurriedly. "And please don't forget to return my trolley," she added.

The reprisals by Saddam Hussein were an awful sight. The Republican Guard rounded up young men—sometimes even women and children—and buried them alive. For years afterward, no one could speak about their mass graves, even though it was common knowledge. People were too afraid to talk. When Dr. Khuzai met with foreigners, she didn't dare to breathe a word about it because Iraqi intelligence agents were everywhere.

The next decade was very hard. Hussein's rule was relentlessly vicious, and the sanctions made daily life a struggle. As the director of a hospital, Dr. Khuzai's salary amounted to about one U.S. dollar a month. To help her family, she worked extra hours in private clinics and hospitals. The hours were tough, but at least she was still serving people through her profession.

She knew university professors and engineers who sold cigarettes or drove taxis just to get by. Many good people started to sell their furniture and belongings, even their windows and doors. Lacking any legitimate way to make money, corruption became rampant. Simply put, everyone had become tainted. If you weren't corrupt, you didn't survive.

The Call to Serve

Late one morning in June 2003, the phone in Dr. Khuzai's office rang. After answering, it took her a moment to recover. She had not expected to hear that the caller was a Major Hope calling on behalf of Director of Reconstruction and Humanitarian Assistance L. Paul Bremer III, administrator of the Coalition Provisional Authority. He asked her to meet with him at two-thirty that afternoon in Baghdad. It was 150 miles away, but she got in the car immediately.

The trip gave her time to reflect on how much had changed in Iraq. Following the country's liberation in April 2003, she had read a survey stating that young widows in Iraq were 7 percent of the population. Many of these widows were as young as 14, some just 10. Often, they ended up living on the street because their families could not support them. Dr. Khuzai decided that it was time to help these women. In May 2003, in addition to her responsibilities at the hospital, she started the Iraqi Widows' Organization and began to look for funds. Perhaps it was for this reason that Bremer had called. Still, how odd it was, after all these years, to be invited into Saddam Hussein's presidential palace.

As she entered the palace, she was flooded with emotion. It was from here, where Bremer greeted her, that so much pain and death had been inflicted on the Iraqi people. In his office, he asked about her background, family, how long she had been in Iraq, and how long she had lived in England. Then he changed the subject.

"Do you know anything about the constitution?" he asked. Dr. Khuzai understood the basic principles of constitutional authority from her life in England. Bremer continued to question her about elections and voting; and Dr. Khuzai did her best to answer him, although she did not understand the purpose of the discussion. Finally, Bremer announced that he had another meeting and asked if she had any questions. Confused, Dr. Khuzai asked, "Why am I here?"

Bremer looked at her and said, "Because you are a strong woman."

When she returned home, her husband asked what Bremer had wanted. She said that she didn't know. Her husband was surprised. "Didn't you ask?" "All he said was that I'm a strong woman," she replied, trying to explain her confusion.

Two days later, Major Hope called to congratulate her. "You've got the job," he said.

"What job?" she asked. "I've already got a job."

She had been appointed as a member of the Iraqi Interim Governing Council. The news stunned Dr. Khuzai, and she explained to Paul Bremer that she needed to discuss the offer with her husband and family. He said he would call her in 48 hours to hear her decision.

That night, the Khuzais had a family meeting. Her husband, four girls, and three boys sat around the table. She told them about the position she had been offered. They could only stare. Her husband said, "Take it."

"How can I take it?" she asked. "I've never even been in politics."

"Well, this is your chance," he replied. "You've been saving the lives of mothers and babies for the last 25 years, but now it's time to help all Iraqis."

Rajaa Khuzai was still filled with doubts, but her husband countered each concern. She said that she didn't know anything about the role; but he told her she would learn on the job. She said she didn't want to fail because she had been successful all her life, as a wife, a mother, and a doctor. Her husband told her that she couldn't know if she was going to fail until she tried.

When Bremer called again 48 hours later, she accepted his offer. On July 13, 2003, the Governing Council was presented on television; and Dr. Rajaa Khuzai was one of three women standing with 22 men.

Difficulties of Leadership

Political leadership has not been easy. There have been many sacrifices, compromises, disappointments, and frustrations. This has left Rajaa Khuzai with moments of doubt. But giving voice to important causes outweighed the difficulties. She knows that she is providing a model for women to follow, and she finds the joys of service to others more than sustaining.

On the Council, the Iraqi men were not prepared to listen to the voices of the women members. But slowly, she has succeeded in getting them to hear her voice. In January 2004, she was in Washington, D.C., being interviewed by reporters. They asked her how Resolution 137 came to be passed by the Governing Council. Embarrassed, she admitted that she had not heard of it. She later learned that it was a bill passed in her absence, which canceled family law, maternity leave, and many other basic women's rights that had existed since 1959.

On her return in February, she lobbied for its repeal. The interim constitution was almost completed, and ceremonies would soon be held. The Council was under tremendous pressure to finish the document in time and present it to the world. But Rajaa Khuzai expressed her strong reservations because of the inclusion of Resolution 137. "I inform you," she said, "that the first woman minister in the Middle East was Iraqi, and she was appointed in 1958. The first woman judge was Iraqi, and she was appointed in 1959, as was the first woman university professor. In the Koran, there is a chapter containing 176 phrases called the Woman's Chapter. It gives defined rights to women. There is no chapter in the Koran called the Men's Chapter. I ask you to reconsider Resolution 137."

There were minutes of silence. Her heart was beating hard. Finally, the president agreed that it should be put to a vote. Fifteen people on the council voted with her, and five voted against her, including one woman.

Dr. Khuzai was happy and proud to see the repeal succeed. The people who had voted against the repeal walked out of the room. That night, Dr. Khuzai started receiving death threats.

Some letters came to her office in Baghdad; others were given to her bodyguard by hand. Her husband received threats at his private clinic, and her family was subjected to them at home.

But she also received wonderful encouragement. Admirers and friends called in their congratulations. Hundreds of e-mails found their way to her from all over the world. She focused on the encouragement and tried to ignore the threats, even as she realized that the dangers were very real.

When the Governing Council debated the makeup of the new national assembly, Dr. Khuzai was adamant about securing a voice for women, whether rich or poor. She asked for 40 percent representation for women. The men countered that even in the United States Congress, less than 25 percent of the members were women. She observed that the United States was already over 200 years old, but this was the newly born Iraq. "We should start out right," she said. They told her she was asking too much and finalized it at 25 percent.

She didn't feel that was enough, but it was a start. It was her secret pleasure that the signing ceremony for the interim constitution was held on March 8, 2004, International Women's Day. Each of the members signed the agreement in turn. Because of the order of names, Rajaa Khuzai was the first woman to sign. Looking at her name in that book, she was filled with pride. She felt a part of history.

Still, that pride was hurt on June 1 of that year when the new Cabinet was formed. Dr. Khuzai had been told that she would be named Minister of Health; but when the formal announcements were made, her name was missing. Six women were appointed as ministers, but none from the Governing Council. In her efforts to secure a voice for women in the Council, her independence and lack of political affiliation made her a controversial choice. Despite her disappointment, she is proud of having 25 women named to Iraq's National Assembly.

"I worked for them," she said. "Now they are here. Whatever role I have, I will work for my people."

New Directions

It was impossible for her to keep up with her practice of medicine. She closed her clinic because of security concerns and no longer works at the hospital. If a terrorist lobbed a grenade into her office, her patients would be killed. The dangers are real for her children, too. Each of them has a driver and a bodyguard. Each has a cell phone and tells Rajaa Khuzai and her husband where they are at all times.

Random violence is still a terrifying reality. Turned back from a checkpoint into Baghdad's Green Zone, her bodyguard drove the car toward the next checkpoint. All of a sudden, a car bomb exploded where they had just been 40 seconds earlier.

Instead of practicing medicine, Dr. Khuzai focuses on humanitarian work now. As a member of the National Assembly, she serves on the Family Committee and the Women's Committee. It enables her to raise important women's issues at every turn. She also travels the world to raise funds for the Iraqi Widows' Organization. In some countries, like Egypt, there is little money to raise, but when Dr. Khuzai meets with other women and sees them smile, she is fulfilled. At the World Bank, she learned about micro loans, the revolutionary approach to sustainable economic development in which people are provided small amounts of credit to create their own businesses. The idea made sense to her, and she brought it back to Iraq to apply it to the Widows' Organization. Despite her concerns that women would not repay the loans, the program has been an inspiring success. She is working to extend the program all over Iraq.

Her joy now comes through these acts of giving. All her life, she realizes, has been engaged by this kind of work. As an obstetrician, her greatest joy came from delivering babies. As a mother, she gave birth to and nurtured seven children. As one of the women who helped found the modern Iraq, she works for others, not herself. In her efforts for the widows of Iraq, nothing touches her heart more than handing over a small piece of clothing or sum of money that will help another human being.

In contrast, Saddam Hussein lived in his presidential palace serving only himself, isolated from the people of Iraq. But Rajaa Khuzai was taught by her father, paraphrasing the words of the "Prophet Mohammed," that the best people are those who help their people.

Today, corruption remains prevalent in Iraq. People in power tend to serve themselves and appoint their family members to important positions. But Rajaa Khuzai hears the words of her father every day in her own memory, reciting from the Koran. As she said, "I think that I have only done small things for my people so far. I need to do more. I am not satisfied with my work." She advises leaders to forget themselves. "If you think only of yourself, you will not help others. Your people deserve whatever you can do for them."

What she is doing now, she said, is not for herself. It is for the people of Iraq—for her children and her grandchildren to come.

Such a Life: The Story of Mikhail Gorbachev and the Breakup of the Soviet Union

We met Mikhail Gorbachev in a comfortable hotel suite overlooking the Pacific Ocean. Talking to this man who had changed the landscape of the twentieth century was disconcerting. There was an entourage of guards and attendants in the room. The former President of the Soviet Union, Gorbachev was preparing for an important speech to world leaders. We were advised that our questions had to be on point, as the president was tired from a long flight.

What made Mikhail Gorbachev take on the tremendous challenge of reforming the Soviet Union? When his nation was at a perilous moment, why did he continue to lead his country toward dissolution when there was a safer and more certain route available in the short term? We weren't as interested in the geopolitical issues as we were the personal ones, although the personal and the geopolitical were all connected in Gorbachev's incredible story. It tells of a peasant boy who was forced through circumstances to become a man at age 10 and lead the largest country in the world at age 54.

As we waited for Gorbachev to join us in a sitting room, we were greeted by his daughter and others in his party, including translators. We felt apprehensive.

Nothing could have prepared us for our first impression. We were taken aback when Mikhail Gorbachev entered the room. Protocol demanded that we all stand up, and that pause allowed us to take a breath and gather our composure. As if on cue, the former president said, "What is your name? I am Mikhail Gorbachev." We exchanged warm greetings and sat down. It was clear that we were in the presence of someone great, even though greatness conveys a feeling that you can't describe.

He was dressed in a plaid shirt, casual slacks, and loafers, making him look like someone's great uncle—nobody's great uncle ever radiated Gorbachev's smile. It made us feel that we were the center of his attention and that he was fully engaged. He exuded a radiance one sees in people who are happy with who they are and what they're doing. We could imagine leaders like Ronald Reagan or Nelson Mandela giving a similar impression.

After exchanging pleasantries, we explained our purpose and what we hoped to learn. We wanted to find out when Gorbachev had first sensed himself as a leader. Was there a point in his youth when he began to be perceived differently than others? Or had some occurrence convinced him that it was necessary to lead? President Gorbachev listened to us carefully but made no comment before beginning his own story. He considered our questions thoughtfully as he spoke about the genesis of his leadership and leading in the face of obstacles.

While there was much he didn't say directly, if we read between the lines we found a leader who chose a different path from what everyone expected of him. Where others saw dangers, chaos, and the end of history, Mikhail Gorbachev saw a new world and worked toward it. His courage, his vision, and his leadership renewed our respect for what he had accomplished.

The Early Years

Great leaders have childhoods which often hold the key to their secrets. In the words of Mark Twain, "Spare me being born in boring times."

Mikhail Gorbachev was not yet 10 years old when World War II broke out. Shortly thereafter his country was invaded by Germany and his simple life changed forever. His formal schooling was interrupted as the country mobilized to support its troops. Nearly 10 million Russian soldiers were killed, many more civilians died, and countless families were torn apart. Gorbachev's childhood was marked by uncertainty. He spent long days in the field doing the work of the men who had been called off to fight.

This took place in a small village near Stavropol in the southern Soviet Union. The cultural influences of this region may have prepared Mikhail Gorbachev for what he would later see as the need for openness. It was a region where Christian and Muslim roots were strong, but there was a deep mutual understanding. By any standard, Gorbachev was "peasant stock." Living on a collective farm, his life was shaped by the Soviet agricultural system. It wasn't until he was 14 years old, when the war had ended, that he attended formal school. He inherited a serious world with little time for fun, where every family was touched by the misery of a continent in ruins.

No one can say for sure what deprivation and adversity does in the formation of leaders, but one often sees a connection between the will to overcome and the will to become someone special. Gorbachev does not dwell on this. In fact, he skirts those times, as a soldier might when he avoids talking about his combat experiences. Following the war, Mikhail Gorbachev joined the Communist Party's youth organization and received a series of promotions to become a youth leader. At age 21, he joined the official Communist Party.

Life for the intellectually gifted Gorbachev changed dramatically by age 19. He left his village to study law at Moscow State University. From that point, he never looked back. He met the love of his life, his future wife Raisa. Their partnership lasted for 50 years until an aggressive form of leukemia took her life in 1999.

Raisa helped him to see that he was destined to lead others. Often, great leaders are able to do more in partnership with another.

After receiving his law degree, Mikhail Gorbachev made an unusual decision to work full-time in the Communist youth movement. He was particularly interested in agricultural policy. His passion and his intellectual curiosity drove him to pursue an advanced degree in agriculture. This catapulted him into a leadership position in the Communist Party. Ultimately, he was given joint responsibility for the agricultural system of the Soviet Union.

From this background, one would never have anticipated that he would break up the Soviet Union and introduce principles of democratization. Every facet of Gorbachev's upbringing and character conformed to Communist ideology. Outsiders might have predicted that Gorbachev would become a traditional leader, disinclined to challenge the assumptions of the society that produced him. Yet he would upset the world to which he was born and win historical acclaim in the face of tremendous criticism.

Mikhail Gorbachev changed the course of history in the Soviet Union and introduced economic and democratic reforms, yet he said he was always a true believer in Communism. In our interview, he reiterated that. He still believes that it is possible to believe in sharing and equality while enabling people to make their own choices. These ideals became his reason to lead, and he has stood by them all his life.

There is no moment that Gorbachev can point to as the day it all became clear. Like so many leaders, his point of view evolved to create who he was. Radical leaders like Gorbachev are often accused of heresy when they realize that the status quo has outlived its usefulness. Each day, such leaders awake with the conviction that they must act to bring about change.

Looking Back at His Life

When hard-line leader Konstantin Chernenko died at 73, melancholy music played on television and radio stations throughout the Soviet Union. The man appointed General Secretary of the Soviet Communist Party took many by surprise. This unusual man would break apart the Soviet bloc and play a major role in ending the Cold War. Yet Tim Sebastian, the correspondent for the BBC in Moscow predicted that Gorbachev would be a traditional Russian leader: "Despite his lively and flexible manner, Gorbachev is still a strict, orthodox Marxist. In no sense has he shown himself to be a liberal."

At the twenty-seventh Congress of the Communist Party of the Soviet Union in February 1986, Gorbachev introduced policies known as *uskorenie* (accelerated economic development), *glasnost* (openness), and *perestroika* (restructuring). By May of that year he implemented the Law on Cooperatives, a radical economic reform that permitted private ownership of businesses. His hope was to improve living standards through worker productivity, giving the Soviet people new possibilities. In a series of swift moves throughout 1987 and 1988, he called for democratization, bringing multicandidate elections into the Soviet political process. He also reduced party control over the workings of government.

In 1988, he abandoned the interventionist Brezhnev doctrine, and thereafter allowed the Eastern bloc nations to determine their own internal affairs. The Soviet press referred to Gorbachev's policies as the "Sinatra Doctrine."

Internationally, Gorbachev met with President Ronald Reagan in Iceland, in an effort to reduce nuclear weapons in Europe. In February 1988, Gorbachev pulled Soviet forces from Afghanistan. Within three years, he had loosened the Soviet hegemony over Eastern Europe, which effectively ended the Cold War.

Around the world, Gorbachev was seen as a heroic leader who had brought sanity to an insane system. At home, Gorbachev was derided for bringing misery to the people of the Soviet Union, although that was the inevitable outcome of market reforms. Some said that he had not gone far enough and others said that he needed to be stopped. Although it seemed that nobody was happy with his leadership, he continued to drive the country toward its better future. In August of 1991, adversaries in the Communist party tried to oust him with a coup. Their attempt failed, but the devolution of power to the Soviet republics accelerated during that period of intense uncertainty.

By the time Gorbachev returned to his office in Moscow, he was president of the Soviet Union in name only. He resigned on December 25, 1991. In 1996, he ran for reelection and received only one percent of the popular vote. This was a rebuke to the changes he had brought into being and a testament to the obstacles he had faced in achieving them.

In speaking with Mikhail Gorbachev, now 74, you hear the tenacity of a man who lived through the torturous years of World War II and through Soviet history under Stalin, Khrushchev, and Brezhnev. All at once, you can see the wisdom learned by a boy who grew up on a collective farm where his father worked at a tractor station, as well as the torment he felt after losing his run for reelection ten years after leaving office. Would he do it again? Gorbachev's reserved smile made us sorry to have asked. Leadership for Mikhail Gorbachev is all about conviction, and leaders don't second-guess themselves.

Gorbachev explained that as a leader, he needed to follow through with the reforms he launched because the consequences of failure were too great. He said, "We have to think of how we are going to live in the new, expanding world. We have to look for answers."

On October 15, 1990, Gorbachev received the Nobel Peace Prize. When we mentioned it, he had the look of a father at his daughter's wedding. Many of those chosen for that august award lead where others can't or won't. As Gidske Anderson, chairperson of the Norwegian Nobel Committee, said in his presentation speech: "The Committee has made this award in recognition of the leading role he [Gorbachev] has played in the radical changes that have taken place in East-West relations. We recognize clearly that his manifold personal contribution in his efforts on behalf of the Soviet Union have proved decisive."

Great leaders are decisive, and Mikhail Gorbachev is such a man. After meeting him, we left with the belief that he remains unfaltering in his underlying principles and values. Anderson also said that there has been a "terrifying waste of intellectual and material resources on both sides of the Iron Curtain." Mikhail Gorbachev was being honored for making a difference.

When asked what gave him the strength as a leader to go against the grain and to lead in a direction that 99 percent of his fellow citizens would criticize, he shrugged and said, "Sometimes leaders have no choice." We believe he meant that the status quo is not an option when there is a clear path to something better.

Today, after the turn of a new millennium, Gorbachev is still forging ahead, pressing on with his belief in *glasnost, perestroika*, and *uskorenie*. He founded the Social Democratic Party of

Russia but resigned in May 2004 when the party's chairman drifted away from its principles. Above all else, Gorbachev is a principled leader who hopes to keep the former Soviet Union on the path to economic and personal success for every citizen. Recently, he has opposed Russian President Vladimir Putin's efforts to replace the election of regional governors with a system where they are directly appointed by the president. With his old adversary Boris Yeltsin, Gorbachev delivered scathing criticism of the plan as a step away from democracy.

Considering Gorbachev's legacy, we are reminded that in 1861, many Americans were in favor of slavery. Abraham Lincoln confronted what prior leaders had ducked and paid a terrible price. When Gorbachev accepted the Nobel Prize, he said, "Immanuel Kant prophesied that mankind would one day be faced with a dilemma: either to be joined in a true union of nations or to perish in a war of annihilation ending in the extinction of the human race. Now the clock has struck the moment of truth." He said that the award is recognition not of him but rather of "innovative political thinking—something of vital significance for human destinies all over the world." Today he says, "I wish I could say the world is safer, but I can't."

In discovering his leadership cause, Mikhail Gorbachev found within himself a passion to liberate the world. He nurtured a belief that things could really be different. In the words of Daniel H. Burnham, director of the first U.S. world's fair in 1893, "Make no little plans; they have no magic to stir men's blood." Sitting across from him on a serene night in San Diego near the shores of the Pacific Ocean, it was clear to us that Mikhail Gorbachev had been prepared to lead all his life. He used every opportunity to develop and share his dream. He crystallized the dream into a simple message—three Russian words—that defined a new Russian spirit. He was the right man at the right time in the right place, and he would convince a world power to do what had to be done. He was asked the toughest question, "Why did you do it?"

He replied with another shrug, saying simply, "I had to."

The Conductor and the Lead Violin: The Story of Hal Kvisle and TransCanada Corporation

Early in his career, Hal Kvisle took a psychological test to assess whether he had leadership potential. He was asked: if you were in an orchestra, which role would you prefer? For those who aspired to leadership, the answer was "conductor." But Kvisle's answer was "lead violin." This was interpreted to mean that he showed promise as a technical research engineer but had limited prospects for management. What the test couldn't show was that Hal Kvisle is both a thinker and a doer. He combines an impulse for action with a refined understanding of what leadership can and should accomplish.

As an engineer and line manager, Kvisle loved getting his hands dirty in work's nitty-gritty. He could also take charge of business challenges when there was a need for genuine leadership. Together, these tendencies have brought Kvisle into formative roles in the energy industry. These culminated in his 2001 appointment as CEO of TransCanada Corporation, a then $25 billion corporation that controls nearly 15 percent of the North American natural gas distribution system. In his leadership rise, Kvisle never had any ambition for control or power. Instead, he found his way to the top because the complex demands of business often call for someone who has the technical skills of the lead violin and the leadership capabilities of the conductor.

Called Upon

When Kvisle was in high school, he had his first experience stepping into a leadership role when the situation demanded it. It was the summer before his senior year. The principal of his small high school in rural Alberta—set in his ways and quick to say no to almost every new idea—had planned to retire after 25 years. Kvisle's father was the vice principal but had no interest in the job. The new principal arrived in June. He was a holocaust survivor from Europe who had wanted to start his life over again in North America. Drawn to Hal's father as a confidante, the new principal spent time at the Kvisles' house discussing the challenges facing the school. He impressed Hal as a man who wanted to make a positive impact.

One day, the new principal asked Hal how the students' union and government council worked. Kvisle shrugged and offered that it didn't really work at all. Nobody was interested in school government and the student union was inept and ineffective. As a result, the school booked terrible bands, and the school dances were a constant disappointment.

The new principal asked Kvisle to consider taking over the student union to make things better. "If you don't do it, who's going to?" he asked.

Kvisle had never wanted to be president of the student council, but the principal's question stirred something inside him. Before the end of summer, he accepted the challenge. None of his close friends were gung ho for school issues, but he led them in forming a party and running a campaign. They swept the elections and took over the student government. That year, under their leadership, things changed. The school held huge dances with some of the top bands in Alberta. The student council organized big fund-raising events for worthy causes, built a student common room, and launched a school newspaper. Kvisle had learned a lesson in how leaders create a positive transformation.

Kvisle studied engineering at the University of Alberta, but with his intellectual bent, he was frustrated by its narrow curriculum. While carrying a daunting engineering course load, he added liberal arts subjects. Within five years, he had finished the engineering degree and was one course shy of completing a joint degree in philosophy. By that time, he had moved to Calgary, Canada's energy capital, for work. Since the University of Alberta would not honor any course work done off campus, he never got that second undergraduate degree. Instead, he began his career at Dome Petroleum. It was the most successful independent energy company in Canada and one of the most active and ambitious in the world.

Kvisle's new job soon brought him to a crossroads in his career. He enjoyed the technical side of engineering, but he saw that many midlevel supervisors had limited management skills. Kvisle saw that success in business was not about his individual performance, but rather the team's effectiveness in meeting objectives. He had the instincts to provide energy and focus to the team's direction. As his high school principal had asked Kvisle, if he didn't do it, who would?

He enrolled in a part-time MBA program to get the skills and credentials he needed to move into management. He was later transferred from Calgary to the small town of Rocky Mountain House, but he continued his studies. For the next four years, he drove to Calgary several nights a week for classes. During the day he was running one of Dome's district operations, with tens of millions of dollars in equipment. And by night he studied management theory. Not only did he obtain a terrific education, but he also became expert at navigating gravel roads in the dark.

His years at Dome were exciting. The company experienced phenomenal growth. Young people with ability and ambition could do extraordinary things there. Jack Gallagher, Dome's charismatic founder, was a dynamic and visionary leader who knew how to motivate his team. "If you're winning, it's easier to win again," he said.

But in 1982, the high-flying company hit a wall. After debt financing a giant acquisition, the energy industry went into a steep decline. The situation went from bad to worse when oil prices collapsed in 1986.

For Kvisle, the crisis gave him his first great opportunity to step up and lead. As a manager, he had created a high-performing team with enthusiastic and motivated people. But suddenly, his department's budget was cut to zero, and he had a team full of effective people with nothing to do. Every morning, they showed up for work to plan projects that would never be funded. The larger corporation, paralyzed by debt, had little grasp of how badly its losses were growing as its equipment and labor went idle.

The company's morale was awful. It had betrayed its employees. Kvisle, as manager of the department, was stuck in the middle. Frustrated, he went to the chief financial officer (CFO) of the company and proposed that he be allowed to go to the bankers and personally make the case for bringing his team back into action. The CFO responded that they'd already tried that argument, and it hadn't worked.

Unwilling to take no for an answer, Kvisle carried his crusade to Howard MacDonald, the chairman and CEO. MacDonald also believed that Kvisle's idea wouldn't fly, but he let Kvisle try it anyway.

Kvisle recognized that the odds were slim; but like the lead violin in the orchestra, he understood the technical issues from the field perspective. He knew the projects inside and out, understood the economics of what they were doing, and could articulate why his department needed to finish its job. Being able to tell that story in a compelling way was critical to making a winning argument. Together with a select group of colleagues, he went on the road and met with Citibank,

Chase Manhattan, and Dome's major Canadian lenders. In the end, his passion and reasoned arguments carried the day. He managed to restore 80 percent of his department's funding.

The Art and Practice of Leading

Despite that success, Kvisle decided to leave Dome when it was poised to merge with Amoco. He didn't have the enthusiasm to see the merger process through, and he didn't want to move to Chicago. As a young leader with a great track record, he realized that he would be giving up a lot by walking out the door; but his choice was clear.

He went to work for Fletcher Challenge, a firm that had been started in New Zealand in the early 1900s by the Fletcher family. It had grown into a worldwide conglomerate that was active in energy, forestry, mining, and other industries. Kvisle came on board to run the Canadian energy assets that he had convinced Fletcher Challenge to acquire. Over 10 years, he built that division into one of the best companies in the Canadian oil and gas industry.

At Fletcher, opportunity rather than crisis ruled the day. This provided Kvisle with the chance to experience and witness the long-term benefits of leadership. One of Kvisle's key mentors was CEO Hugh Fletcher, whose intellectual curiosity made a big impact on Kvisle. Fletcher strove to find the right course of action and to understand the key value drivers. Then he could determine what changes a company needed to make to take advantage of those trends. This was a vast undertaking, given the complexity of the industries Fletcher was involved in and the geographic range of the company. It required deep analysis and introspective thinking. Kvisle appreciated his intellectual rigor and incorporated it more deliberately into his own leadership style.

The benefits accrued. Just as he had done earlier in his life, Kvisle did not motivate his people with a gung-ho approach. Instead, he described the key value drivers and objectives for the team. He also explained how much was possible when people extended themselves. He provided direction, insight, and advice. Then he got out of the way. His success confirmed his belief that good leadership is not an esoteric, ethereal undertaking. Nor is it manipulative, Machiavellian, cheerleading, or political. It is a pragmatic, hands-on, and common-sense endeavor with a long-term view.

As a manager, Kvisle knew that people needed to be told what to do and taught how to do it. As a leader, he learned how best to organize them, leverage their talents, and give them room to achieve their own success. The long-term impact of his leadership came from enabling people to excel at their jobs in such a way that the company could enjoy the benefits.

After 10 years at Fletcher Challenge, Kvisle's leadership energy was sapped. He felt frustrated and cross-threaded with the leadership in New Zealand. As a result, he felt he was doing a poor job leading his own team. While he might be earning a living by coming to work every day, to continue doing so was counterproductive to the organization and to himself. His enthusiasm to outperform was gone.

A change, however, was as good as a rest. Among the situations available to him, TransCanada Corporation intrigued him at an intellectual level because of its moves within the energy industry. He was hired as a senior vice president and soon experienced firsthand some very effective leadership in action.

Doug Baldwin, one of the board directors and a former CEO of Imperial Oil Resources, became interim CEO of TransCanada. He brought a rigorous and disciplined Exxon style of leadership to the company. With this approach, employees learned to never waiver from common sense in assessing situations before they proceed with determination. Soon, Baldwin gave TransCanada a crash course in "Exxonism." He took the complex strategy of the company, and broke it down into pragmatic pieces.

After 18 months, Hal Kvisle took over as president and CEO. When he joined the company he hadn't aspired to the top role, but the opportunity for leadership presented itself again. He could now bring to bear his intellectual curiosity and rigor, his pragmatic focus on common sense, and his personal connection with people.

The company had major challenges. Baldwin had reduced its employees from 7,000 to 6,000, but they were still overstaffed. When Kvisle organized his first senior management meeting, there were 250 people at the senior director and vice president levels. Kvisle soon brought that number down to 50 and the overall organization down to fewer than 3,000. He did it in such a way that the people leaving the organization did not feel as though they were being rejected and the people staying did not feel demoralized. Instead, he carefully and honestly explained that the company needed to change, and change meant a big shift in personnel.

The next challenge was a creative one. To Kvisle, TransCanada was a small company with great opportunities, but it seemed set in its ways. Rather than jumping at the first solution that came along, he wanted people to consider new ideas and look at a range of possibilities. The range of possibilities around any decision was always wider than people believed. A company operates in a complex business environment and must make decisions after considering a broad range of input from business, political, environmental, and social perspectives. Believing that people tend to behave as their leader does, Kvisle tried to make a model of his curious, broad-minded, and analytical approach to assessing potential pros and cons.

He remembered how powerfully intellectual curiosity had been fostered at Fletcher Challenge. Hugh Fletcher's father brought people to his family dinner every Sunday afternoon to engage in high-minded debate. Kvisle wanted to instill that spirit at TransCanada. He had to stop himself from grappling too deeply with day-to-day issues. He still has the same love for the technical challenges that led him to answer "lead violin" in his leadership assessment.

In recent years, the company has reported record levels of earnings and profitability. It's an exciting time to be involved in the energy business. TransCanada Corporation is providing its employees with an opportunity to accomplish things on a grand scale and really have an impact on their corner of the world.

The Third Period

Kvisle believes that leadership is about the long term. In a crisis, a battle, or an emergency, leadership is situational or incident-based. But leadership in business is more strategic and farseeing. An effective leader must be capable of intuitively knowing what an organization needs—whether it's discipline, direction, or innovation—to break out of mental boundaries. The leader needs to adapt to what is required.

Communication ability is also critical. Can you capture the heart and soul of your team while instilling them with energy and excitement? Part of that communication means engaging employees to successfully organize the company, conveying messages that get people on the bandwagon, and demonstrating success so their commitment is confirmed. A leader must also be a source of calm and inspiration. And a leader needs to be a model of pragmatism, common sense, and drive. Many people have the ambition for leadership, and they try to exhibit the right qualities to live up to the role. Kvisle believes that such a demonstration has to be genuine. The leader must have an authentic commitment and genuine interest in what's best for the company, not what's best for the leader.

Why lead? Hal Kvisle recognizes that he can make an important contribution through achievement. He gains his greatest pleasure as a leader from dealing with complex challenges, seizing an agenda, and guiding a group to success. It still amazes him how much good one can accomplish by accepting the responsibility of leadership.

What's next for Kvisle? He knows that some day his interests will turn to other things. He has a ranch and loves to spend time with his family and friends. But he could also get excited about some entrepreneurial venture. When your leadership energies are depleted, it's time to find a new area of interest. A Canadian, Kvisle uses a hockey analogy to describe life. The first period of the game is from ages one to 25, the second period from 25 to 50, and the third period from 50 to 75 plus overtime. Every successful hockey player knows that it's critical to play well in the third period. You have to have the same passion at the end of the game as you did at the beginning, and you must be capable of going into overtime if necessary. Being 60 years old should be the most interesting time in your life.

Leadership that Is Not Safe: The Story of Benazir Bhutto and the Struggle for Pakistan

Benazir Bhutto, the former prime minister of Pakistan, was a remarkable twenty-first century leader. A statuesque woman, she had a grand appearance and a regal aura. One was struck by the force of her viewpoint. There was no question as to where she stood. At age 35, she became the youngest and the first woman to lead a modern Muslim nation. Her strong leadership and uncompromising positions ultimately led to her being removed from her post. She never accepted this and resolved to return, even in the face of great danger. When she returned to run for office, she was the target of an assassination attempt. Within three months' time, she had been killed by militants opposed to her candidacy.

Her family was a strong influence in propelling Benazir Bhutto to leadership. From the age of nine, her father, Prime Minister Zulfikar Ali Bhutto, introduced her to the leading politicians and made sure she was well educated. She studied at Harvard and Oxford, where she learned the political landscape of the West. Living and studying in the United States made her conscious of the civil rights struggle.

Her life changed in 1977 when martial law was declared in Pakistan. Her father was placed under house arrest. After spending two hard years in prison, he was hanged. During this time, both of her brothers were killed.

"Having no choice," was how Benazir Bhutto described her decision to take action. This choice without a choice seems to have been the one that fired her passion and commitment to be the leader. It ultimately led to her assassination in 2007.

In 2005 and 2006, she told us the story of her quest to answer the question *Why lead?*

"I was a shy girl who led an insulated life," she said. "It was only when I came to Oxford and Harvard that suddenly I saw the power of people. I didn't know such a power existed. I was determined to go back home and try changing things."

From 1979 to 1986 she lived under house arrest at home and in exile abroad. In 1986, she returned to Pakistan and entered politics. She emphasized the need to heal past wounds and put an end to the deep divisions in Pakistani society. She stressed reducing discrimination between men and women and launching health and education reform.

She said that she would like to be remembered for overturning a military dictatorship and promoting democracy. However, she concluded, "I found that many people opposed me simply on the grounds that I was a woman."

When she discussed leadership, she expressed confidence that she would again serve Pakistan's nearly 150 million people. We learned that she did not see leadership as an entitlement. She was on an ongoing quest to become a better leader. She explained that as a young girl, she had no role models. She learned how to lead as a woman in a man's world. In the beginning, she didn't know what she had to do. She just knew she had to do it.

In her presence one felt the intensity of her convictions. And yet she expressed her beliefs with a calm that wouldn't force those beliefs on you. She knew why she was leading and stated her point of view clearly.

Leadership by Circumstance

In her own words, Benazir Bhutto explains how she arrived at the door of leadership. We quote them directly and without commentary, in reverence to her beliefs as a leader.

I am asked often how, as a Muslim woman in a traditional society, I became prime minister of Pakistan. I would say that it was not a decision I took to enter politics. I would say that I was propelled on the road of leadership by circumstances beyond my control. The gauntlet of leadership was thrown down before me and I had no choice but to pick it up.

Once I picked it up, I focused my life and energy on bringing democracy and human rights to my people. I found that leadership is demanding and it is difficult and it can be sad. Like life, it often demands difficult decisions. I had to choose between family and duty, and I had no real choice. The stakes were too high to allow obstacles to prevent success. I learned that often personal happiness was pushed aside out of necessity in pursuit of my political goals. It was sad, but it was necessary.

Leading by Passion

For me, my leadership was born of a passion that became a commitment—a commitment to an idea, to principles, to fundamental human values. My commitment to democracy, to human rights, and to modernity helped me walk the high mountains of success as well as the low valleys of imprisonment and exile. Leadership demands a price from an individual, and it also demands a price from the family. It has not been an easy life for me, but women often have to make difficult choices—choices we sometimes wish we were not forced to make, but must live with the consequences for better or for worse.

As a child of my age in the late '60s, I was influenced by the social ferment around me. I grew up at a time of student power and student protest. Across the world, from Paris to Washington, students were taking to the streets to make their voices heard. This was an important factor in my youth. This was a time of white minority rule in several parts of Africa. The fight against apartheid shaped the philosophy of my commitment to stand up for a principle and to be counted standing up for that principle.

It was also a time when the women's movement was gaining strength and powerful women role models were coming to the fore. Kate Millett had just written her book *Sexual Politics* and Germaine Greer and Gloria Steinem were speaking out for women's rights. The women's rights movement empowered and emboldened me.

It was also a time of war. American forces were engaged in Vietnam and students from my campus had to go off and fight that war. Many of them did not want to do so. It was a time when Robert Kennedy epitomized an age with his idealism and his support for the rights of the underprivileged. These important steps helped shape my outlook on life. They helped me focus on making the decision to fight injustice, to promote freedom, and to safeguard the rights of the weak and the dispossessed.

I was in America during the Watergate crisis and the impeachment proceedings against President Nixon. During Watergate, I saw the awesome power of the people to change policies, to change leaders, and to change the course of history. I marveled at how people could bring down a government. I lived in a dictatorship. Those criticizing the president of Pakistan ended up in prison, and here in America those criticizing the president were bringing him down.

From Harvard I went to Oxford in England, and there the British politicians in power were threatening to throw all Asians into the sea. While I was at Oxford, the

Conservative Party chose a woman, Margaret Thatcher, as leader of the opposition. The idea of the first British woman prime minister became an intense topic for student discussions. Many people believed that the Conservative Party could never win an election simply because it was led by a woman.

At Oxford, I became the first female foreign student to be elected as president of the Oxford Union. It was there that I learned to debate, to gain the confidence to speak before an audience, to focus my energy on attaining specific goals, and to fight and beat the odds. It was there that I learned to refuse to accept 'no' for an answer and, in the words of Bobby Kennedy, to ask, "Why not?" I had been told that as a foreigner I could not become president of the Oxford Union.

I had been told that as a woman I could not win the presidency of the Oxford Union and should not run. But I did run and I did win. And I learned to overcome my fear of losing. I learned to overcome fear. I learned to take risks. I learned never to give in when the task seemed formidable or impossible.

My Return to Pakistan

I returned to Pakistan in 1977 hoping to join the Foreign Service. My aim was to become ambassador to Washington. I thought I would give the best parties with all the people I knew from Harvard.

But within a week, my life changed dramatically. A military coup took place in Pakistan. I was awakened by my mother in the early hours of the morning. My father was the prime minister and army tanks had surrounded the prime minister's house. Our family huddled together and for hours we did not know whether we would live or die.

My thoughts went to the prime minister of Bangladesh, who had been assassinated with his entire family.

We did survive the night. My father was taken away by the military. He was released by the courts but re-arrested and finally hanged amid international outrage. A few hours before his murder, my mother and I went to his death cell to see him and to bid him farewell. It was there in that final meeting that I decided that I would fight for democracy and fundamental human rights in Pakistan. During the long night of military dictatorship, which lasted 11 years, my mother and I were imprisoned time and again. My mother was beaten, charged, and denied proper treatment. Today she suffers from a form of Alzheimer's, which doctors say came on by the head wound.

I spent nearly six years behind bars, often in solitary confinement. During the summers, it was unbearably hot; and during the winters, it was brutally cold. The conditions of the cell were primitive—mosquitoes, flies, cockroaches, dust storms, and dryness were constant companions, as were loneliness and a lack of communication with the outside world. By the time I was allowed into exile through international pressure, I was anorexic. My hearing and eyesight were affected forever. My face muscles hurt when I talked, as the years of imprisonment and silence had atrophied them.

Through this dark night of terror, young men were lashed for raising the slogan, "restore democracy." Others were imprisoned, tortured, or hanged. But the flame of freedom was never extinguished. It lived on—fed by the sacrifices of so many.

My family background and the long years of imprisonment made me a rallying point for the democratic movement. I returned to Pakistan in 1986 and was welcomed by millions of Pakistanis who lined the route from the airport and demanded an end to dictatorship. When I got married and was expecting my first child in 1988, the military dictator called for elections. He thought a pregnant woman could not campaign. But she could, and she did, and she won. My election broke the myth that a woman could not be elected prime minister in a Muslim country. It was a severe setback for the forces of fanaticism that wished to build a theocratic society not only in Pakistan but across the Muslim world. And it stirred a debate about gender, religion, and politics.

The lead Muslim scholar in Saudi Arabia issued an edict against my election. He said I had usurped a man's place in society and that I had to be removed. But there were other religious scholars who supported me. I especially remember the religious scholars in Egypt, Syria, and Yemen. The religious scholar in Yemen said that Islam permitted a woman to govern a Muslim country, and he referred to a passage in the Muslim religious book which describes the rule of Queen Sheba in laudatory terms noting that her reign brought prosperity to her people.

The fanatics in Pakistan weren't convinced by the scholar in Yemen. They were deeply upset at my religion. They dreamt of spreading the ideological frontiers of Islam through Pakistan, into Afghanistan, into central Asia and then onto the shores of Europe. They turned to Osama bin Laden for help. They called him back from Saudi Arabia because he had been fighting in Afghanistan. After the Soviets left, he went back to Afghanistan. They said, "We need your help. This woman has usurped a man's place in society. We need your help to continue our struggle to spread the ideological frontiers of Islam." And he gave

$10 million to purchase the loyalties of parliamentarians who were loyal to me.

Still today, the fanatics who believe in a war between Islam and the West fear my popularity and the strength of my party. They believe that a democratic Pakistan at peace with its neighbors and itself internally is a threat to their war against the West. They were the ones that twice destabilized the governments that I led. It was during the eclipse of my government that the Taliban seized all of Afghanistan, and it was only after I was overthrown in 1996 that Al-Qaeda was established in Afghanistan; and set up camps to train, recruit, and arm young men from across the Muslim world. Two years after my overthrow in 1998, Osama bin Laden declared war against the West on the soil of Afghanistan; and three years later, the World Trade Centers were attacked in 2001.

My husband, Asif Ali Zardari, was arrested on the night my government was overthrown on November 4, 1996, and served nearly 10 years in prison, even though he was never convicted of a single crime and the courts repeatedly ordered him released. He was 42 when he went to prison and was finally released from prison at age 52. He has since suffered a heart attack. They took away the best years of his life. Each time he was acquitted, he was re-indicted under more absurd accusations. I was told he would be freed if I announced my retirement from politics. But I knew that my duty to my people came first, for the sake of my children and all the children of Pakistan.

My duty to Pakistan's democratic struggle is one baptized in blood, for during this struggle my father and both my brothers were killed. Their legacy focuses my drive. Their spirit empowers me. I have come too far to turn back.

My Family

I have three children. My youngest was three when the government was overthrown. It's difficult explaining to little children why their father can't be there and why their mother has to keep on the move. I empathize with single mothers. It's tough holding down a job and looking after small children without a father. I chose my children's schools. I took them to hospital when they fell down and needed treatment. I sat with them with their fevers and helped them with their homework. And I had to be there when the tooth fairy called. And through the years, as the older ones became teenagers, I learned about Harry Potter, Buffy the Vampire Slayer, and Eminem.

I believe my own educational opportunities provided life and career choices to me that were denied to most women and certainly almost all women in the developing world. But my experiences at Harvard and Oxford taught me that if women are to be defined by their own abilities, they need an education that empowers them.

As the prime minister of Pakistan, I appeared before the joint session of the U.S. Congress in 1989. In that address, the most meaningful line for me was my simple message to the women of the world. That message is comprised of three simple, powerful words: "Yes, you can." I urge women all over the world not to accept the status quo, not to accept no for an answer. It is critical for women, whether in California or Kabul or Kirkuk, to refuse to accept traditional roles and traditional constraints, acquiescing to the tradition dictated by men like those of the Taliban. A tradition of sublimation of mothers and daughters is unacceptable.

In the East and the West, we must reject the notion that leadership and femininity are contradictions. I recall the words of Lady Margaret Thatcher, a leader I much admire. She said, "When a woman is strong, she is pushy. But when a man is pushy, aah, he is a great leader." We have made progress, smashed many glass ceilings. There are still others left to break. We can focus our drive on overcoming obstacles and we can achieve objectives. I chose focus. I chose action. The greatest obstacle to progress for women in the third millennium is the bigotry of groups like the Taliban and the fanatics that declared war on America. We fight against terrorism and we fight against the bigotry and intolerance that confine and constrain and victimize the generations ahead.

The solutions will not be quick and simple; but if we focus our energy, refuse to be distracted from what is important, act decisively and bravely, and refuse to accept arbitrary constraints, then in the end our single-mindedness can wear down even the strongest enemies, even the highest barrier. We shall prevail if we insist on reclaiming our religion from the fanatics who distort it and use it to subjugate women and keep our people ignorant.

Today in Pakistan, the wall of repression has descended across the people; the cause of human rights is set back decades, as is the cause of women's rights. The question is: will we let tyranny succeed? I say no. This new century must be an era where honor and dignity are protected in peace and in war, where women have economic freedom and independence, and where women are not defined simply by who their fathers are or who their husbands are, but by their own achievements, where they are equal partners in peace and in development. The question before us is whether we will fight for what we believe, whether we will risk our personal comfort to confront bigotry and intolerance and inequality. For in politics, business, art, and academia, there will always be the pressure of what is convenient, to follow the path of least resistance, to do what is safe, and to do what is conservative.

Leadership Lessons

I have learned leadership is not rooted in safety. Leadership is the product of boldness. And so, do not be timid and do not surround yourselves with those who are timid. Don't do what is necessarily popular today. Do what is right. I know that modern leaders now take polls to decide what they need to do. But 60 years ago, a great American president, Franklin Roosevelt, used polls not to decide on policies, but to learn all he had to do to persuade the public to lead the people on the path he believed to be right.

The forces of dictatorship murdered my father two decades ago, and I still vividly recall the dark and tragic days when he languished in a prison cell, living in inhumane conditions with the world helpless to stop his murder. But he remained courageous to the end—even in the hours before his death—because he was the consummate leader. And in the last letter he wrote to me, he quoted Robert F. Kennedy, himself a victim of assassination, quoting the poetry of Alfred Tennyson. For me these words are important.

In 1979, from the horror of his death cell, my father wrote that every generation has a central concern whether to end war, erase racial injustice, or improve the conditions of working people. The possibilities are too great and the stakes too high to bequeath to the coming generation only the pathetic lament of Tennyson: "Ah, what shall I be at 50 if I find the world so bitter at 20?" Even at this time of war, even more at this time of tyranny in my nation, I say, let us not be bitter because it diverts us from what we must do to build a better world. Leaders lead. Remember that. Whether it is in politics or in business, don't be afraid to stand out and don't be afraid to stand up. Go forth and lead. Remember that time, justice, and the forces of history are on your side.

Forces of History

Few of us will ever know what it is to visit a father who is unjustly imprisoned, to experience exile, or to feel the anguish of a loved one's death because of a leadership commitment. But regardless of what is at stake, Bhutto's message is clear: "Leaders lead." They don't give in to the fear of losing or lose sight of the reason for the struggle.

Benazir Bhutto remained committed. She was resolute, strong in her vision, focused on her intent, and certain that she would rise again to regain her office. Her commitment to democratic ideals and her unyielding position on equality for women pitted her against powerful religious leaders and the Pakistani military. She lived in danger for who she was and for what she stood for. Yet she spoke out every day, determined to create fairness in a not-so-fair world as a woman leader: doing what needed to be done; paying the price.

Fathers and Sons: The Story of Ara Hovnanian and the Hovnanian Legacy

Ara Hovnanian is an interesting and captivating leader. Raised in his family's home-building business, he has a youthful appearance and an old soul. As a testimony to his business acumen and leadership skills as CEO, he has taken his family's already successful firm, Hovnanian, to 20 times its volume and 100 times its sales revenue. Today, Hovnanian is a Fortune 500 company, and one of the largest home-building firms in the world.

Ara is a second-generation leader. His father founded the business as a young immigrant from the Middle East, arriving with three children and little means. As a facet of industry, family businesses have been relatively neglected in the field of leadership study. Yet more than 80 percent of the businesses in the world are family-led. Such leaders are not like the leaders from institutional organizations. Their apprenticeship program starts at the dinner table where the stories of the day are told with great color and emotion. The trials and tribulations are personal to everyone there. Bitter disappointment as well as satisfaction are experienced every day by each member of the family. It is what makes these leaders unique.

The Hovnanian family is rich in culture. Their values and principles guide their decisions every day. Ara Hovnanian talks every day to his father, Kevork Hovnanian, who is still chairman in his eighties. While their accumulated net worth would allow them lavish lifestyles of leisure, these men work 80-hour weeks. They lead with the passion and the commitment that creates unstoppable momentum in their company.

There was a never a question that Ara Hovnanian would lead the business. Although he was told that he could do whatever made him happy, the business was his destiny. He was raised on it. On Saturdays when other children were off with friends, Ara and his dad would make site visits to the communities they were building. Ara watched his father's interactions with everyone, asking questions, giving instructions, encouraging, and correcting. The footsteps Ara had to follow were large indeed.

Ara's road to leadership and his *Why lead?* decision is embedded in a family dream that began a world away. That story starts with a young man whose parents were immigrants themselves, in flight from another country.

Fleeing Home

Kevork Hovnanian climbed the stairs to the roof deck where his young family slept out in Baghdad's dry, hot summer nights. Kevork, a cautious and thoughtful man, listened carefully to the sounds of the city. He felt safe in the country to which his parents fled from Turkey in 1915. They almost didn't make it. Thousands had died in Turkey. It had left the Hovnanian family with a persistent feeling of never being completely safe that remained for years.

A soldier, the 35-year-old Kevork slept with a pistol under his pillow to protect his wife and three children. One would think it was unnecessary in the Iraq of 1958. The company that he had founded was doing great. His firm Dilja Construction and Saraji Trading Company had grown from nothing into the largest road-building company in Iraq, employing 1,400. As he lay down next to his young wife and looked up at the stars, he thanked God as he did every night. His last thought on this day was that he had learned how to build and lead a business, bringing him enough success to ensure a bright future for his two daughters and son.

What he didn't know that on this day, July 14, 1958, his world would change forever. He would be forced to flee Iraq, much like his parents had fled Turkey 40 years before to escape the Armenian genocide.

At 5 a.m., Kevork awakened before the first light. He was sure he had heard gunshots in the distance. He raced to the street, revolver in hand, where he met his neighbor Fadhel. The neighbor shouted, "We won. The revolution is over."

Kevork immediately looked down. He was grim. If what he heard was true, then the Baath party had taken over the government. His worst fears had been realized. They had seized control of the palace, executed the royal family, and taken over the army. He felt a sense of dread as he walked back into the house. It was now a country with an unclear future, and he knew instinctively that his business was doomed. The construction business is always the first to suffer during times of instability.

Over the next few days the truth unfolded. The pro-Western Hashemite monarchy was no more. King Faisal's grand white palace with its white-pillared entranceway was captured. The King, Prime Minister Nuri as-Said and many others were dead. The royal guard had been destroyed. It had been a bloodbath.

Within days, Kevork and his three brothers made plans to flee what seemed certain to become a dangerous environment for Armenian citizens.

He remembered thinking it as a kind of manifest destiny. Like his parents who had fled the terror of the Armenian genocide a generation before, he now had to find a safe haven for as many family members as he could get out. Although his parents had masked their despair in a veil of silence, they felt a deeply ingrained stigma of being forced out of their own country, persecuted, and endangered. There was no question in Kevork's mind. He had to get his family out of harm's way. This was the only right and clear decision possible.

He had little time to consider that he was ruined financially. They contacted relatives in the United States in search of a safe haven. Although their future was promising, it was also frightening. Without funds and a formal education, he felt scared and helpless. Starting from scratch seemed like a huge hill to climb, but he resolved to be optimistic and to let nothing stand in the way. He would never give up. Never.

True leaders tend to overcome life's twists and turns and find a pathway back after having their dreams swept away. Leaders of family businesses that pass from generation to generation always face adversity. Kevork was practical: he had to make his hard luck his good luck. He had to stay strong for his family, his brothers, and his son. He knew it was going to be a difficult road.

Coming to America was exhilarating and humbling. Having nothing after having so much left him feeling listless, almost depressed. He would spend hours just walking. He tried every angle in his mind. He still believed in his dream: that one day he would get back to his business. In the early days after arriving in New Jersey, he refused to take handouts. He needed to be independent. He didn't want just any job. He wanted one that would lead him back to the dream that he had left.

He bounced ideas off his wife, who continued to reassure him with the comforting words, "Things will work out. You can do it again." It was what he needed to hear, and it reinforced what he would always know to be his God-given gift: the ability to keep his dream in sight and to never look back.

One spring day, Kevork and his brothers found a 20-acre parcel of property in New Jersey. As they looked over the land, the dream returned with a new twist. This time, they would create a homebuilding company. None of them knew how, but from that moment on, the Hovnanian family became the story of the little engine that could—chugging along, looking ahead, moving forward. Through ups and downs, trials and tribulations, the family stuck it out. Together they survived shaky markets, political shifts, and financial mistakes. Few could have foreseen a future of headline-making success, and Kevork would never have made such a prediction. He couldn't take his eyes off what was necessary to make it happen every day.

Over time, the dream became real. The market was right. Suburban life was expanding everywhere. And their idea was to provide every family a good home at an affordable price.

Like so many family-led businesses, the Hovnanians took great pride in what they did for their customers. Perhaps the reason family-led businesses outperform companies led by non-family owners is that people with their name on the door operate at a higher level of intensity.

In fact, naming the company was one of the defining moments in the Hovnanian family history. Kevork was insistent that the company be called Hovnanian. His brothers objected, saying it would be too hard to remember. Kevork's response was "All the better." He considered the family name distinctive. He persuaded his brothers that this name—and the pride they took in their work—would hold the company together for generations to come.

Leadership Legacy

Today Hovnanian is led by the boy who was two years old when the family fled Iraq along with their road construction business. He's the same boy whose Armenian grandparents fled Turkey to stay alive. As Ara tells his story, it is clear that he had all the advantages, as well as the awesome responsibility, of knowing that one day he would take the helm. He would have to measure up and be as good as these resilient new Americans who had built a business from nothing and made it thrive. But there was never a question that he would someday be the leader of this company. He knew it during those Saturday morning company inspections when he was barely out of his child's car seat. He knew it in the summers when he worked as a laborer. He knew it when he rooted out saw inefficiency to help build houses with higher productivity and innovation.

Ara's leadership journey began during the hours that he spent with his father, Kevork. He doesn't remember the specifics of their conversations, but he does remember the intimacy. For two summers in high school, he took jobs working their construction projects. As a laborer, he saw firsthand how disorganized house building could be at that time. He felt that introducing innovative techniques would create more speed and less waste. At age 16, he took a summer course in real estate and started selling houses on weekends.

Although a graduate of the University of Pennsylvania's Wharton School, Ara nonetheless started at the bottom in his family's commercial construction division. There he learned the art of planning and developing shopping centers, offices, and even mini storage facilities. However, destiny intervened. The number two person under his father left the company and a search began for a replacement. One evening, Ara's father offered him the position. Ara was shocked. This would be a job for a seasoned professional.

Asked what it was like to take on such a big job so young, with his father as his direct superior, Ara replied: "I have always had my father as a boss. It was a lot of pressure—a crazy and busy time, but I learned and luckily did more things right than wrong. My father taught me a lot early on. Although I had been thrown into the fire, I was having a great time."

He had been well prepared and things worked well for him for a time. His instinctive assumptions about the business were right. If he focused on processes, things would consistently improve. He was becoming an able manager, but not yet a leader.

Some things can't be taught in advance. They have to be learned at the right time, in the right way. For Ara, one of the first and biggest leadership lessons he learned was moving from being a hands-on doer to letting himself delegate. When the company began to grow and acquire other businesses, Ara found that in order to lead other managers, he would have to learn how to step back. "The leaders of the companies we had acquired would never have tolerated my managing them. In fact, the only way to keep them was to find a way to maintain their interest and enthusiasm."

The second lesson he learned was when to dive in and when to stand clear. "I loved homebuilding—all of it—including the designing and planning of communities, the advertising and the selling," he explained. "I was a hands-on manager, involved in every detail." He realized that his leadership style was not being embraced by his people. He was too opinionated and he was micromanaging as opposed to leading. "In a way, leading is like letting go," he said.

Eventually, he put his people's spirit and excitement ahead of his vision of creating easily repeatable, documented, teachable, systemized processes. He admits that at times he still feels the need to manage. It's hard to resist, he adds with a smile and a shrug.

Ara tells his story modestly. His great lesson is that leadership is about learning. He knew that he had to develop his own leadership style and that he needed help to do it. He enrolled in an immersion leadership program where he got intensive coaching, with input from his direct reports, his board, and his father.

During the program, one of the instructors said, "As a leader, you know that there are times when you have to march up a hill in a battle, the flag in your hand. When you get to the top of the hill and put the flag in the ground, you want to be able to look around you and know that your troops are there beside you."

Ara learned that leadership is about letting go of preconceived notions and being there for your team. He is heavily invested in developing and supporting leaders at every level in the company. He continues to spend time honing his leadership style and still searches for personal learning opportunities to grow. He unabashedly admits that you have to let go so that you can learn to lead, if you love the business.

As in the past, dinner at the Hovnanian family home is full of discussion. His children hear the stories that engage them. The business never stops. In answering the question *Why lead?* Ara said, "I love it. My dad is 82, and he still loves it. Few people can call their fathers every day and talk to them about a business that they really love."

Perhaps Ara's eldest son would have taken over his own leadership legacy. That he didn't is one of the tragedies the family has experienced. Alton Hovnanian lost his life in a boating accident when he was only 15 years old. An innocent island camping trip ended horribly. Alton was a special boy, unaffected by the success of his family. He was principled, caring, intelligent, curious, a natural-born leader, and loved by his classmates. His parents were tortured by their loss; but they told themselves that they must not allow their grief to keep them from appreciating the beauty of their son's life.

In a twist on the way that leadership is usually passed from father to son in a family business, Ara finds himself inspired by Alton's death to rededicate himself to his firm and family.

"My son Alexander," Ara said, "is interested in joining the company at some point." He recalled that at seven years old, Alexander began talking about ownership, offering advice to both Ara and his father about control. We can only wonder what he is thinking now as he looks at his father and grandfather—two leaders who care about the well-being of everyone involved in this family enterprise.

Chapter 8

Because It Was Right

These last stories tell of leaders who seem to lead from a place entirely outside themselves. They lead by example, living in a way that inspires others to share, grow, and become leaders themselves. The source of their energy and conviction comes from their desire to help or to heal. Perhaps it is their willingness to change the world for the better or to touch the souls of others. Many of these leaders did what they did "because it was right." The leaders who most clearly fit this category—Erin Gruwell, Jane Simington, Mike Towers, Swanee Hunt, Pat Mitchell, and Mohandas K. Gandhi—led principally because deep down they made a hard choice.

Included here are two high school teachers who are out to make the world a better place. Some would question whether they are leaders. We felt that their work preparing young leaders is important. After all, many leaders in other chapters refer to teachers who taught them to believe in themselves and gave them the courage to lead. These teachers do it because they believe wholeheartedly in building the next generation. You will see the nobility of those who teach the leaders of the future and their clear link to those leaders.

There are also nontraditional leaders who became leaders of leaders. Their fingerprints can be found on movements that truly create change. Gandhi led a movement that liberated a billion people, while the far-reaching voices of Pat Mitchell and Swanee Hunt educate the world through the media.

What differentiates these leaders is that they have each given up something to get back something they seek. Like Gandhi, these leaders did not start out to be what they became. Their destinies were to lead so others can be leaders.

Teach One to Teach Another: The Story of Erin Gruwell and the Freedom Writers Diaries

Erin Gruwell's outlook on life changed during the 1992 Los Angeles riots sparked by the Rodney King case. She was living in a sheltered Los Angeles suburb, and expected to attend law school. She watched news reports of children throwing Molotov cocktails and carrying television sets out of broken store windows. At that moment, Gruwell decided to choose the classroom over the courtroom. She felt a need to change the conditions that generated such violence in young people.

No one could have foreseen the incredible odyssey that began a year later, when Erin Gruwell walked into her first high school classroom in the city of Long Beach, California. Many of her 150 students had been written off by the education system, but she helped them write a book, graduate from high school, and attend college. She traveled the world with her students, met political leaders in Washington, D.C., drew philanthropic leaders to her cause, and changed lives.

Gruwell's tenacity and dedication to her students is chronicled in the book *The Freedom Writers Diary: How a Teacher and 150 Teens Used Writing To Change Themselves and the World Around Them* (Doubleday Random House, 1999). Gruwell's inspiring story was dramatized in the 2007 motion picture *Freedom Writers*, starring the acclaimed actress Hilary Swank as Gruwell.

Erin Gruwell represents a new generation of leaders who see themselves as social entrepreneurs. They use the kind of passion, vision, and strategic thinking that we have seen in other leaders who have made an impact on the world.

Classroom Survival

Gruwell was required to work as a student teacher for a semester during graduate school. A teacher one year away from retirement would become her mentor at the school, but he provided her with no guidance on her first day. Instead, he gave Gruwell a stack of books and some paper and told her to meet him in the teachers' lounge at the end of the day.

Stepping into her classroom for the first time, Gruwell discovered a roomful of self-proclaimed gangsters. Erin was 23. She faced a class of 30 16-year-olds. One of her students, Sharaud, sauntered in bouncing a basketball. He was a large, tough boy who had reportedly threatened a teacher with a gun and had pledged to make the new student teacher burst into tears before the semester was done.

One day, a student drew a picture of Sharaud and passed it around the room. The other students laughed hysterically. When Sharaud saw it, he looked as though he was going to cry. Gruwell stormed over and grabbed the picture. To her horror, she saw a crude racial caricature of Sharaud with big lips. Her reaction was instantaneous. For the first time since she had started teaching, Gruwell screamed at her students. She railed against racism and the damage such cruelty can do, saying, "Don't you know this is how the Holocaust began?"

To her astonishment, none of her students had ever heard of the Holocaust. Gruwell knew that violence and death were very much a part of her students' lives, so she then asked how many in the room had ever been shot at. Nearly every hand went up. In fact, there had been 126 murders in their community that summer. From that moment on, Gruwell understood that her mission as a teacher would be to throw her classroom plans away and make tolerance the core of her new curriculum.

The turnaround was almost immediate. Her students were used to putting on masks of anger, disdain, and toughness.

They described their neighborhood as a war zone and felt that the color of their skin made them a target of violence. Many of them had seen loved ones murdered. Many had fathers, brothers, and uncles in prison. One girl had been to more funerals than birthday parties, and one of the boys sensed that a drive-by shooting was about to take place whenever he saw a low-riding Chevy drive down the street.

These students had learned how to suppress their emotions to seem bold and larger than life. In turn, Gruwell had put on a mask of her own to pretend that she wasn't afraid to swim in a sea of sharks. Teachers aren't supposed to let their guard down. They're not supposed to get angry or cry. But like a parent driving a car and reaching over to protect a child at a sudden stop, Gruwell responded to her classroom's need instantaneously. Her innate passion unlocked the passion and authenticity of her students. They benefited from a powerful teachable moment when a crude racial caricature scrawled on a piece of paper was exposed to the light.

Gruwell saw that her students were capable of juxtaposing the pain they had experienced in their lives with terrible tragedies like the Holocaust in Europe, the genocide in Rwanda, the ethnic cleansing in Bosnia, or the racist violence that plagued southern states in the United States. One student said her curriculum—as he folded it into a paper airplane and threw at it her—was filled with dead white guys in tights. So she changed it and changed its emphasis. A book like Harper Lee's *To Kill a Mockingbird*, (Lippincott, 1960) which dealt with racism and violence, came alive for those students in the context of their own lives. Since the Holocaust was unknown to them, Gruwell tried to get copies of Anne Frank's *The Diary of a Young Girl* (Doubleday, 1952), for her class. Her principal gave her a blank look and told her the budget had been exhausted until next year. The librarian told her "those kids are too stupid

success. Many students are no longer dropping out, joining gangs, using drugs, or getting pregnant. They're reading books and engaging with society.

Gruwell believes that her success as an education leader has been all the greater because she surrounds herself with "people who are smarter and more savvy than me with bigger talents than I have." Collaboration has been critical in everything she does. Her objective is to change hearts and minds by getting people to open up to a world they wouldn't normally consider. "As a teacher, I've always felt that I had to be humble enough to be a student at the same time," she said. Education can be a reciprocal process. By engaging her students in learning, Gruwell learns as well. She believes that there lies a parallel between teaching and leading.

"Great leaders have to be humble enough to learn from those they are leading," she explained. Gruwell believes that when you're walking straight ahead without looking back, you may not realize that nobody is following you. A leader, like a teacher, must listen to and get to know the people they want to help. You can't just be an expert on learning materials. You need to be an expert on individuals too.

Gruwell gets her greatest joy as a teacher and leader in accomplishments of the people she's been privileged to teach. "Watching my students become authors and stand in front of a group of kids and tell their story, watching them graduate from college and give speeches, is awe inspiring. To see kids who lived in homeless shelters and carried guns now carry a pen to sign autographs—there's nothing better." Her work is meaningful to her because she believes that each act of teaching passes the baton to another person. "I believe in 'Teach one to teach another,'" she said. In turn, her students have learned to channel their own passion and integrity. With that strength,

Gruwell believes, "They can go back into the ghetto and lead their families out. They can go into a prison and talk to their cousins and relatives and say, 'Follow me. I know how to get out of here.'" One of her students convinced his father, an inmate at San Quentin, to leave his gang life behind and to go back to his school for his GED.

In our society, Gruwell stated, "People don't always realize the power of one." When Anne Frank's family was under threat, Miep Gies hid them from harm for as long as she was able. Gies did not consider herself a hero for what she did. Rather, as she put it when she visited Long Beach, "I simply did what I had to do because it was the right thing to do." Gruwell believes the same attitude should call individuals to action whenever they are confronted with injustice. When someone believes in something, they need to back up that belief with integrity. During the civil rights struggles in the 1960s, one of the prevailing arguments against activism was that "things have always been that way." The same passivity paralyzes people today in the face of inner city violence, poverty, and inequality in education. Gruwell looks at leadership as an opportunity to stand up and challenge the belief that things can't change.

One of the most powerful tools Gruwell uses in her educational campaign is what she calls the "Trojan Horse." When she was asked to testify before Congress about race and education, she realized that the best way to make her case would be to bring along three of her students. Inviting her students to testify gave them access to decision makers, while also exposing those decision makers to the voices of those most affected. In all her leadership activities, Gruwell believes that understanding comes from bringing people together face to face.

The Social Entrepreneur

Gruwell describes herself as a "social entrepreneur." She uses the passion, resourcefulness, and vision of an entrepreneur to run her nonprofit organization, the Tolerance Education Foundation, to bring people and resources together for a common cause. She draws on a network of lawyers, accountants, business leaders, and board members to provide specialized services. Like the founder of a start-up, she funnels 80 percent of the income she makes from speaking and consulting engagements back into her organization.

She also feels a strong spiritual connection to her work, which reinforces her physically and emotionally. She never feels exhausted or sick, despite her draining schedule of teaching and working during the day, running her nonprofit and writing books at night, and traveling many days out of the month. She has the zeal and the passion of a religious devotee, spreading her philanthropic message to any who care to listen. Her message is simple: People who lack advantages can realize their potential if they are treated like unique individuals who deserve respect, generosity, and love.

Erin Gruwell, while still in her thirties, can claim remarkable leadership accomplishments. That she has changed so many lives for the better makes her highly remarkable as well.

If Not Now, When? If Not You, Who?: The Story of Jane Simington and the Journey to the Sacred

Since she was a little girl, Jane Simington knew she was supposed to be a leader. The eighth of eleven children growing up on a farm in Canada, she couldn't stop asking questions. She had much she wanted to ask her father, but he was busy on the farm. The best time to catch him was first thing in the morning, when he went out to tend to their cows. So, at 4 a.m., she would join him on those morning walks to the barn so she could discuss her goals and life. There were no distractions at that time of day—he was all hers. That set the stage for her life of boundless energy and fighting for what's right.

In her years of healthcare work, she helped others learn how to handle crises and showed them how to turn fear into faith. But that had not prepared her for a phone call she received one morning.

The voice on the other end said only, "There has been an accident." Simington didn't want to hear the rest. She heard that her son had been killed. He had been ripped from her heart and the words tortured her soul.

The accident happened in the woods where Simington remembered him at his happiest. But happiness had suddenly ended for her. It had been replaced by depression that brought her life to a complete standstill. She shut down emotionally and physically. "I stayed in this dark night," she said, "until I finally came up with some answers to the *why* questions—answers that fit for me about my place in the world. I had to convince myself that the greatest gift that I had to offer was hope."

And so Jane Simington began her book, *Journey to the Sacred* (Taking Flight Books). She wanted it to connect these answers in a new way, to provide a pathway to growth. It was meant to be read by others, but writing it allowed her to live again.

After 10 years of research, note–taking, and rewriting, the book became her point of power. When she wrote its last words, she cried her last tears and felt finished with her grief.

She decided to be a leader again and try to help the world. The power of leadership, she learned, comes from taking the blinders off and being yourself. That's when people know you're a leader.

Beginning the Path

Simington had a loving childhood. Her mother encouraged her education and sent her to a Catholic boarding school. In college, she graduated after three years with a diploma in nursing. On graduation day, she felt disappointed because she felt she hadn't learned to heal people yet.

Her nursing career was intense and varied. She went from the emergency room into palliative care and then into geriatric care. She later went into management and became an educator and a board member. She had a nagging feeling, however. She didn't believe the health care profession was addressing the primary causes of illness. Something was missing.

Simington earned a degree in psychology. Although she found a psychologist's knowledge and skills useful, she did not find any answers. She returned to nursing and earned another degree in science. She also discovered the writings of Martha Rogers, a physicist and nurse who studied energy fields. Simington was fascinated by this new view and started exploring holistic medicine. She became the first health-care practitioner in Canada to examine the effectiveness of therapeutic touch, which heals by changing the balance and flow of human energy. This technique has gained wide acceptance.

When Simington's son was killed, she felt as if her own life had stopped. She experienced the emotional darkness of serious depression. In her despair, she lost her leadership ability and turned inward. She knew that leaders have to face outward, yet deep down she felt trapped. Contending with her own crisis was different from teaching others how to deal with theirs. She narrowed and intensified the emphasis of her academic studies to focus on healing. In truth, she was searching for her own healing.

She began to study alternative approaches to healing. Although Western medicine is focused on physical illness, many non-Western cultures view spirituality as a crucial part of health. Simington realized that she knew nothing of the spiritual world. Her beliefs were being challenged, and few of them were holding up under the fire of life experience. She explored other religions and others ways of believing. She earned a doctorate studying the concepts of spirituality and spiritual well-being. The University of Alberta hired her, and she began to tiptoe back into the world.

Her first significant healing work took place at a women's prison. Simington knew that to touch the souls of the female inmates, she would need to use soulful techniques. She was familiar with the research that saw a correlation between the brain's right hemisphere and healing. She also knew how much her own brain's right hemisphere had done for her creative endeavors of music, dancing, drumming, visualization, and guided imagery. She believed that creativity was her soul's voice, and thought that teaching creativity to the prison's traumatized and grieving women might give voice to their souls, too.

Ironically, those women became teachers and guides to her. They taught her about trauma, abuse, grief, sorrow, regret, and shame. They taught her about love, beauty, and soul. "The right-brain strategies I provided them gave their souls voice," said Simington, who added, "in turn, they have given voice to the awareness growing within me." In another project, she provided workshops for aboriginal groups.

The stories told by these traumatized women were so powerful that she decided to record them on video. When she showed the video to potential backers, there would be a long silence and then the clapping would begin. Simington found herself crying. It was as though all of the pain of the past few years had been worth it. She had finally come back into the world.

Those experiences gave Simington the courage to finish her book. She had been working on it during many pain-filled years, but her thoughts had been muddled. After making the video, she knew how the story needed to unfold. She finally finished the book *Journey to the Sacred.* The time had come for her to show the world what she had learned. She would use her own pain and healing to make a radical difference.

Leadership Healing

As a counselor, a great deal of Simington's healing work is done for other leaders. She knows that such people are subject to difficult personal challenges. Yet when something bad happens in their lives, it can be a stimulus for change and growth. She is direct, focused, and aligned in her approach. Listening intently to what a grieving person tells her, Simington tries to relate it to another story. Instead of telling people what to do, she helps them see what they are not seeing.

One leader told her, "If I had to do it over again, I would have become a medical doctor." Sensing the authenticity of that person's yearning and the opportunity it presented, Simington asked, "Why not now?" The person protested that age 46 was too old to start medical school.

"How many years would it take?" Simington asked.

"I'd be 52 when I finished," the leader answered.

"So," Simington suggested, "won't you still be 52 in six years anyway?"

Many of Simington's stories come from her experiences in the aboriginal world. The rituals, morals, and folklore of Native North Americans are imbued with art, music, and metaphor. She uses their stories as templates to help leaders and others with their own spiritual lives.

Simington's mission is to bring a new model of care to people emotionally trapped by their belief systems, political systems, psychological circumstances, economic systems, and even health care systems.

She began to understand these spiritual cages when she worked with women incarcerated in federal penitentiaries. She saw that their experiences were similar to those of the elderly, who feel trapped in institutionalized care facilities. Lack of freedom comes not just through confinement in a physical structure surrounded by barbed-wire fences. The imprisonment of the human spirit is caused by the intense feelings of entrapment one experiences when forced to exist under the control of others. When our bodies are no longer ours to command or when we feel smothered by shame, fear, guilt, or regret, then the soul is in bondage, and its energy wanes.

Such withering happens in workplaces, schools, and homes. It is the opposite of creative energy. It can be remedied in an environment that respects all people and nurtures spiritual well-being.

Her personal grief allowed Simington to reach beyond herself and listen to the spiritual struggles of others. She learned to recognize such a journey as a "soul walk." Most of us, she believes, insulate ourselves from the problems of others. But when we are blind to the problems around us, we feel justified denying the human need to care for others.

When Simington took off her own blinders, she was able to acknowledge her problems and connect with the problems of others. She believes that leaders waste a lot of energy reinforcing their own assumptions, which increases their isolation from others. Leaders are most vulnerable when things are going smoothly, because there is no need to reexamine their beliefs. Ultimately, however, all leaders face challenges to their world view. Only when they are threatened do they see that the world is not what it seems. By overcoming life's wounds, leaders can experience real spiritual growth. They will gain insight that lets them develop new beliefs and new ways of leading that are outside of themselves and aware of the needs of others.

In her professional life, Simington has been a teacher, a mentor, and a leader. Since writing her book and healing herself from her unfathomable grief, she entered a new level of leading. She is aware that doing exactly what she is supposed to be doing gives her incredible personal power. She is living her life with purpose and passion, and feels that she is fulfilling some kind of destiny.

That journey, she now recognizes, did not just start with her son's death but with the nagging feeling that there could be better approaches to health care. She knows that while it is possible for an individual to ignore such nagging, it would be a mistake to do so. At those rare moments when she feels her energy flagging, she hears a little voice in her head asking, "If not you, who? If not now, when?"

Teaching Power: The Story of Mike Towers and Westford Academy

As we interviewed hundreds of leaders, we kept hearing about the power that teachers wield in awakening an awareness of leadership and its possibilities. Our research would not be complete without delving into the lives of some of these extraordinary teachers. It is not surprising that we discovered such teachers to be leaders in their own right. They create vision, share achievable dreams, and motivate students to reach top performance in and out of school.

Today, teacher leadership is a well researched subject. Ten years ago, there was a transformation in leadership studies that recognized teachers for their leadership characteristics. Although teachers have always been team leaders, department chairs, and administrative executives, such hierarchical leadership is secondary to their leadership of students. Teacher leaders make a difference in the lives of their students.

One of the more exhaustive scholarly investigations on teacher leaders was conducted by Lieberman, Saxl, and Miles in 1988. They suggested that teacher leaders operate differently than other teachers in the ways they build trust and develop rapport—while performing all the customary duties of teaching. Such individuals also spend significant time with students outside the classroom.

We found one such teacher in a suburban high school in Westford, Massachusetts. Mike Towers teaches English and theater, working around the clock on student theater productions. Outside of Broadway or Piccadilly Circus, you couldn't find a more poignant production of *Les Miserables* than the one staged at Westford Academy in 2004. Mike Towers gets his students to reach beyond what would be expected to produce the extraordinary. His impact on other people is impressive.

Towers told us why he works night and day and why his students are willing to work late after school, making sets and rehearsing. He told us how he ended up at Westford Academy and how he drives successive classes of high school students to stage one masterpiece after the next.

Connecting and Belonging

Mike Towers doesn't see himself as a traditional leader, but understands that he operates in a leadership capacity. When he spoke, he quickly explained the essence of his own leadership and mission.

> When I was a child, I was driven by things that still drive me today. Those are the things that I focus on in my teaching. The first thing that mattered to me was belonging. I always wanted to belong, to be part of something—a group of people. Connecting with people became my mission. An important part of what I teach is that you have to treat all people well. That's my motto or mantra, and that's how I live and teach. These three words, 'Treat people well,' are the most important for me.
>
> I started performing in grade school. The theater shaped my life. From these experiences I learned that teaching goes hand-in-hand with the responsibility for shaping lives. At a young age, I learned that my goals must include touching and connecting with others. Performing was a good way to do that. My interpersonal skills made me feel good, and they made other people feel good. For me this was success.
>
> My family had a profound influence, which continues to this day. I grew up in Maryland in a military family. My father is now a retired Air Force Lieutenant Colonel.

We were lucky that my father knew how consistency and stability would impact the family. I still don't understand government policies that require families to move every two to three years. My father was savvy enough to transfer himself back and forth between Andrews Air Force Base and the Pentagon.

After five tours, they finally caught on to what he was doing and forced us to move. So for eight years we lived in Maryland, where we all attended a Catholic elementary school. My family was very structured and strict, characteristics that made my father a good military officer. He was not much of a communicator; however, when he did speak, he was very clear.

My mother is almost desperate to connect in a positive way. I call her the Mother Theresa of Lowell. She works in the Lowell Public School System. Her mission is touching, shaping, and changing lives anyway she can. That's become a big part of who I am. I see my mother as a saint and myself as an ordinary guy.

We moved from Maryland to Massachusetts in 1984. That's when I started at Westford Academy, where I teach now. When I arrived at the school, I was just five feet tall and weighed 95 pounds. The Academy had 900 students, and I knew no one.

Being the smallest in the class affected me in many ways. We underestimate how self-perception and leadership is influenced by stature. Although I wanted so desperately to be part of people's lives in a positive way, it was hard for me because I was little. I was always hoping there would be some magic potion that would make me grow. I was looking for it in every magazine out there.

I was very conscious of charisma. I believed that I had charm, but I also recognized my inadequacy. In fact, as a youngster, I considered myself an underdog in everything I did. But being short made me work harder too. I tried to learn to laugh at myself, asking what people would want from me. It was hard for me to be a short person, but I looked at it as a challenge. I enjoyed challenges, and I welcomed them.

So, I took my five-foot frame and started to network, not because I was a politician but because I wanted to be part of this new community. I got involved in many activities. I was on the soccer team, wrestling team, and tennis team and performed multiple theatrical productions a year. It was a way to connect and learn. Athletically, it was hard to compete at my size. There were times I couldn't match up. I worked hard. I was undaunted. In my sophomore year I was elected president of the class and had a good academic, athletic, and performance record.

I felt successful. I worried that people would accuse me of being driven by popularity. That wasn't the case. I just enjoy people and want to belong. I'll talk with anybody. I draw on people. I pride myself in having no prejudice or age discrimination. I tell kids all the time how much they have to offer.

When I graduated from Westford in 1988, I wanted to attend Boston College; but I was wait-listed. So I went to St. Anselm's College in New Hampshire instead. That's where I faced my greatest challenge and experienced a turning point in my life.

When I got to Saint Anselm's, it was a rude awakening. Although I was much taller, at 5 feet 11 inches, I didn't feel like I belonged. I didn't make friends. I had never before failed to connect. I moved into a room with two other guys who had been best friends in high school. They only wanted to be together and I was clearly the third wheel.

I was trying to make friendships, but they saw me as an obstacle.

I started acting out. I struggled. It affected me emotionally. I tried to continue to do all the things that had worked in the past. I ran for class president and lost. I tried out for the first play but didn't get in. I tried out for soccer but got cut. I tried out for tennis, my strongest sport, but fell off the team. It was an emotional whirlwind. I was struggling everywhere. Academically, I struggled for a year. It was the darkest time of my life. I didn't return to Saint Anselm's.

I want every student or person that I now know to learn how to avoid such a negative experience. Whether I'm teaching math, theater, or English, I find ways to help students better understand how they can develop and use skills and experiences to protect themselves from negativity. I instill in every student a sense that one must build character to build relationships. Character is the building block, the energy, and the aura they need to be strong enough when they find themselves in tough predicaments. In life each person must have the strength and courage to combat life's struggles.

I feared that the things I had built in my life had been taken away from me at St. Anselm's; but I found that this was false. I didn't need to be the captain, number one, or president. What I needed was the patience to find friendship in people who produce a love of life, a love of living, and a love for others. I realized that my failure to cope was impeding my need for belonging and contribution. This was real leadership. Once I understood this, I found my way back to school and reapplied to Boston College. This time I was admitted. The lessons would stay with me for life, fortifying me to become a true contributor.

Full Circle

I always knew I wanted to be a communicator. But when I was at Boston College, I realized I was going to be not a lawyer but an actor. After college, I went to New York City and pursued acting professionally. I had some success and acted off-Broadway and on television. I was happy with my work but not happy with my purpose.

When I was working as a bartender between stints, I got my first sense that I had to do more for others to fulfill my life. At the bar, I saw true addiction. We had drug addicts, alcoholics, homeless people, and veterans as customers, and this disturbed me greatly. People would come to me with a check on which they were supposed to live. They'd ask me to cash it and then drink it away. They were living in cardboard boxes across the street in the park, and I was serving them in a bar.

I never considered myself a writer, but I started to write about my experiences, particularly with addiction. I went home in 1994 and told my mother I was moving to California to start my life as a writer. I was going to write for TV in order to communicate and connect. Then I got a call from the Westford Academy principal, who had been my principal. He wanted to meet with me. Of course, I visited him. When we met in his office, he told me that he knew I was in town and had heard what I was planning for myself. He wanted me instead to become a teacher at Westford.

Something about his vision for me had a big impact. I was 23 years old. I worked as an assistant in my first year and sat with the kids all day long, whether in study halls or office detention. As the same time, I was still writing. But I began to feel as though I was successfully communicating with people and reaching them on all fronts. Students could come and talk to me about algebra, or about their best friend who'd been drinking and driving, or about relationships, or about addiction, or about writing a speech for president of the class. I felt that I had something to offer. I was connecting and making a difference and impacting people.

That was the springboard. I started humbly, making $7,200 that year with a degree from Boston College and no classroom experience. I had to develop. When a math slot opened, I became an aide in the classroom. I started to shape my skills and understand what I was put here to do. From math, I went on to English; and then I built the theater program. That brought my career full circle. Teaching math opened the door for me to teach something I was truly an expert on.

At times, I question whether I can or should keep leading. Once, because of a disagreement over an administrative issue, I even resigned. I worked somewhere else, but missed teaching, even though I was making twice the money at half the hours. I realized I was in the wrong place and no longer doing what I was meant to do. So I went back. It's all I can and should do.

I still hope to be a writer and an actor of sorts. I get frustrated when I look at the world and see things I wish I could address on a larger scale. Ideally, some day I'd like to be a writer who has had an impact on others for what I've written and be known for a production as a director or performer. But being a teacher and a leader at Westford Academy and managing a successful theater arts program means that I'm making a difference.

I define my own leadership differently than you might expect. Working intimately with students, often one-on-

one, I believe that I teach power. I'm not talking about the power of politicians or those in charge, but rather the power to shape, change, and impact others' lives in small or large ways. I ask my students to embrace that power because I know I have it. But I don't have any more than they do.

It's power when I smile at you and make you feel good. It's power when I say hello to you in the hallway and make you feel that you belong. I try to teach kids to know their own power. Theater is wonderful for that. What better way to come to terms with your own power than by acting on a stage in front of a live audience? Theater is about the relationship between a performer and an audience. I believe that life should be all about making connections with other people, too.

Becoming Swanee Hunt: The Story of Swanee Hunt and Harvard's Women and Public Policy Program

From Cambridge, Massachusetts, home to influential political leaders and thinkers since the time of the founding fathers, Swanee Hunt walks from Brattle Street to Harvard's John F. Kennedy School of Government, where she teaches and directs the Women and Public Policy Program. She is focused on influencing policies that affect women and the women who shape public policies. Her program supports research, teaching, and publishing, while mentoring women, training executives, and advancing women's leadership in public service.

Before Harvard, Swanee Hunt was better known as the U.S. ambassador to Austria. For four years, she went above and beyond the call of diplomatic duty, focusing on the war in the Balkans as few U.S. leaders had, hosting negotiations and international symposia to secure peace. She became well known as a humanitarian from her project to restock the destroyed national library in Sarajevo. She also worked extensively with Bosnian women and religious leaders, helping them to unite after the divisions of war. Her book *This Was Not Our War: Bosnian Women Reclaiming the Peace* (Duke University Press, 2004) collects the thoughts of 26 women caught in the Bosnian conflict. When she represented the United States in Austria, Swanee Hunt became an intellectual leader for women in post-Communist Europe.

Even before becoming an ambassador, she'd had plenty of training for such a leadership role. A tireless civic leader and philanthropist, Hunt has received honors from groups as far ranging as the Anti-Defamation League and the Institute of International Education. She has contributed scores of articles and has gained acclaim as a world-class photographer. Her photograph "Sarajevo Soccer Field," which had been turned into a makeshift graveyard, is in the permanent collection of the Brooklyn Museum in New York City. Her diverse interests include a musical composition, "The Witness Cantata," which has been performed throughout the United States. She also holds two master's degrees and a doctorate in theology.

Swanee Hunt's record as an ambassador is well documented. What we will focus on is where Swanee Hunt comes from. The Hunt name, like that of Getty or Rockefeller, is legendary in the U.S. oil business. Swanee Hunt and her 15 brothers and sisters came from a politically conservative family led by her father H.L. Hunt, who had been recognized as one of the 10 wealthiest men in the United States.

What caused her to stand out from her family members and social peers to advocate progressive causes? As our interview commenced, Swanee Hunt said, "Maybe you should look at my new book if you want to learn more about my life as a leader."

After our discussion, a chapter called "Roots" in her then-unreleased book told the full story. Everyone is a product of a specific family. Growing up in an unusual family, Swanee Hunt successfully forged her own life, demonstrating a true leader's path-changing ability.

Multiple Families

Swanee was not born a Hunt. Her mother Ruth was born in 1917 and grew up poor in Oklahoma. Ruth's father, Walter Ray, and his wife, Grace, went by buggy and wagon to Arkansas to start a better life. When tuberculosis claimed Walter's life, Grace raised her children by herself. Swanee's mother got a firsthand education in how she would do the same later on.

As the youngest of five children, Swanee's mother benefited from having four siblings who were already working. Considered gifted in many ways, Ruth wrote poems with the titles "Gee

Whiz" and "No Siree" that were published in the hometown newspaper. She became a proficient typist, which would change her life. She was a straight-A student, and her siblings pushed her to go to college. At 17, she was a freshman at Oklahoma State University, but her enrollment took opportunities away from her brothers and sisters, so she quit school. She moved to Shreveport, Louisiana to live with her sister Swan. Swan later married a Mr. Lake. Ruth's sister loved to introduce herself with, "Hello, I'm Swan Lake." She became Swanee's namesake.

Shortly after moving in with her sister, Swanee's mother took a job at a law firm that represented much of Louisiana's oil interests. Swanee describes her mother as a pretty brunette with a unique personality that immediately connected with people. One day, a tall man came into the office. Something about him instantly attracted Swanee's mother. She took notice, and so did he. He was also 29 years her senior and married with six children. She didn't know any of that at the time, but she found out later that one of the children was older than she was.

One night, Swanee's mother didn't come home to her sister's apartment. Less than a year later, she was being kept in an apartment in New York and delivered a baby out of wedlock by herself. Being a devoutly religious woman, one can barely imagine how she felt.

Swanee would be the fifth of the children born out of wedlock to Ruth Ray and H.L. Hunt. They lived in a tiny home just down the road from some of the wealthiest families in the country. Swanee's life was not tragic; but it was troubled. It was masked by affluence, wrapped in power, and secret pockets of sadness. It was a world filled with lies, with one lie always leading to another. To Swanee, the biggest lie of all was that of a pious mother who had children with a fictitious husband known as "Mr. Wright." She never divulged the true name of the children's father.

The only man that Swanee knew as a child was a gentleman who came over for dinner on Thursday nights. The children would dress up in their Sunday clothes, a tablecloth would go on their kitchen table, and Ruth would fix up her hair and put on her prettiest dress. This Thursday-night visitor cut an impressive figure when he arrived: six feet tall, fair-haired, and broad shouldered. He always appeared with a starched shirt, pressed pants, straw hat, and large cigar. He had a special way about him. As Swanee put it, "We knew he was important, and Thursdays was the most important day of the week."

When Swanee was seven years old, the family stopped talking about the fictitious husband, Mr. Wright. The man who visited on Thursdays lived in a mansion up the street. In 1955, Lyda, his wife and mother of his six children, passed away. Two years later, Swanee and her family moved into the big house known as Mount Vernon with their new father, H.L. Hunt.

Life as a Hunt

In many ways, life in the bungalow was happier than life in the mansion. In the bungalow, there was music and play and constant laughter. In the big house, Swanee recalled, "I got lost wandering. I'd never been in a home where the first and second floors were connected by three stairways and an elevator." Her father stopped her in the hallway and asked, "Which one are you?"

For years, she tried to figure out the relationship between her mother and father. Eventually, it dawned on her: the man who came on Thursdays was her real father. One day, she asked the cook about her father's divorce from Lyda. She had assumed that a divorce had happened because the only way to have children was through marriage. It was then that she first heard the word *illegitimate.* That described the kind of child Swanee was. "Honey," the cook explained, "they were never divorced."

Legitimacy eventually came. "A year later," Swanee remembers, "my mom and dad went out one afternoon all excited. Mother was really dressed up." The next day at school, the teachers rewrote their names. Swanee was no longer Swanee Wright, she was Swanee Hunt. Over the years, the children from the two Hunt families came to know each other. Life moved on. But those were confusing times for young Swanee.

Through the 1960s, Swanee tried to deal with the stress of an obsessive father who was possessive of his wife's time. There were days when her father tried to methodically break down her mother's spirit. From time to time, her mother confronted him with a list of his girlfriends. Swanee's three sisters developed a deep resentment for their father, but her mother defended him, saying that he didn't know how to show love. There were no gifts and few smiles. In contrast, Swanee's mother had been constantly and spontaneously generous. But the atmosphere of the big house changed everything. Swanee remembers the children virtually raising themselves.

Energetic and full of enthusiasm, Swanee began to work at Hunt Oil Company at 13. One day, she courageously confronted her father: "Why do you go out with other women? You're married to my mother. That's not right. You shouldn't do it."

He replied, "You don't know what you're talking about. King Solomon had 700 wives—it's in the bible." That was the last time she talked to him about his indiscretions. He continued to sire more children with other women. Her mother turned to prayer.

H.L. Hunt was born in 1889, and by his own account was a genius. He described a violent father and a mother who taught her son at home. He left the family farm itching to find his way in the world and build an empire. After he became a success, H.L. Hunt promoted his philosophical and political positions. He wrote daily newspaper columns and a series of books. One was the utopian novel *Alpaca* (H.L. Hunt Press, 1960), which espoused the theory that voting privileges should be granted in proportion to wealth. He believed that everyone could and should do just what he had done. In a world in which the families like the Hunts got whatever they wanted, it was a powerful and oppressive set of beliefs.

Breaking Away

Swanee Hunt could have been influenced by her father, as several of her brothers had been, but her heart followed her mother's spirituality and caring. After high school, she took a religious path and studied theology. She set a course to look for solutions to the world's iniquities.

By the mid 1970s, she tried to distance herself from her father, who she said "was so out of touch, I could avoid being in his sight and, therefore, mind." She told us that her father expected his children to line up for his politically conservative causes. As she was finding her own way, she learned of her father's secret *third* family. This made a profound impact on Swanee's point of view. As we talked with her and learned of her zeal to give back, we became more understanding of her sense of social justice.

Swanee Hunt did not rely on her wealth and status as a platform. Instead, she spent years studying and practicing good works. While attending university, she fell in love with a handsome young man who was also intent on becoming a religious leader. He was her first love. She spent years trying to keep a family together, but her life experiences made this a challenge she couldn't overcome. The end of her marriage proved to generate even more energy. She continued to hone her skills of writing and speaking.

Over the next two decades, Swanee Hunt became a civic leader and philanthropist in her adopted city of Denver, where she focused all of her resources on social justice. There she led community efforts for the governor and two mayors to improve public education, affordable housing, and mental health services. She cofounded the Women's Foundation of Colorado, which raised a $10 million endowment promoting women's economic self-sufficiency. She spent 12-hour work days reaching out to needy causes.

She was remarried with a family by 1993, when she was appointed ambassador to Austria. She describes her swearing-in ceremony as: "A squirmy, gaggle of children holding little American and Austrian flags sat cross-legged on a muted-rose carpet around the stage. My family-oriented swearing in was a first for the U.S. State Department. Mother gazed lovingly up at me as she held the bible on which my hand rested. Vice President Al Gore led me in taking the oath of office."

When she began her remarks, she commented with relief that her mother did not have to explain to her father the liberal democratic path she took to her ambassadorship. As she said, "Our family's desire to change the world has been an essential component in my life. I have spent much of who I am—time and energy, health and wealth—trying to figure out how to have the greatest impact on others."

Even in breaking away, she was still a product of her roots. Like many leaders, Swanee Hunt has taken the disadvantages of childhood and resolutely turned them into strengths. In her book, she describes this transformation with the eloquence of a poet and the curiosity of a historian:

> My father was a brilliant, eccentric, oil-patch "wild-catter", who drilled for black gold on a hunch and a

prayer. My inheritance isn't just company stock, but also genes and family lore replete with adventurers exploring new territory, relying on their vision and cunning to create institutions and businesses where none existed. Dad's trailblazing led to my penchant for striking out into the unknown taking on intractable social problems. My mother's religious devotion became my own brand of evangelism, a determination to save others from hell on earth.

I'm often asked how I wound up so different from my parents' conservative ways. I don't fully accept the premise. Sure, my persuasions diverged from my parents'. But I've been more surprised by how many of their bedrock attitudes and inclinations are fundamental to my thinking and actions—particularly their insistence that every person is responsible for changing the world. My roots have allowed me to launch out on my own, to the inner city of Denver, the imperial halls of Vienna, and the rubble-strewn streets of Sarajevo. Wherever I've ended up, my folks have come along.

Swanee Hunt has spent her life trying to be a leader who could add the value she believed was in her. She is tireless in her work, and renowned in her determined, perfectionist style of leading. Privately, she said she is "trying to hold onto my father's best and let the rest slip away." She thinks about her father this way: "While our relationship was painfully lacking, he meant the world to my mother—and she meant the world to me."

Say Yes, then Figure Out How: The Story of Pat Mitchell and the Public Broadcasting Service

In March 2000, the Public Broadcasting Service (PBS) announced the appointment of Pat Mitchell as president and chief executive officer. They pointed out that Mitchell brought to the post a distinguished background as network correspondent, award-winning producer, television executive, and college-level educator. *Forbes* magazine hailed her as one of the most influential executives in the entertainment industry. The PBS announcement also mentioned her membership on prestigious boards and councils, including the Council on Foreign Relations, board membership of United Way of America, Sundance Institute, and the Women's Leadership Council at Harvard's Kennedy School of Government. It referred to her lectures on leadership and the role of media in society. She has given testimony before the U.S. Congress and Britain's House of Lords. It also noted that she had been a magna cum laude graduate of the University of Georgia, where she earned a master's degree in English literature.

Pat Mitchell's story is about becoming the highest-ranking woman leader in the media industry. As CEO and president of PBS, she led a member organization that reaches nearly 90 million people each week through on-air and online content. This private, nonprofit corporation founded in 1969 reflects the social and economic makeup of the nation. The presidency of PBS was described as "a burnout job" by Mitchell's predecessor, John Swope. Rumors and whispers in the press made it clear that the success of PBS was dependent upon a person who could consolidate what the member stations had in common, rather than tending to disagreements. It was not going to be easy. It would require a master at bringing about change, someone who could recreate the vision of public broadcasting in America.

Heidrick and Struggles, a prestigious executive search firm, sought out the best candidate. Mitchell was selected from among 10 top media executives, some with much more experience. How the board and the search committee reached that decision in unknown. The press announcement stated that Mitchell was very close to delivering the "total package of desired qualities." What Pat Mitchell brought to the table is a story that's worth telling.

Formation of the Total Package

Pat Mitchell was born on her grandfather's farm. Her mother was alone and her father—right off the farm himself—was a private serving in the army. Her early years were typical for army families. Moving from base to base, she had had multiple addresses by the time she entered the third grade. She believes that this experience was part of her development as a communicator, and a critical factor for successful leadership. "I learned quickly that you only have a few days when you are a new girl in a new school, particularly when you don't have an accent to match the place you live. You have to adapt, become intuitive and instinctive—operating on a timeline that others don't have to live by." There was trauma associated with losing friends and moving on; but it allowed her to gracefully adjust to change.

By Mitchell's her early teens, her mother was no longer willing to move. She convinced her husband to return to the place where they had grown up. They moved for the last time to their new home in Swainsville, Georgia. A town of about 5,000 then and 5,000 today, it was just 30 miles away from the farm village where they had met. For the first time, Mitchell could stay in one place to finish high school in a small town.

One teacher, Shirley Reid, influenced Mitchell in a remarkable way, and became her role model. "She was someone I wanted to look like, dress like, sound like, be like, be as smart as—as well as being in control." Reid had come to Swainsville right out of college. Mitchell remembers her as being attractive and articulate. "She was everything I wanted to be. I remember her wardrobe, and the way she walked—poised, wonderful, and cosmopolitan. She was my gateway to the outside world."

Mitchell worked with this teacher on plays and debates, realizing that there was more she could become. She recalls, "This wonderful teacher helped me to focus on creating dreams." Shirley Reid made her aware of her potential. By this time she was set on a course that would take her beyond Swainsville. As clear as this was to her, she was unsure of how to do it. She remembered that her father used to say, "If you are so eager to get out, your only ticket is education." The message was clear. The family had limited economic means, and no one in her family had ever been to college. She set a course to make that dream come true.

At various times, those formative years allowed her to sort through choices and adapt. She knows that circumstances will always create opportunities and obstacles. In the south in the 1960s, there were few careers for young women. Although she decided to be a lawyer, her parents steered her toward nursing or teaching. Finally, her father simply said no—she should teach. She earned a drama scholarship to the University of Georgia. There she switched to teaching and earned a degree in English literature. She continued on to graduate school because she wanted to teach at the college level.

During this time, she got married. On the day she received her master's degree, her son was born. In the morning she was on stage receiving her diploma and that afternoon, she was in the delivery room—just barely making it in time. She continued to study while she taught at the university, but ran out of time and options as she faced a divorce, limited funds, and single parenthood. She had to suspend her studies just as she was about to do her doctoral dissertation.

She grew up believing that young women didn't have to have a BS or a BA but rather had to have an MRS. That was expected. For the first time in her life, she had to admit to herself that this wasn't exactly what she had planned. She decided to leave the South and the cocoon of the university where she had spent the past nine years. But she wasn't ready to leave teaching—with a young child, it was the perfect career. She moved to Richmond, Virginia and took a job at Virginia Commonwealth University. That same year, the students burned down the English building where she had her office.

Mitchell describes it as a great time. Rioting spilled onto the streets. It was the height of the student revolution. Reporters descended on the campus, referring to it as an epicenter for revolution. Her inquisitive mind and her need to understand opened up a larger vision about the world, and it formed her opinion about journalists.

One day, she asked a writer for *Look* magazine: "How do you put a story together?" He offered her the chance to help put the story together. When she did, *Look* offered her a job in New York. She accepted but hedged her decision by getting the school to agree to a leave of absence. She needed a way to come back if she had to. In the back of her mind, she figured she'd be gone for just a year.

News Maker

She found herself in New York working for a large magazine as a researcher and writer. New York opened her eyes. For the first time, she said, "I really had a life I would not have ever seen for myself, except in my dreams."

Just as she was falling in love with her life, the magazine went bankrupt. Now she was unemployed, broke, and under-experienced for anything except teaching. Worse, it was October, and the prime teaching positions were filled. She went home to her apartment as the news was still sinking in. She had to dig deep into the adaptability she had developed early in life.

She resisted her first instinct to return to Georgia, where she could afford to live and pick up some job to tide her over. She talked to everyone she knew to try to keep herself on course. She was willing to take on anything and turn it into another advancement step.

One evening, a friend called and said, "Why don't you sell a story to NBC?" He offered to introduce her to the news director. During the interview, she sold him on the idea of doing a story for them.

"When he asked me to do the first story, I had no idea what that meant, but I said yes, of course. One thing I had learned in my life was to say yes and figure out how to do it later." As she returned home, she realized that although she had no clue what she had just said yes to, a new world had opened up. She would be paid not as an employee but as a franchise. She rounded up a camera crew and went out the next day. She learned as she went and put the story together. She laughingly remembers the sound man saying, "Hold the mic this way," and then admonishing her to look toward the person to whom she was talking. She made it up as she went along.

Fortunately, she had hired the right crew. When the story aired, she was so dreadful that they cut her out, but the story was good.

She was hooked on the media. She had discovered a new way of sharing information. She had also opened up a new way of teaching. She understood that the story she had reported and produced was being watched by millions of people. This was a

"A guy named Ted Turner noticed our work and I went to Atlanta to talk about some of the projects we had on our plate. One of them was the history of women in America." Although they had tried to sell it to every network and cable company, they had all said no. Ted Turner asked if the stories they wanted to tell were in the history books. Mitchell said they weren't. Turner said, "Okay, let's do it."

This led to a relationship that changed her life again. She was offered the job to run the documentary division at Turner Broadcasting System. She found herself back in Georgia, where she never thought she'd return, producing 500 hours of documentaries a year.

When Time Warner merged with CNN, she spent another three years doing some of the best work of her career. Turner had a huge influence on her as a leader. "He is a total iconoclast, a genius, a visionary. There aren't that many leaders like him in the world. So, to work closely with him was a leadership lesson that changed my life." Each time she met with Turner in his office, she looked at the sign on his desk: "Lead, follow, or get out of the way." Mitchell said that it's no joke. "He leads, you follow, or you get out of the way." But his leadership style for her included complete trust. He believed in her and gave her the power to execute.

Moreover, he gave her what she needed to do her job. There were no excuses, and embedded in her memory are the words, "Never dull." She never knew what to expect when she would be called to Turner's office to hear his next big idea. "Carrying out some of his great big ideas was the thrill of a lifetime. I was part of an entrepreneurial company where all you had to do was say yes to an idea, and the next thing you knew it was a channel—a 24-hour series on the Cold War." She interviewed over 600 world leaders, and that film is now the basis for courses at Yale, Princeton, and Harvard.

Leading the Confederacy

After the company was sold, she had no interest in staying. Ted Turner was the reason she stayed there. She valued every bit of the time. She was thinking that she might go back to teaching when she got the call to consider becoming CEO at PBS. She knew that this might be the right thing. "I admired what they did, but I didn't know very much about how it worked." After a series of interviews, she was offered the job and found herself sitting in Washington, D.C., leading the nation's only public broadcasting service.

Immediately, she knew that this would be a far cry from the fast-moving, decision-making environment of Ted Turner's world. Now she had to work with 350 independent stations. "This is a leadership challenge beyond all other CEO challenges in the media business," she said. "You lead by consensus, influence, and example." All of her experiences had been in top-down environments. She immediately recognized PBS as a "confederacy." She describes being president of PBS as "running for the presidency of PBS every day except there never is an election." She doesn't downplay the day-to-day challenges facing CEOs in the other media companies, but there are more variables at play for a publicly sponsored broadcaster. In some respects, it's like being a university president: There are a lot of powerful constituencies. Again, her past experiences came to the fore to assist her. Traditional corporate leadership skills just wouldn't work.

When we asked Pat Mitchell why she continues to lead, she replied, "I am driven by the need to positively influence people's lives. That's what drew me to teaching, and that is what drew me to TV. And that's what keeps me in the media up to this point. We have enormous power. I worry deeply about the way this power is being used and misused around the world. I sit in an institution whose mission is to use media for good—no matter how tough the challenges are. I am driven by that goal and the vision and mission that we can create programming that informs people in ways that changes their lives or opens their minds or strengthens their community. We do that everyday. So no matter how tough it may be to get resources or how tough the battles may be on Capitol Hill, I am driven by what we actually do. It keeps me on the front lines."

Had her vision of her own leadership style changed greatly? She said that it has evolved naturally through different responsibilities. "When you are running a small company where everything depends on you, you think about your leadership and your responsibilities in a different way. The most evolutionary thing for me in the last six years has been that every day as a leader here, I use the experiences of every other job I have ever had. You take skills with you to every job."

What's vital, Mitchell thinks, is having the confidence to take the risks necessary to grow into a role. "I never had a television course in my life, but I just stood in front of the camera and used my teaching skills. So, you transfer. In this job I use my teaching skills, my reporting skills, my documentary skills, my leadership skills, and the skills I learned working for Ted Turner. Every day I get to use part of what I have had in my own set of experiences—and that is very powerful."

Every day, she said, "I am learning something new. I still learn from observing other leaders, and I think about leadership from the point of view of my staff and the point of view of the whole institution. I think about all of us running media companies right now. We are like those who run other companies; but we are particularly challenged as leaders. We need to lead through specific changes that will transform our industries. There are no easy answers."

In Mitchell's life, she didn't wait for the answers before she dove in. She stepped into the void and discovered the answers along the way.

Be the Change You Wish to See in the World: The Story of Mohandas K. Gandhi and the Social Revolution of Passive Resistance

The final leader in our book is Mohandas K. Gandhi, the Indian nationalist icon who died in 1947.

We were drawn to him for many reasons. Doing philanthropic work in India, it was impossible not to think of Gandhi and the human rights advances he led over a half century ago. Without political power, religious office, or personal wealth, Gandhi affected hundreds of millions of lives and helped a great nation to be born. He did it not for personal gain, but to make the world a better place. His nonviolent approach to protesting social wrongs has been emulated by some of the greatest leaders of our own time. Gandhi's leadership has been invoked by Martin Luther King Jr. in the U.S. civil rights movement and Nelson Mandela in ending apartheid in South Africa.

Gandhi embodied the higher principles that we had observed in the leaders we interviewed for this book. Many of those leaders told us that leading effectively required them to live their values so their followers would feel the authenticity of those values.

Gandhi's transition from an ordinary idealist to someone who had great personal magnetism came about when he determined that one needs to "be the change you wish to see in the world." Many of the leaders we interviewed also spoke about the real fulfillment of leadership arising not through status, wealth, or achievement, but through the act of selflessly serving others. Gandhi was adamant that he did not sacrifice his health or wealth for others because he was averse to enjoying life. He said that serving others gave him the most joy and fulfillment.

As Gandhi showed, the trials and satisfactions of leadership are not limited to one's achievement. The trials and satisfactions of leadership point to universal themes from which all of us can benefit from and learn to seek out.

Early Career

Gandhi was born in the Indian town of Porbandar in 1869 to a family that was active in local government but had no great wealth or power. Physically small, he was not interested in sports or school and preferred to be alone. What he lacked in physical or academic ability, however, he seemed to make up for with a strong moral sensibility. Whenever there was a game or a dispute or a misunderstanding, the young Gandhi found himself in the role of arbiter. He settled differences and focused on what he would later call the "search for truth."

He was wed in an arranged betrothal at age 13, and the marriage would last over 50 years. Even as an adult, he still floundered in school. He continued his studies in England, where he was inspired by the prosperous nation's great opportunities. He broadened his studies widely and obtained his law degree. He did his best to fit in by acting like an English gentleman, but he failed to make a strong impression. He did, however, learn a lot about the English people, and that knowledge would help him in the colonial confrontations to come.

Making little headway as a lawyer, Gandhi and his family moved to South Africa, where he set up practice. Under the South African system of racial segregation, he had one of his first life-shaping experiences. Gandhi was riding in a first-class train compartment when a white man who joined his compartment, refused to spend the night in the same space as an Indian. Gandhi was told by the authorities to move to a third-class berth, but he refused to do so. The train conductor then removed Gandhi from the train. He spent the night in a railway station, contemplating the anger and humiliation of discrimination.

Over the next quarter century, Gandhi worked for racial justice in South Africa. He developed his concept of *satyagraha* (peaceful civil disobedience) and tried to live his own life with increasing simplicity and strong moral authority. He argued legal cases, engaged in protests, was beaten, sent to jail, and became an advocate for important causes. Once a shy man, he grew comfortable speaking before the public and leading others. As his reputation grew, he still felt no sense of fulfillment or accomplishment. He was distressed that others didn't follow his ideas more closely. He concluded that he needed to be more exemplary in leading a moral life.

Influenced by the writings of John Ruskin, Leo Tolstoy, and Henry David Thoreau, Gandhi left his law practice in Johannesburg and moved his family to the countryside, where he would focus on health and medical care issues. In the first decade of the twentieth century, he founded Tolstoy Farm. It was a cooperative where all members of the community worked together, functioning as an extended family and living according to Gandhi's moral principles.

Gandhi believed that he needed to purify his own spirit before he could make demands of others. This moral approach to living extended into the public sphere, where his increasing opposition to racial segregation was demonstrated by leading protest marches and publicly burning his registration card. At all times, he counseled his followers to resist unjust laws but never to become violent. He didn't see such resistance as passive but believed he affirmed life by personally exemplifying truth, justice, and human rights.

By the time Gandhi returned to India he was 45 and already widely known for his nonviolent ideology. He would need all of his experience and personal strength in the struggle to come.

Injustice in India

Beginning in the 1600s, India had become increasingly dominated by the British. The British East India Company, a private firm with a royal decree to trade freely in Asia, initiated the British presence in India. The densely populated country was highly divided politically and came under the rule of British merchants, civil servants, and military. The British East India Company remained in charge until a series of violent and bloody revolts forced Queen Victoria to revoke the charter and assume the title of Empress of India. Thereafter, the British ruled the giant country through a series of viceroys. Even so, those revolts kindled Indian nationalism and dreams of independence.

Wherever Gandhi went in India, crowds gathered around him to receive his blessing. He became a political force after he forged an agreement in a major labor dispute. Despite heightened tensions, Gandhi found a solution that was satisfactory to both employers and employees. In this, he invoked the principles of *satyagraha.* He first got the employees to pledge nonviolence and then fasted until both sides came to terms.

Gandhi would use this approach again and again in the ensuing years. He was able to motivate others to aim for a higher goal by appealing to them spiritually. He showed courage and fortitude by putting his own life at risk to demonstrate his principles with unwavering conviction. Intransigent opponents found this quiet, righteous certitude impossible to combat. Inevitably, Gandhi's words and his deeds focused attention on the day's social issues and created incredible momentum for change.

Gandhi conducted his own life in a manner that resonated deeply with the Indian people. He dressed simply and acted with genuine humility. He cooked his own food, was a strict vegetarian, and lived an ascetic life. In the eyes of the public, he was indisputably a great man, but one who had come to live among them without the trappings of power. Moreover, his words always matched his deeds. His self-sacrifice enabled others to live more selflessly. Gandhi spoke tirelessly about the virtues of a moral life and the necessity of nationhood to overcome the injustices of colonialism. He also taught that we should hate the sin, not the sinner. This helped to free people from anger for their oppressors and to engage in nonviolent resistance. To Gandhi, attacking another person was like attacking yourself. In the same way, showing love to another was an expression of love of oneself.

The next dramatic event in Gandhi's political activism became known as the Salt March. In Indian history, it could be seen as the emerging nation's Boston Tea Party. Salt was necessary for daily life in that hot climate. The British government had a monopoly on salt production and prohibited Indians from making their own. The final blow was the imposition of a salt tax. Gandhi had anticipated that such an event would globally publicize the injustice of British rule. He organized a 240-mile march to the sea where, according to British regulations, picking up a grain of salt residue would be illegal. At first, few people marched with Gandhi, but their numbers grew dramatically.

Indian and British politicians alike couldn't understand this mode of protest, and they were confounded by the effect it had on the local populace and the watching world. Gandhi spoke at every rest spot to elaborate on his message of justice and moral principle. After 24 days, the procession finally reached the sea and Gandhi walked into the water to pick up a lump of salt. As simple and even anticlimactic as it seemed at the time, that act spawned protests all over India. The British were under increasing pressure to allow home rule. To reassert control, they threw countless protesters and political leaders in jail. They had temporarily stopped the rebellion, but their moral authority had been destroyed.

In response, the British hosted a conference in London to discuss constitutional reforms. Gandhi returned to England as a conquering hero, adored by British crowds, celebrities, and the press. "I have come here to win freedom," he said. He did not want dominion status for his nation, he wanted outright independence. For the tottering British Empire, it was a provocative message indeed. The Indian factions played into British hands by bringing their internal squabbles to the conference, which reinforced the British belief that strong authority was needed to govern people who couldn't govern themselves.

Gandhi called this setback "the most humiliating day of my life." He returned to India with two realizations. One, that Britain would not leave India voluntarily out of any sense of moral justice, and two, that Hindus and Muslims, the main Indian ethnic groups, would not work together for independence without extraordinary leadership. With those certainties, Gandhi picked up where he had left off. He led protests, fasted, and strived to make the goal of a morally principled independence a reality for everyone.

When World War II began, everything changed. The once-mighty British Empire was drained of resources in the fight with Germany, Italy, and Japan. The people of India did not relent in their drive for independence. Soon, it became a question of when, not if, their goal would be achieved. After the war, Louis Mountbatten, the British Viceroy of India, was charged with managing the transition to home rule. Tensions between Hindus and Muslims worsened as the reality of independence drew closer. Gandhi's message of nonviolence was ignored as the death toll climbed. Undeterred, he visited town after town, preaching moral principles and trying to stem the violence by putting himself in harm's way.

With the terms of home rule finalized, India was scheduled to declare its freedom on August 15, 1947. But in Gandhi's eyes, the astounding achievement contained the mark of failure. Instead of the Indian subcontinent uniting as one nation, the discord between Hindus and Muslims had led to partition and the creation of Pakistan as a homeland for the majority of Muslims. Although jubilant commemorations were scheduled in the new capital of New Delhi, Gandhi was distraught. Instead of marking the day, he traveled to Calcutta, where Hindu-Muslim violence continued to rage. Even though the British were vanquished, Gandhi was still protesting the injustice of violence and hate.

Gandhi's tactics worked. On the day of independence, a year of communal rioting halted. The Hindus and Muslims of Calcutta began to speak and work with each other again. The peace did not last, however. Two weeks later, riots broke out again while Gandhi was staying at the home of a Muslim. He vowed to fast until civility returned, and the impact of his words was felt almost immediately. In shame, those who had led the riots visited him to beg forgiveness. They brought with them a signed pledge that no such violence would erupt in Calcutta again. Only then, did Gandhi break his fast. Even though riots would continue in other Indian cities, Calcutta would live up to its promise.

Gandhi returned to New Delhi to try to squelch the rioting there. Much of the anger in India came from word of the repression of the new Hindu minority in Pakistan. Gandhi wanted to travel to Pakistan to assist them, but New Delhi was still in turmoil. Once again, Gandhi began a fast, promising to break it only when and if the violence stopped. And once again, the leaders of the riots came to Gandhi with a pledge to protect the life, property, and faith of the Muslim people. Gandhi broke his fast.

There was an attempt on his life two days later. While praying and speaking to a small group, a bomb was thrown in his direction. It exploded without harming anyone, and Gandhi continued to speak after only a brief interruption. But he knew that his life was in danger and his time was short. Extremist Hindus hated Gandhi for preaching tolerance and love of Muslims and for thwarting attempts at violence and revenge.

Ten days after the bomb, Gandhi arrived to speak before a large crowd of followers. A young Hindu stepped forward and started to bow as though genuflecting, but then pulled out a handgun and shot Gandhi in the heart. He died with the name of God on his lips.

A Legacy of Leadership

As a political leader, Gandhi's accomplishments were extraordinary. With no power other than his own moral authority, he helped lead a movement that brought freedom to one-fifth of the people in the world. He did so without resorting to violence or threatening its use, and led others to resist such temptation. He knew never to begin a cycle of revenge that could never be stopped and that demeaned the human soul.

As a moral leader, Gandhi's accomplishments were just as profound. Early in his activist career, he came to believe that he did not have the right or the credibility to work for the ethical betterment of others unless he himself led an exemplary life. His quest for personal purification, though directed inwardly, had a powerful effect on others. To Gandhi, this was not so extraordinary. He saw *satyagraha* as simultaneously purifying and asserting the spirit. He also knew that he could win over skeptics with acts of self-inflicted suffering, which he displayed through his simple lifestyle, his meager belongings, his willingness to put his life in danger, and his many fasts in the cause of peace.

Gandhi directed his political and moral leadership toward specific goals. He had capabilities and tools at his disposal. He devised strategies and formulated messages, and his acts were consistent with his words. In this, Gandhi was the greatest of political or business leaders. His disavowal of money, belongings, and status was one thing; but he also sacrificed his health and ultimately gave up his life for the cause in which he believed.

What kind of compassion and self-sacrifice could bring a man to such extremes? The answer lies in Gandhi's own words. He saw service not as a sacrifice but as a fulfillment of the self. It was something to be done in full knowledge of the satisfaction and joy it brings. "Service can have no meaning unless one takes pleasure in it," he wrote. "Service which is rendered without joy helps neither the servant nor the served, but all other pleasures and possessions pale to nothingness before service which is rendered in a spirit of joy."

In these words we heard echoes of many other leaders' sentiments. Most started their careers for personal reasons—a drive for money, a need to overcome humble beginnings, a desire to be special. But many of these self-focused people found their greatest satisfaction not in personal gain but in service to others.

If leadership is a journey, then often its ultimate goal seems to be personal enlightenment. In this Gandhi spoke wisely as well. "The best way to find yourself," he said, "is to lose yourself in the service of others."

PART III
Conclusion

In this final part of the book, we return to the questions we posed at the end of Chapter 3, The Leadership Discussion: *Why lead?* and *When is enough, enough?* These initial questions extend beyond the realm of leadership to touch on issues of the meaning and purpose of life and whether they can be fulfilled through leadership. As Warren Bennis stated, the process of leadership is really the same process as becoming a fully integrated human being.

Our journey to India provided a fertile environment for asking deep questions about life and leadership's impenetrable complexities. What did we discover from our trip to India and our journey of inquiry around the world through the lives of successful leaders? What qualities, intentions, and character did those leaders possess that made them so successful and enduring? Part of that journey took us from the intellect to the heart and from the ego to the soul. As one successful leader said,

"Those that lead from the head and the ego are not effective leaders. It's when you lead from the heart and the soul that you lead with wisdom and have greater impact."

On our journey of inquiry to answer our original two questions, we discovered a third question: *What is the next level of leadership-- the one that takes a leader beyond "enough" and creates sustainable meaning and purpose?* In finding the answer to this third question, we discovered that there are really two levels of leadership, which we describe as conditional (level 1) and unconditional (level 2). *Conditional leadership* is mostly based on achieving your own objectives. *Unconditional leadership* is transformational—your purpose is no longer simply about you and your personal goals. It is about a greater purpose. We discovered that the journey from conditional to unconditional leadership is one that magnifies a leader's effectiveness and success and creates more meaning, joy, and sustainability in the experience of leading. And we discovered that the very question of "enough" can be a catalyst to making the transition to unconditional leadership.

Sri Narayani Amma's messages were universal and not specifically about leadership. But what we found is that they had unique application to some of the key issues of leadership. The concept of the journey from happiness to joy is a different way to look at leadership, its impact, and its experience. The insight seems paradoxical, but it is also simple and profound. Chapters 9 and 10 present the conclusions of our journey, with Chapter 10 addressing the most important insight we gained: the transformational insight of unconditional leadership that provides a meaningful answer to the question *"Why lead?"*

Chapter 9
Leadership Insights from the Journey

As the variety of these stories indicates, there are no clear-cut or pro forma paths to becoming a leader. The spark that kindles leadership remains a mystery, but it is very clear that all the leaders we studied created purpose, set definite pathways, and pursued their goals tirelessly. Who can predict whether the trauma of a disadvantaged youth will inspire someone to rise above those challenges and to rise above the ones that follow? Consider Henri Landwirth's journey from a concentration camp survivor to a successful entrepreneur. To imagine the influence that a sense of personal mission can have on a young person, consider Jim Lewis, who carried his goals on a list in his pocket for 60 years.

We all have dreams for ourselves. What gives some people the drive to make those dreams happen—and bring others along with them? A quest can also begin later in leaders' lives, bringing their leadership to different levels by linking vision with passion. Wasn't this Mary Robinson's story? Suddenly, an ordinary leader gains eloquence and personal magnetism while engaging committed followers in a surprising new venture.

Others, like Mikhail Gorbachev, became leaders because they simply could not say no. What drove a farm boy to change the geography of the world? Isn't this true for so many leaders who are asked to take the helm? It is a well-known fact that

George Washington wished he could return to his farm Mount Vernon, but chose instead to lead.

There seems to be little chance that leadership could arise in a vacuum, for all these leaders were actively engaged. What makes one person in the crowd step forward even when it is dangerous or unsafe? But time and again, a leader emerges when most needed, and sometimes from surprising sources. Gandhi sacrificed an easy life to make the world a better place. Leadership that arises from values or spiritual conviction is often the easiest to grasp, because the purity of intention is so clear. It is very difficult for most of us to imagine making the sacrifices necessary to devote one's self to a greater cause, which could even consume one's very life.

Early Changes

Many of the leaders we interviewed were given great opportunities to do things early in life. While they seemed to become leaders partly through personal drive, they were also challenged to do more than others did at an early age. Henri Landwirth survived the Holocaust. Rajaa Khuzai survived Saddam Hussein. Mikhail Gorbachev and Ron Greene both took responsibility for running their family farms at an age when most children don't take responsibility for their own laundry. Even traditional business leaders like Claude Lamoureux and Larry Strecker handled one assignment after another to stretch their abilities and put them into positions of greater leadership responsibility. The spark of leadership may be widespread in many people, but it's kindled by rarer circumstances.

Being Tested

This doesn't mean that a leadership path is always taken at an early age. People can assume leadership later in life after circumstances give that leader a distinctive voice. But leadership is not simply an inspiration or a calling. It requires well-honed technical and emotional capabilities. Mary Robinson prepared herself for leadership by rising to the top of her class and then going to Harvard Law School. Leaders may be born or discovered early, but they do not become effective leaders without being tested. They fare better after they fail and learn from their mistakes. Anthony von Mandl's business grew after every adversity.

Making Choices

Leaders frequently throw themselves into the deep end where they are forced to take on more than they can handle. They must have survival skills to thrive despite the odds and hold things together during times of transition.

Leaders make the choice to lead. Early on, a leader can make that choice without realizing its full implications. Who can forget Rafiah Salim taking a train to school and eventually finding her way to the United Nations? Leaders may seek the glory or the rewards of leadership and underestimate the required sacrifice, burden, cost, and dedication. And the next time a leadership choice arises, do they choose to lead once more? For the most part, the leaders that we wrote about made the choice to lead over and over again. We conclude that *leadership is a continual set of choices.*

It seems that the question *Why lead?* had different answers at different times in our leaders' lives. For many leaders, the meaning of their leadership evolved. This fluctuating sense of meaning shows the importance of reflection and self-awareness. Leadership experts like Warren Bennis advise leaders to keep a diary and to think deeply on the challenges and issues in their lives. If a leader is aligned with his purpose, then his leadership has greater impact. It is also more sustainable because it is more closely linked with what the leader finds meaningful.

Leadership Principles

Apart from the question *Why lead?* there is an enormous amount of leadership advice and insight to be had from these leadership interviews. We believe these insights are a major "take away" value of the book. We gleaned seven principles or insights that are helpful in understanding leadership. The greater one's mastery of these principles, the more capable a leader one can become. We also formulated seven questions that will provide a personal perspective on each of these principles.

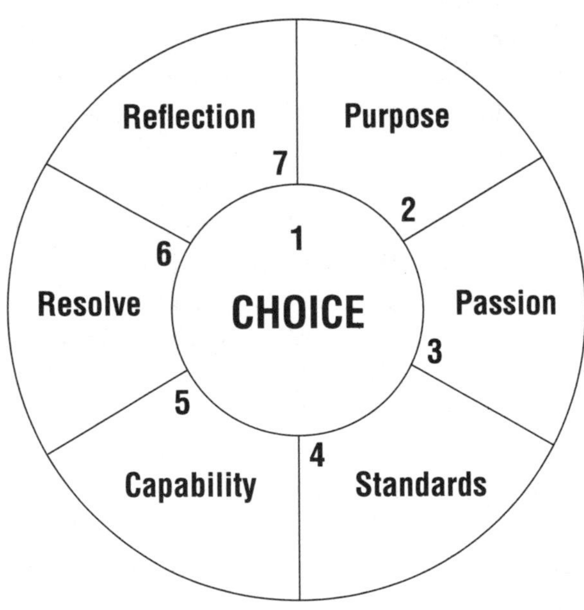

Figure 9.1 Seven Leadership Principles

There is also an eighth principle—a transformational principle that we call *unconditional leadership*. It magnifies the impact of leadership based on the preceding seven principles. The eighth principle is the focus of Chapter 10.

Principle 1: Choice

Leadership is a choice, an act of the mind and the will. It is a choice that leaders make when they answer the question *Why lead?* It is not a choice that is made once. It is a continual commitment that leaders make to themselves over and over again. A leader can make the choice to lead without realizing the full implications of that decision. Leaders who want the glory, the status, or the rewards of leadership often underestimate the sacrifice, the burden, the cost, and the dedication required. Yet, generally, leaders make the decision to lead over and over again.

Question 1: *Have I been clear about my commitment to lead?*

Principle 2: Purpose

Leaders must have a clear sense of purpose. With a clear sense of purpose, leaders can set goals aligned with that purpose. Their plan often looks like a blueprint to others. A sense of purpose in some leaders can be intense enough to create a sense of personal destiny. They create a feeling that they are not ordinary or are meant for special achievements. Most are motivated early on by a desire to be rich, successful, or accomplished. They can transcend those needs and gain satisfaction from helping others reach the same kinds of objectives.

Question 2: *Can I state my purpose for leading in one sentence?*

Principle 3: Passion

Leaders create achievable dreams that others want to share. Leaders' tremendous passion for their goals is articulated in a way that transmits passion and that connects emotionally with others. They keep the dream alive by approaching it with a committed team. A leader's passion can compel others to make things happen. Leaders believe that the very nature of life is accomplishment. Some future leaders are lost in their early years until they recognize the one thing that needs to be done. They focus their passion and energy on making these things happen.

Question 3: *Do my passion and dream compel me and others to "go for it"?*

Principle 4: Standards

Leaders have ideals, integrity, values, and standards. Some leaders lead from a place that is entirely inside themselves. They lead by example, living in a way that inspires others to grow into leaders themselves. The source of their energy and conviction often comes from their values. All the leaders' stories show a strong drive for improvement or even perfection. High-impact leaders work with intensity and conviction. This can sometimes make their leadership role frustrating and even lonely.

Question 4: *Am I leading with integrity and high standards?*

Principle 5: Capability

Leadership takes great fortitude, development of character, and depth of capability. The challenges facing leaders don't lend themselves well to textbook solutions. A breadth of personal and professional experience and development is helpful in preparing leaders for the challenges they face.

Question 5: *Do I have the maturity and the breadth of experience to handle the challenges of leadership?*

Principle 6: Resolve

Leadership requires incredible resolve and fortitude, and no leader is immune to failure. Without a deep sense of determination, no leader can stay the course through the inevitable setbacks and failures. Even when others have given up on the dream, leaders expend great energy on finding ways to rekindle the flame. They never let up until they reach their dream. Leaders may be born or discovered early, but they do not become effective leaders without being tested. They often do better after they fail and learn from their mistakes. Leaders seem continually to make the choice once again to throw themselves into the fray, where they are often forced to take on more than they can handle. It requires special survival skills to thrive despite the odds and hold things together while managing difficult transitions.

Question 6: *Will I have the commitment and strength to weather the setbacks and recreate the dream?*

Principle 7: Reflection

Leadership is not only an inspiration or a calling; it requires technical and emotional capabilities that need to be honed. Some level of failure usually follows success, and success almost always follows failure—if leaders are able to maintain their momentum. Leaders learn and grow continuously from both success and failure, but they refrain from assigning blame. They are naturally curious about the world and want to learn what they can about every new challenge or opportunity. They discover possibilities that others have failed to unearth. As they are driven to question the world, leaders are also driven to question themselves. Such self-reflection is the source of self-awareness, development, and personal growth. It also helps leaders to gain the most from each experience, good or bad.

Question 7: *Am I using the lessons I have learned to correct course and direction and improve my leadership skills?*

Chapter 10
Why Lead?—The Answer

When you think you are helping others, it is not true. You are actually helping yourself. This is because, at the level of the soul, we are all one. Through helping others, you connect with your soul and that is the source of joy.

—Sri Narayani Amma

Beyond the seven principles, the final, transformational principle is service to others. One can have mastered the seven principles and be an enormously talented leader, but without the eighth principle, a limited one.

Unconditional Leadership: Transformational Leadership through Service to Others

Principle 8: Service

Service to others magnifies the experience of all the leadership capabilities mastered at level 1. Through service, a leader's impact is magnified, as are the meaning, joy, and sustainability of his or her leadership experiences.

Question 8: Do I find meaning, purpose, and joy in what I choose to do?

Level 2 leadership was evident to varying degrees in each of the leaders we interviewed. Unconditional leadership relies on all the capabilities of level 1 leadership, but is transformational through a simple but fundamental difference: focusing on others rather than on one's own agenda. Some of the capabilities at level 1 touch on this theme indirectly, as all leaders work with and through other people. The quality and value of these interactions is critical, and emotional intelligence and trusted influence are important capabilities. However, unconditional leadership places others first. The impact of this shift in orientation is what can take a good leader to greatness.

Conditional leadership is based primarily on achieving your own objectives. In its initial stages, leaders tend to set personal goals and professional objectives. They define their success in terms of achieving specific results. The route to success requires facing difficult or challenging situations and exercising faith and fortitude to achieve a certain level of professional and financial success. This provides a certain sense of satisfaction or happiness. Achievement at this level can be very important

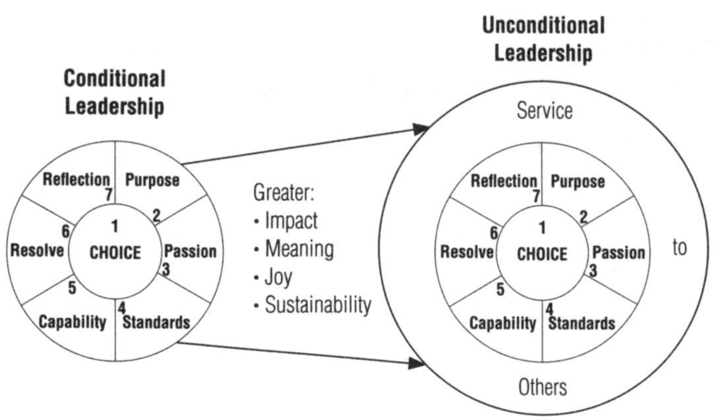

Figure 10.1 Leadership with a Higher Purpose

in creating a solid platform from which to go further. This level of achievement and success can be rewarding in itself, but there is more that can be attained.

One of the key transformational events in leadership is recognizing that there is more to be gained beyond the initial goals. There is a pathway to a second, higher level of leadership. That level is unconditional. It is no longer just about you and your goals. It might be defined as *leadership with a higher purpose.* Leaders who experience this see new possibilities and reach higher levels of success and impact. They are also more fulfilled.

This shift is more challenging than it sounds, but its practical value is priceless. This change in orientation is really the path of personal growth and transformation. It may sound simple but it takes considerable work and commitment. Mac Van Wielingen highlighted this difficulty when he said, "The challenge in leadership is to detach yourself from your own interests and look to the needs of the organization."

Hal Kvisle echoed this theme: "The leader must have an authentic commitment and genuine interest in what's best for the company, not what's best for the leader." And John Keane added another perspective: "You will truly succeed when others want you to succeed." How do you act as a leader to have others invest in your success? By helping others to succeed by putting their interests first.

Culture is an important part of creating the right environment for this way of operating to flourish. John Hammergren stated his belief clearly: "Some people argue that execution beats strategy every time. But I believe that culture beats execution every day. Culture is formed by a leader's ability to build trust; and the key for future leaders, as they grow and expand their responsibilities, is to develop a capacity to move between an 'I' and a 'we' perspective."

Service to others was one of the critical distinguishing features of many of the great leaders we interviewed. Larry Strecker, the leader most visibly struggling with *enough,* is considering work in a nonprofit or a church. He said, "Leadership gives you more leverage to make a difference in people's lives."

Pat Mitchell expressed a similar view in her management style when she said, "You lead by consensus, influence, and example. I am driven by the need to positively influence people's lives."

On a similar theme, John Coleman stated, "In running a business, I came to realize that more than money, people wanted to have great experiences." John Lloyd's perspective is that "leadership is about people. If you put people first, they will be loyal and support you." Jim Lewis, looking back on a life as a highly accomplished executive, realized that what drove him and what gave him the greatest satisfaction was not personal gain but the people around him: "It was never about me. I did it for you."

Henri Landwirth, having seen more pain than many of us can imagine and having achieved much success as well, fills the emptiness in his life by devoting himself to very sick children and the homeless. Landwirth's favorite quote is by Churchill, cited at the beginning of this book: "You make a living by what you earn, but you make a life by what you give." Landwirth's view is, "No one was ever honored for what they had but only for what they gave."

Erin Gruwell, foregoing a more traditional achievement-oriented career, became a teacher who changed the lives of her students, and enriched her own life beyond limits: "I became their student as well as their teacher." Mike Towers, another teacher, described the essential quality of leadership to which all teachers should aspire: "What teacher leaders do is to make a difference in the lives of their students."

Rajaa Khuzai, frustrated by the external limitations of her service as a medical doctor and a politician, pours herself into helping others. When asked how she was able to play such a prominent role in her country, she said, "Because I never think about myself, I only think about others."

Paul Brainerd, having achieved incredible success in business, now extends his knowledge and capability to others in well-picked philanthropic projects that represent a new model for philanthropy. The meaning and the joy he experiences in that role are captured in his favorite expression: "The difference between work in business and work for others (philanthropy) is the difference between a handshake and a bear hug."

Just as remarkably, the political leaders Benazir Bhutto and Mikhail Gorbachev have demonstrated that serving others goes well beyond any concern for self. After all, would either of those leaders have led in such dangerous times if personal gain had been their motive? This view is underscored particularly poignantly in the case of Benazir Bhutto, given her tragic assassination in Pakistan while trying to help her people. She experienced great hardship, but nonetheless stated: "Let us not be bitter because it prevents us from building a better world."

Gorbachev's commitment to destiny is reflected in the simple response to the question, "Why did you do it?" He said, "I had to." Mary Robinson, who led Ireland through difficult times, offered another perspective that highlights the resolve leaders need: "Leaders want to be liked, however doing the right thing is always more important."

Gandhi sublimated the importance of personal attainment to the importance of serving others. It gave him such joy and satisfaction that it seemed to nourish him physically. Gandhi's famous quote, "Be the change you wish to see in the world," is displayed prominently at the Kennedy School of Government at Harvard.

We see this notion of fulfillment through service to others as something that is important for a leader personally, while also being practical, even profitable. It is not merely a more "noble" way of leading. It is a formula for advancing a leader's impact.

As Anthony von Mandl said, "A service orientation—the opposite of narcissism—is necessary for long-term success." Hans Zulliger stated his philosophy of leadership clearly, "It is important [that] successful leaders see themselves as servants of society, unwilling to exploit their success." He further said, "It is important to focus on projects that raise consciousness for life and humanity."

Claude Lamoureux emphasized that leading in this way is a full contact sport: "I believe in MBE—management by example. If an organization needs lots of work done, then its leaders have to work hard." For entrepreneurial leaders who have created successful self-sustaining organizations, Ron Greene observed, "Whether you understand it or not, in building a company, and in creating that opportunity for others, you are serving others. And if you are successful, it is others who make a good leader great."

Finally, Ara Hovnanian offers this perspective on one element of successful leadership and perhaps a transition that needs to occur: "In a way, leading is letting go."

This diverse group of leaders expressed similar views on the need for a social conscience and responsibility, views that have contributed to their success. Rafiah Salim from the United Nations attributed her success to continuing to ask one question: "How can I help?" Jane Simington, a healer, challenges us all by asking, "If not you, who? If not now, when?"

Swanee Hunt takes the challenge one step further and, in an appropriate reflection of her own journey, said, "Every person is responsible for changing the world." The dynamic balance between service and success is an astounding force capable of driving organizations to even greater heights while contributing to a greater good.

Leading is never easy. The personal and physical price of level 1 (or conditional) leadership can be heavy. It is full of negatives. Some days, it may seem that nothing is right. Leaders feel a sense of frustration and futility as setbacks and sacrifices add up. This creates pressure and stress, causing many leaders to lose their focus. The challenges of leadership and life are too great, and the happiness and meaning derived solely from the ego are too small to sustain us.

Enough—A Catalyst to a Higher Level of Leadership

In many of our stories, the leaders have a hard time saying no. It seems that their psychological makeup and the relentless demands of their roles pull leaders away from their objectives. They are left asking themselves, "Is this really worth it?" They may also wonder, "Why am I doing this?" and "When is enough enough?" *Enough* is defined here not just materially, but in the myriad ways that the ego is sustained and fed through power, achievement, and recognition.

We asked hundreds of leaders *Why do you lead?* and found that the question revealed more truth than a battery of assessment instruments. Sometimes the *Why lead?* question stopped leaders in their tracks. And it was easy for us to see that they were either struggling for happiness around their initial objectives or already more purposeful now that they had raised the ante to a second level of leadership. These leaders had no trouble verbalizing why they do it.

through others. You can't operate in the realm of joy in a sustained way until you get outside yourself. It's not about you. Many philosophers, statesmen, leaders, and spiritual teachers have taught this message. Helping others is what all great leaders do.

Personal fulfillment happens by experiencing the lives and the happiness of others firsthand. It is not about sacrificing your health, security, or happiness for others. Fulfillment is not a way to rationalize taking a caregiver role or becoming a martyr. There needs to be a balance in each person's life between work and service, between happiness and joy. If you have a wonderful job that gives you everything you need, that is positive. But don't limit yourself, for there is even more to be gained.

Just as *enough* is a point that people must reach for themselves, so too is joy. Joy is worth its weight in gold as a higher leadership goal.

Leadership is a major responsibility, and all leaders are obliged as providers to care for the needs of themselves and their families. Level 2 leadership is not aimed at self-sacrifice or self-denial, although every leader knows those feelings. It's about being more effective and influential by pursuing your passion for leadership. In Level 2 leadership, one pursues a higher purpose through personal growth and service to others.

As you discover your own style, you will realize that by reaching out to others, you will be rewarded more than you can ever imagine. That is what great leadership is really about—attaining your true potential through serving others.

My Personal Experience: A Reflection by Phil Swift

I had to learn some hard lessons of leadership firsthand. As a young leader, I was obsessed with numbers, measurable objectives, hard data and rational logic. As a student, I excelled in math and philosophy. As a business leader and entrepreneur, I was analytically astute. My assessment of a company's worth was generally precise and rational. With hard work, talent, and some luck, my success in business went far beyond my original ambitions.

As I exceeded my professional and financial objectives, more of the same didn't seem like enough. I began to adopt a less logical, more intuitive approach to life and business. I was still a seeker looking for the more important insights. Our lives and businesses are very complex. I studied math, philosophy, and business, earning an MBA. I'm familiar and even comfortable with complexity. But I came to feel that the real answers should be simple.

The truth, I believe, is simple; and the messages of great leaders are simple and clear.

After leaving India, I had much to contemplate. Months later, the solution came to me. After wrestling with the concept of *enough*, I made a decision that was as unimaginable a few years ago as it was obvious and natural now. Having concluded that I had enough for my family, I would dedicate the future growth in my business activities and much of my time and resources to the service of others.

Once I made that decision, my interest in business was renewed. Success in business was no longer just personal, it now had greater meaning and scope. Before, I was working too hard to generate more; now I was working in order to share the benefits with others.

I found satisfaction in contributing to important projects in India and to various projects in my own community. In doing so, I achieved a kind of peace.

Even the most difficult day at the office no longer seems so draining and empty. Whenever I am stressed with business issues, I find that revisiting these principles and connecting with those who are serving others enables me to feel an incredible fulfillment that I don't get from work alone. The integration of my leadership in business with my service to my family and to others—has made my life more whole.

INDEX

A

Achievement orientation, 22
Adobe Systems, 144, 145
Advertising, 121, 122
Affiliation orientation, 22
Afghanistan, 193, 212, 213
Africa, 172, 209
Air Force Academy, 131
The Alchemist (Paulo Coehlo), 103
Aldus, 142–144
Alpaca (H.L. Hunt), 256
Al-Qaeda, 213
American Hospital Supply, 66–67
American Nurses Association, 106
American Nurses Credentialing Center (ANCC), 106
Amma, Sri Narayani, vii, 11–13, 15, 18, 19, 21, 22, 25, 26, 280, 289, 297
Amoco, 201
ANCC (American Nurses Credentialing Center), 106
Anderson, Gidske, 194
Annan, Kofi, 73, 77
Anti-Defamation League, 251
Apartheid, 209
Apple Computer, 142
ARC Financial Corporation, 10, 24, 83
Armenian genocide, 220
Armstrong, Lance, 69–70
Arthur Andersen, 161
"Asian Flu," 43
AT&T, 163
Auschwitz, 54
Austria, 149–150, 251, 257

B

B2B Magazine, 125
Baath party (Iraq), 220
Baghdad, Iraq, 182, 186
Baldwin, Doug, 202–203
Bangladesh, 211
Bank Negara Malaysia, 72
Bank of Montreal, 150
Banks, 113–114
Basketball, 95–97
BBC, 93, 192
Beirut, Lebanon, 99
Bell Helicopter, 94
Bennett, Gail Cook, 48
Bennis, Warren, 3, 26, 64, 90, 283
Bertram, Bob, 48
Bhutto, Benazir, 4–5, 31, 175, 206–217, 293
Bhutto, Zulfikar Ali, 206, 210–211
Bin Laden, Osama, 212–213
Bordeaux, France, 153
Bosnia, 231
Boss, being a good, 46
Boston College, 246–249
Boston Gas, 161

Bouey, Gerald, 48
Boy Scouts, 110–111
Brain, 239–240
Brainerd, Debbi, 147
Brainerd, Paul, 127, 140–147, 293
Brainerd Foundation, 146
Brazil, 134
Bremer, L. Paul, III, 181–183
Brezhnev, Leonid, 193
Brezhnev doctrine, 192
Britain (*see* United Kingdom)
British Columbia Liquor Control Board, 152
British Empire, 274
Buchwald, Art, 58
Buddhism, 72
Burnham, Daniel H., 195

C

Calcutta, India, 275
Calgary, Alberta, 40, 86, 199
California, 151
California Cooler, 155
Canada, 151, 152, 154, 158, 199, 201
Capability (as principle of leadership), 286
Central Catholic school (Lawrence, Massachusetts), 96
Chase Manhattan, 201
Chennai, India, 9–10
Chernenko, Konstantin, 1920
Children, 23, 61
China, 134
Choice (as principle of leadership), 285
Choices, making, 283–284
Christianity, 72, 190
Churchill, Winston, vii, 23, 30, 292
Ciba-Geigy, 112
Citibank, 200
Civil rights movement, 269
Clark's Great Canadian Cider, 154–155
CNN, 2664
Coehlo, Paulo, 103
Cold War, 192, 193, 266
Coleman, John, 81, 82, 118–127, 292
Coleman, Linda, 120, 121, 125
College of the Holy Cross (Worcester, Massachusetts), 97
Commitment, 208
Communication, 204–205
Communist Party of the Soviet Union, 190–193
Computer industry, 160
Concept Resources, 40
Conditional leadership, 280
Conservative Party (United Kingdom), 210
Cooper, Gordon, 57
Corporate governance, 51–52
Corruption, 180, 181, 187
Council on Foreign Relations, 259
Couzy, Bob, 97
Creativity, 239, 241
Cronkite, Walter, 57–58
Cycling, 69–70

D

Darling, Larry, 40
Democracy, 211–212
Denbury Resources Inc., 44
Desktop publishing, 140, 142–143
The Diary of a Young Girl (Anne Frank), 231–232
Dignity U Wear, 62
Dilja Construction and Saraji Trading Company, 219
Disney World, 57, 58, 60
Diwaniyah, Iraq, 177, 179, 180
Dome Petroleum, 199–201
Dot-coms, 68, 124
Dysfunctional behavior, 23
Dyslexia, 120, 126, 233

E

East India Company, 272
Edison, Thomas, 30
Egypt, 212
Ellison, Larry, 143
Energy industry, 16, 36–43, 86, 1975, 199–204
England (*see* United Kingdom)
"Enough," 3, 25, 62, 104, 127, 136, 280, 295–297, 299
Enron, 52
Entrepreneurship, 163–164
Episcopal Hospital (Philadelphia, Pennsylvania), 105
Ethical Globalization Initiative, 166, 172
European Union, 169
Everybody Wins (book), 69–70
Exxon, 202, 203

F

Faisal, King (Iraq), 220
Financial goals, 136
Firing employees, 45–46, 87, 138
Fletcher, Hugh, 201
Fletcher Challenge, 201, 202, 204
Forbes magazine, 259
Foundation for the Third Millennium, 116
Frank, Anne, 231–234
Freedom Writers (film), 229
The Freedom Writers Diary (book), 229, 232
Frito-Lay, 132, 133

G

Gallagher, John, 199
Gandhi, Mohandas K., 30, 227–228, 269–277, 282, 293–294
Gates, Bill, 143
General Dynamics, 56–57
General Electric, 163
Germany, 150, 274
Gies, Miep, 232, 234
Give Kids The World, 58–62
Glasnost, 192, 194
Glenn, John, 58
Global Institute for Leadership Development, 18, 25, 64
Goals, 24–25
Gorbachev, Mikhail, 31, 175, 188–196, 281, 282, 293
Gorbachev, Raisa, 190–191
Gore, Al, 257
Governing Council (Iraq), 183–186
Great Potato Famine, 166, 167
Green Zone (Baghdad, Iraq), 186
Greene, Ron, 33, 35–44, 282, 294
Greer, Germaine, 209
Grove, Andrew, 63
Gruwell, Erin, 227, 229–236, 292
Gulf War, first, 101, 177, 180

H

Halliday, Denis, 75
Hammergren, John, 63–71, 291–292
Happiness, joy vs., 12–13, 297–298
Harkins, Phil, 15, 18–19, 21–27, 102
Harvard Club, 162
Harvard Law School, 167
Harvard University, 86, 160, 206, 207, 210, 214, 251, 259
Havel, Vaclav, 25–26
Health care, 105–106
Heidrick and Struggles, 260
Heinsohn, Tom, 97
Hinduism, 72
Hiring employees, 87, 161
Hockey, 45, 205
Hofstadter, Robert, 112
Holiday Inn, 57–59
Holocaust, 230, 231, 282
Home-building industry, 2186, 220–221, 224
Homeless people, 62
Hope, Major, 181, 183

House of Lords, 259
Hovnanian, Alexander, 225–226
Hovnanian, Alton, 225
Hovnanian, Ara, 175, 218–219, 222–226, 294
Hovnanian, Kevork, 218–223, 225, 226
Hovnanian (firm), 218
Human rights, 215
Hunt, H.L., 252–258
Hunt, Lyda, 254
Hunt, Swanee, 227, 228, 251–258, 295
Hunt Oil Company, 255
Husky Energy, Inc., 43
Hussein, Saddam, 177, 179–181, 187, 282

I

"I CARE," 68
IBM, 160, 163
Iceland summit, 193
ICLIF (*see* International Center for Leadership in Finance)
Imperial Oil Resources, 202
Independence, 35
Independent Petroleum Association of Canada (IPAC), 36
India, 162, 269, 272–276, 279, 300
Indonesia, 43, 85, 134
Information technology (IT), 164
Institute of International Education, 251
Integrity, 41, 43
International Center for Leadership in Finance (ICLIF), 73, 78–79
International Wine and Spirit Competition, 155
International Women's Day, 185
Investor relations, 43
IPAC (Independent Petroleum Association of Canada), 36
Iran, 92–94, 99–100
Iraq, 177–187, 219–220
Iraqi Widows' Organization, 182, 186
Ireland, 76, 129, 166–172
Irish Labor Party, 168–170
Islam, 73, 75, 190, 212–213, 274–276
ISO 9000 standards, 114
IT (information technology), 164
Italy, 274

J

Japan, 274
Jersey Shore Medical Center, 106
Jobs, Steve, 142, 143
John Deere, 131–132
Journey to the Sacred (Jane Simington), 237–238, 240
Joy, happiness vs., 12–13, 297–298

K

Kahanoff, Syd, 39–40
Kansas State University, 131
Kant, Immanuel, 195
Keane, John, 129, 159–165, 291
Keane, Marilyn, 161
Keane Inc., 159, 161–163
Kelowna, British Columbia, 149, 154
Kennedy, John F., 57
Kennedy, Robert F., 209, 210, 216
Khrushchev, Nikita, 193
Khuzai, Rajaa, 175, 177–187, 282, 293
King, Martin Luther, Jr., 30, 269
King, Rodney, 229
Koran, 184, 187
Krakow, Poland, 53–54
Kuala Lumpur, Malaysia, 73, 75, 76
Kuwait, 180
Kvisle, Hal, 175, 176, 197–205, 291

L

Lakeland, Florida, 57
Lamoureux, Claude, 33, 45–52, 282, 294
Landwirth, Fanny, 53
Landwirth, Henri, 33, 52–63, 281, 282, 292
Landwirth, Margot, 53, 55
Landwirth, Max, 53
Leaders, 21–27
Leadership timeline, 24
Lee, Harper, 231
Leo, Brother, 96–97
Level 2 leadership, 290, 298
Levels of leadership, 280
Lewis, Jim, 81, 82, 92–102, 281, 292
Life-altering events, 66
Lincoln, Abraham, 195
Lloyd, John, 81, 82, 103–108, 292
Long Beach, California, 229, 232, 234
Long Island, 160
Look magazine, 262–263
Los Angeles, California, 151, 152
Lowell, Maryland, 245

M

MacDonald, Howard, 200
Macintosh computers, 142
Magnet Recognition Program, 106–107
Maine Department of Transportation, 119
Malayan Banking Berhad (Maybank), 73, 76–77
Malaysia, 73–76
Management by example (MBE), 50–51, 294
Management by objectives (MBO), 50
Mandela, Nelson, 189, 269
Marine Corps, 104–105
Mark Anthony Wine Merchants, 158
May Department Stores, 133
MBE (*see* Management by example)
MBO (management by objectives), 50
McAllister, J.F.O., 166
McClelland, David, 22
McKesson, John, 63
McKesson Corporation, 63–64, 67–68
McNabb, B. G., 56–57
Media, 263–264
Medland, Ted, 48
Meridian Health, 106, 107
MetLife, 46–47, 49
Mike's Hard Lemonade, 156
Millett, Kate, 209
Minneapolis Star Tribune, 141
Mission Hill winery, 149, 155
Mitchell, Pat, 227, 228, 259–268, 292
Morality, 273
Moscow State University, 190
Motivation, 13, 21
Mountbatten, Lord, 274
Muslims (*see* Islam)

N

Nasdaq, 124
National Assembly (Iraq), 185, 186
Native Americans, 241
Natural gas, 197
Natural Resources Entrepreneur of the Year, 35
NBC, 263–265
New Delhi, India, 275
New York, New York, 46
New York Stock Exchange, 44
New Zealand, 155, 179, 201, 202
Nixon, Richard, 209
Nobel Peace Prize, 194, 195
Nonprofit organizations, 146
Nonviolence, 272
Northern Ireland, 169, 171
Nursing, 106–107, 238

O

Ogilvy, David, 51
Ogilvy & Mather, 51
Okanagan Cider Company, 154
Okanagan Valley (British Columbia), 148, 156
Oklahoma State University, 253
Olcott, Chester, 63
Ontario Teachers' Pension Plan (OTPP), 47–50, 52
Optimism, 163, 164
Orlando, Florida, 58, 60
OTPP (*see* Ontario Teachers' Pension Plan)
Oxford University, 206, 207, 209–210, 214

P

PageMaker, 142
Paget, Bob, 37–38, 41, 42, 44
Pakistan, 206–215, 217, 275
Passion (as principle of leadership), 285–286
Payless ShoeSource, 130, 133–138
PBS (*see* Public Broadcasting Service)
Peedam (retreat), 10, 11, 15, 18–19
PepsiCo, 132
Perestroika, 192, 194
Personal fulfillment, 298
Petroff, Neil, 48–49
Philanthropy, 144–147, 293
Poland, 53–54
Polls, 216
Poole, Bucky, 96
Power, 267
Principles of leadership, 284–287, 289
Public Broadcasting Service (PBS), 259, 267
Publishing, 141
Purpose (as principle of leadership), 285
Putin, Vladimir, 195

Q

Queen's University Belfast, 76
Quinn, John, 58

R

Racism, 230, 231, 270–271
Ray, Grace, 252
Ray, Ruth, 252–255
Ray, Walter, 252
Raytheon, 93, 98–101
Reagan, Ronald, 189, 193
Recycling, 154
Reflection (as principle of leadership), 287
Reid, Shirley, 261
Rejection, 171
Renaissance Energy Ltd., 35–38
Renaissance Resources Ltd., 40–44
Republican Guard, 177, 180, 181
Resolution 137 (Iraq), 184
Resolve (as principle of leadership), 286–287
Retirement, 135–137
Rico, Rich, 122
Risks, taking, 268
Robinson, Mary, 129, 166–173, 281, 283, 293
Rockefeller, John D., 30
Rockwell International, 93, 94, 100
Rocky Mountain House, Alberta, 199
Rogers, John, 169, 170
Rogers, Martha, 238
Roosevelt, Franklin, 216
Ruskin, John, 271
Rwanda, 231

S

Said, Nuri as-, 220
St. Anselm's College, 246–247
Salim, Rafiah, 33, 74–80, 283, 294
Salt March, 273–274
Sarajevo, Bosnia, 251

Satyagraha, 271, 272, 276
Saudi Arabia, 98–100, 212
Savak, 93, 94
Schweitzer, Albert, vii
Sea World, 58
Seagram, 153
Sebastian, Tim, 192
Sebastian winery, 152
Self-sacrifice, 276–277
September 11, 2001, terrorist attacks, 124, 213
Service (as principle of leadership), 289
Service to others, 44, 269, 277, 290, 294, 299–300
Sexual Politics (Kate Millett), 209
Shaw, George Bernard, vii, 26
Sheba, Queen, 212
Silicon Valley, 124
Simes, John, 155
Simington, Jane, 227, 237–242, 294
Sin, 273
Slavery, 195
Social Democratic Party of Russia, 194–195
Social entrepreneurship, 229, 236
Social Venture Partners, 145–146
Software development, 159, 161
South Africa, 269–271
Soviet Union, 188–194
Sports, 45, 47
Stalin, Joseph, 93, 193
Standards (as principle of leadership), 286
Stanford University, 110, 112
Starlight Motel (Cocoa Beach, Florida), 57
Stavropol, Russia, 190
Steinem, Gloria, 209
Stewart, John, 16, 83, 86, 89
Strecker, Larry, 129–139, 282, 292
Sun Oil, 39
Sundance Institute, 259
Sustainability, 114–115
Swainsville, Georgia, 260, 261
Swank, Hilary, 229
Swift, Cindy, 15
Swift, Gabriel, 15
Swift, Morgan, 15
Swift, Phil, 10, 11, 22–26, 44, 83, 86, 89
Swope, John, 259
Syria, 212

T

Taiwan, 134, 138
Teaching, 229–235, 243–244
Tehran, Iran, 92–94, 99
Temple University, 105
Tennyson, Alfred, 216–217
Terrorism, 124, 166, 172, 213, 215
Tested, being, 282–283
Textron, 94
Thailand, 43
Thatcher, Margaret, 210, 215
Theater, 244, 250
This Was Not Our War (Swanee Hunt), 251
Thoreau, Henry David, 271
Tichy, Noel, 24
Time Warner, 266
Timeline, leadership, 24
To Kill a Mockingbird (Harper Lee), 231
Today show, 265
Tolstoy, Leo, 271
Tolstoy Farm, 271
Toronto Stock Exchange, 41
Tour de France, 70
Towers, Mike, 227, 243–250, 292–293
TransCanada Corporation, 197, 202–204
Transformational leadership, 289
Transformational shift, 3
Trinity College, 167

"Trojan Horse" campaign, 234
Trust, 141, 170
Turkey, 220, 222
Turner, Ted, 266–267
Turner Broadcasting System, 266
Twain, Mark, 189
Tyco, 52

U

Unconditional leadership, 280, 291
United Kingdom, 169, 179, 270, 274
United Nations, 73, 74, 77–78, 166, 172, 180
United States, 110, 151, 185, 206, 231
United Way of America, 259
University of Alberta, 198–199, 239
University of British Columbia, 150
University of Calgary, 38, 85
University of Georgia, 259, 261
University of Malaya, 76
University of Minnesota, 66, 140
University of Oregon, 140
University of Pennsylvania, 223
University of Western Ontario, 85
U.S. Congress, 185, 214, 233, 234, 259
U.S. Navy, 160
U.S. State Department, 257
Uskorenie, 192, 194

V

Van Wielingen, Mac, 16, 81–91, 291
VIA, 118, 119, 122–127
VIA Group, 125
Victoria, Queen, 272
Vienna, Austria, 149–150
Vietnam War, 140, 167, 209
Virginia Commonwealth University, 262
Vision, 26, 83, 140, 156–162, 164, 165, 217, 224, 229, 236, 243, 248, 258, 262, 268
Von Mandl, Anthony, 129, 148–158, 283, 294
Voyager Petroleum Ltd., 39–40

W

Walt Disney Company, 58, 59
Warnock, John, 144
Warren Bennis Award, 64
Washington, George, 30, 282
Watergate crisis, 209
Welch, Jack, 23, 24, 63, 70
West Point, 131
Westford Academy, 243–246, 248–249
WestJet Airlines Ltd., 44
Wharton School, 223
"Whatever," 22
Wilson, Margaret, 48
Wine business, 148–158
Winfrey, Oprah, 265
"The Witness Cantata" (Swanee Hunt), 2520
Woman to Woman (television show), 265
Women, 208, 210, 212
Women's Foundation of Colorado, 257
Women's Leadership Council, 59
Women's rights, 172, 184, 209, 214–215
World Bank, 186
World War II, 53–55, 85, 189–190, 274
WorldCom, 52

Y

Yeltsin, Boris, 195
Yemen, 212

Z

Zardari, Asif Ali, 213
Zulliger, Ann, 117
Zulliger, Hans, 81, 82, 109–117, 294

ACKNOWLEDGMENTS

There are many people we wish to recognize and thank for their contribution to this book. It is difficult to be exhaustive, as in many regards, this book is the result of a lifetime's journey and one involving many leaders.

The greatest tribute and gratitude must go to Sri Narayani Amma for the guidance and enlightenment that inspired this book. We also recognize and thank a good friend, Dr. Badri Rickhi, who introduced us to Amma.

We are enormously grateful to the leaders we interviewed for this project. They offered their time and allowed us to tell their stories, often sharing personal and intimate aspects of themselves. We thank them for their willingness to open up. The power of the *Why lead?* question led us to important conclusions around leadership development.

Keith Hollihan's involvement and contributions were critical. He was instrumental in working with us to take early drafts and ideas and turn them into a professional manuscript. The involvement of our good friends Ruth Decary and Margaret Bard—both authors in their own right—was enormously helpful. They helped stress test and clarify ideas, narrative, and conclusions. Judith Cardanha and Theresa Deal exhaustively edited the entire book.

We wish to thank our many friends and colleagues whom we burdened with endless requests to review drafts of the manuscript. We want to recognize Father Shawn Aaron, Bill Andrew, Amy Decary Scissons, Charles Gulizia, Valda Harris, Gordon Hasick, Susan Healy, Jim Hume, Mary Anne Hutchings, Nancy Jacklin, Ian Kennedy, Brendan Marshall, Karen MacDonald, Jennifer Mack, Walker McKinley, Jeni Quigg, Badri Rickhi, Cheryl Smith, Nancy Smith, Jeff Storwick, Jennifer Stubbs, Pat and Kelly Whelan, and Pam Wilhelms. We would also like to thank Michael McInnis, Mark Wiseman, and Brad Zumwalt for assistance in arranging some of the interviews. I (Phil Swift) would also like to thank my mother, Phyllis Swift and my brothers Chris and Stephen Swift for their support and encouragement.

This book and the journey would not have been possible without the business partners and colleagues at ARC Financial Corp to whom we are greatly indebted. A very special thank-you to Susan Wrigley who was with us every step of the way on this project, transcribing and editing every interview, through completing the full manuscript and endless edits. Also to Ellen Rosenberg who worked selflessly to help us along the way.

We are forever grateful to B.G. Dilworth for successfully navigating us through the publication process and making the arrangements with Mary Glenn at McGraw-Hill, who proved to be a guiding force in all matters of the publication.

Most of all we want to thank all those who kindly gave their time to be interviewed and added their wisdom in pursuit of the *Why lead?* question. Without their stories this book would not be possible. For the following, we wish to extend our special thanks and sincere appreciation for allowing their stories to be told.

Benazir Bhutto (in memoriam)
Paul Brainerd
John Coleman
Mikhail Gorbachev
Ron Greene
Erin Gruwell
John Hammergren
Ara Hovnanian
Swanee Hunt
John Keane
Rajaa Khuzai
Hal Kvisle
Claude Lamoureux
Henri Landwirth
Jim Lewis
John Lloyd
Pat Mitchell
Mary Robinson
Rafiah Salim
Jane Simington
Larry Strecker
Michael Towers
Mac Van Wielingen
Anthony von Mandl
Hans Zulliger